Philip Henry Gosse

The Romance of Natural History

Philip Henry Gosse

The Romance of Natural History

ISBN/EAN: 9783744692649

Printed in Europe, USA, Canada, Australia, Japan

Cover: Foto ©Thomas Meinert / pixelio.de

More available books at **www.hansebooks.com**

THE ROMANCE

OF

NATURAL HISTORY.

BY

PHILIP HENRY GOSSE, F.R.S.

AUTHOR OF "AQUARIUM," "HISTORY OF THE JEWS," "RIVERS OF THE BIBLE,"
"NATURAL HISTORY OF BIRDS, MAMMALS, REPTILES," "THE OCEAN,"
"POPULAR BRITISH ORNITHOLOGY," ETC. ETC.

With Elegant Illustrations.

BOSTON:

GOULD AND LINCOLN,
59 WASHINGTON STREET.
NEW YORK: SHELDON AND COMPANY.
CINCINNATI: GEORGE S. BLANCHARD.
1864.

PREFACE.

———

THERE are more ways than one of studying natural history. There is Dr Dryasdust's way; which consists of mere accuracy of definition and differentiation; statistics as harsh and dry as the skins and bones in the museum where it is studied. There is the field-observer's way; the careful and conscientious accumulation and record of facts bearing on the life-history of the creatures; statistics as fresh and bright as the forest or meadow where they are gathered in the dewy morning. And there is the poet's way; who looks at nature through a glass peculiarly his own; the æsthetic aspect, which deals, not with statistics, but with the emotions of the human mind,—surprise, wonder, terror, revulsion, admiration, love, desire, and so forth,—which are made energetic by the contemplation of the creatures around him.

In my many years' wanderings through the wide field of natural history, I have always felt towards it something

of a poet's heart, though destitute of a poet's genius. As
Wordsworth so beautifully says,—

> "To me the meanest flower that blows can give
> Thoughts that do often lie too deep for tears."

Now, this book is an attempt to present natural history
in this æsthetic fashion. Not that I have presumed constantly to indicate—like the stage-directions in a play, or
the "hear, hear!" in a speech—the actual emotion to be
elicited; this would have been obtrusive and impertinent;
but I have sought to paint a series of pictures, the reflec-
tions of scenes and aspects in nature, which in my own
mind awaken poetic interest, leaving them to do their
proper work.

If I may venture to point out one subject on which I
have bestowed more than usual pains, and which I myself regard with more than common interest, it is that of
the last chapter in this volume. An amount of evidence
is adduced for the existence of the sub-mythic monster
popularly known as "the sea-serpent," such as has never
been brought together before, and such as ought almost
to set doubt at rest. But the cloudy uncertainty which
has invested the very being of this creature; its home on
the lone ocean; the fitful way in which it is seen and lost
in its vast solitudes; its dimensions, vaguely gigantic; its
dragon-like form; and the possibility of its association
with beings considered to be lost in an obsolete antiquity;

all these are attributes which render it peculiarly precious to a romantic naturalist. I hope the statisticians will forgive me if they cannot see it with my spectacles.

The Illustrations are drawn for the most part by Wolf, and engraved by Whymper: they will speak for themselves.

P. H. G.

ToRQUAY. 1860.

CONTENTS.

I. TIMES AND SEASONS.

II. HARMONIES.

VI. THE MINUTE.

VII. THE MEMORABLE.

VIII. THE RECLUSE.

XI. THE UNKNOWN.

XII. THE GREAT UNKNOWN.

List of Illustrations.

ROMANCE OF NATURAL HISTORY.

I.

TIMES AND SEASONS.

" To everything there is a season;" and, in its season,
everything is comely. Winter is not without its charm,
the charm of a grand and desolate majesty. The Arctic
voyagers have seen King Winter on his throne, and a full
royal despot he is. When the mercury is solid in the
bulb, to look abroad on the boundless waste of snow, all
silent and motionless, in the very midst of the six-months'
night, must be something awful. And yet there is a glory
and a beauty visible in perfection only then. There is
the moon, of dazzling brightness, circling around the
horizon; there are ten thousand crystals of crisp and
crackling snow reflecting her beams; there are the stars
flashing and sparkling with unwonted sharpness; and
there is the glorious aurora spanning the purple sky with
its arch of coruscating beams, now advancing, now receding, like angelic watchers engaged in mystic dance,
now shooting forth spears and darts of white light with
rustling whisper, and now unfurling a broad flag of crim-

A

soned flame, that diffuses itself over the heavens, and is reflected from the unsullied snow beneath. These phenomena I have seen during many years' residence in the grim and ice-bound Newfoundland, and in still sterner Canada. There, too, I have often witnessed the

> . . . . " Kindred glooms,
> Congenial horrors !" . . . .

that the poet apostrophises, when

> . . . . " The snows arise, and, foul and fierce,
> All winter drives along the darken'd air."

A snow-storm, when the air is filled with the thick flakes driven impetuously before a blinding gale, rapidly obliterating every landmark from the benighted and bewildered traveller's search on a wild mountain-side in Canada; or on the banks of Newfoundland when a heavy sea is running, and floes of ice, sharp as needles and hard as rocks, are floating all around—is something terrible to witness, and solemn to remember.

Yet there are gentler features and more lovable attributes of winter, even in those regions where he reigns autocratically. The appearance of the forest, after a night's heavy snow in calm weather, is very beautiful. On the horizontal boughs of the spruces and hemlock-pines, it rests in heavy, fleecy masses, which take the form of hanging drapery, while the contrast between the brilliant whiteness of the clothing and the blackness of the sombre foliage is fine and striking. Nor are the forms which the *drifted* snow assumes less attractive.

Here, it lies in gentle undulations, swelling and sinking; there, in little ripples, like the sand of a sea-beach; here, it stands up like a perpendicular wall; there, like a conical hill; here, it is a long, deep trench; there, a flat, overhanging table; but one of the most charming of its many-visaged appearances is that presented by a shed or outhouse well hung with cobwebs. After a drift, the snow is seen, in greater or less masses, to have attached itself to the cobwebs, and hangs from the rafters and walls, and from corner to corner, in graceful drapery of the purest white, and of the most fantastic shapes.

The elegant arabesques that the frost forms on our window-panes, and the thin blades and serrated swords of which hoar-frost is composed, are beautiful; and still more exquisitely charming are the symmetrical six-rayed stars of falling snow, when caught on a dark surface. But I think nothing produced by the magic touch of winter can excel a phenomenon I have often seen in the woods of the transatlantic countries named above, where it is familiarly called silver-thaw. It is caused by rain descending when the stratum of air nearest the earth is below 32 deg., and consequently freezing the instant it touches any object; the ice accumulates with every drop of rain, until a transparent, glassy coating is formed. On the shrubs and trees, the effect is magical, and reminds one of fairy scenes described in oriental fables. Every little twig, every branch, every leaf, every blade of grass is enshrined in crystal; the whole forest is composed of sparkling, transparent glass, even to the minute leaves of the pines and firs. The sun shines out. What a glitter of light! How the beams, broken, as it were, into ten thousand fragments, sparkle and dance, as they are reflected from the trees! Yet it is as fragile as beautiful. A slight shock from a rude hand is sufficient to destroy it. The air is filled with a descending shower of the glittering fragments, and the spell is broken at once ; the crystal pageant has vanished, and nothing remains but a brown, leafless tree.

But all this is the beauty of death ; and the naturalist, though he may, and does, admire its peculiar loveliness, yet longs for the opening of spring. To his impatience it has seemed as if it would never come ; but, at last, on some morning toward the end of April, the sun rises without a cloud, the south-west wind blows softly, and he walks forth, "wrapt in Elysium." Life is now abroad : larks, by scores, are pouring forth sweet carols, as they hang and soar in the dazzling brightness of the sky; the blackbird is warbling, flute-like, in the coppice; swallows, newly come across the sea, are sweeping and twittering joyously; the little olive-clad warblers and white-throats are creeping about like mice among the twigs of the hedges ; and, ha !—sweetest of all sounds of spring !— there are those two simple notes, that thrill through the very heart,—the voice of the cuckoo !

Here, too, are the butterflies. The homely "whites" of the garden are flitting about the cabbages, and the tawny "browns" are dancing along the hedge-rows that divide the meadows; the delicate "brimstone" comes

bounding over the fence, and alights on a bed of primroses, itself scarcely distinguishable from one of them.
On the commons and open downs the lovely little "blues"
are frisking in animated play; and here and there a still
more minute "copper"—tiniest of the butterfly race—
rubs together its little wings, or spreads them to the sun,
glowing with scarlet lustre like a coal of fire.

The beetles are active, too, in their way. The tiger-
beetle, with its sparkling green wing-cases, flies before our
footsteps with watchful agility, and numerous atoms are
circling round the blossoming elms, which, on catching
one or two, we find to belong to the same class; the dark-
blue *Timarcha*—the bloody-nose—is depositing its drop
of clear red liquid on the blades of grass; and if we look
into the ponds, we see multitudes of little black, brown,
and yellow forms come up to the surface, hang there for
a moment, and then hurry down again into the depths.
And then come up the newts from their castle in the mud,
willing to see and to be seen; for they have donned their
vernal attire, and appear veritable holiday beaux, arrayed
in the pomp of ruffled shirt and scarlet waistcoat. The
frogs, moreover, are busy depositing their strings of bead-
like spawn, and announcing the fact to the world in loud,
if not cheerful strains.

The streams, freed from the turbidity of the winter
rains, roll in transparent clearness, now gliding along
smooth and deep in their weedy course through "th' indented meads," where the roach and the dace play in
sight, and the pike lies but half-hidden under the pro-

jecting bank; and now brawling and sparkling in fragmentary crystal, over a rocky bed, where the trout displays his speckled side as he leaps from pool to pool.

The willows on the river margin are gay with their
pendant catkins, to whose attractions hundreds of hum-
ming bees resort, in preference to the lovely flowers which
are already making the banks and slopes to smile. The
homeliest of these, even the dandelions and daisies, the
buttercups and celandines, are most welcome after the
dreariness and death of winter.

"Earth fills her lap with treasures of her own;" and
even "the meanest flower that blows" has, to the opened
eye, a beauty that is like a halo of glory around it. Yet
there are some which, from the peculiarities of their form,
colour, or habits, charm us more than others. The ger-
mander speedwell, with its laughing blue eyes, spangling
every hedge-bank—who can look upon it, and not love it?
Who can mark the wild hyacinths, growing in battalions
of pale stalks, each crowned with its clusters of drooping
bells; and interspersed with the tall and luxuriant cow-
slips, so like and yet so different, filling the air with their
golden beauty and sugary fragrance, without rapture?
Who can discover the perfumed violet amidst the rampant
moss, or the lily of the valley beneath the rank herbage,
without acknowledging how greatly both beauty and
worth are enhanced by humility?

If in this favoured land we are conscious of emotions of
peculiar delight, when we see the face of nature renewing
its loveliness after winter, where yet the influence of the

dreary season is never so absolute as quite to quench the activities of either vegetable or animal life, and where that face may be said to put on a somewhat gradual smile ere it breaks out into full joyous laughter—much more impressive is the coming in of spring with all its charms in such a country as Canada, where the transition is abrupt, and a few days change the scene from a waste of snow to universal warmth, verdure, and beauty. I have observed, with admiration, how suddenly the brown poplar woods put on a flush of tender yellow-green from the rapidly-opening leaves; how quickly the maple trees are covered with crimson blossoms; how brilliant flowers are fast springing up through the dead leaves in the forests; how gay butterflies and beetles are playing on every bank where the snow lay a week before; and how the bushes are ringing with melody from hundreds of birds, which have been for months silent. The first song of spring comes on the heart with peculiar power, after the mute desolation of winter, and more especially when, as in the country I speak of, it suddenly bursts forth in a whole orchestra at once. The song-sparrow is the chief performer in this early concert; a very melodious little creature, though of unpretending plumage.

Much of all this charm lies in the circumstantials, the associations. It may be that there is something in the psychical, perhaps even in the physical condition of the observer, superinduced by the season itself, that makes him in spring more open to pleasurable emotions from the sights and sounds of nature. But much depends on association and contrast: novelty has much to do with it. Everything tells of happiness; and we cannot help sympathising with it. We contrast the ζωή with the θάνατος, and our minds revert to ἀθανασία. Here *is*, where before there *was not*, at least for us; and this is novelty. The hundreds of rich and fragrant violets that we find in April are not less rich in hue or less fragrant in odour than the first; yet the first violet of spring had a charm that all these combined possess not. We can never hear the cuckoo's voice, we can never mark the swallow's flight, without pleasure; but the *first* cuckoo, the *first* swallow, sent a thrill through our hearts which is not repeated.*

Akin to this is the rose-coloured atmosphere through which every thing in nature is seen by childhood and youth; to whom the robin's breast appears of the brightest scarlet, and the sloe and blackberry are delicious fruits. Love nature as we may,—and one who has ever wooed can never cease to love her,—we cannot help being

---

* Darwin, writing of the Australian forest, observes:—"The leaves are not shed periodically: this character appears common to the entire southern hemisphere, namely, South America, Australia, and the Cape of Good Hope. The inhabitants of this hemisphere, and of the inter-tropical regions, thus lose perhaps one of the most glorious, though to our eyes common, spectacles in the world,—the first bursting into full foliage of the leafless tree. They may, however, say that we pay dearly for this by having the land covered with mere naked skeletons for so many months. This is too true; but our senses acquire a keen relish for the exquisite green of the spring, which the eyes of those living within the tropics, sated during the long year with the gorgeous productions of those glowing climates, can never experience."—*Nat. Voy.*, (ed. 1852,) p. 433.

conscious, as "years bring the inevitable yoke," of such
a sadness as Wordsworth has described, in that Ode which
—rejecting, of course, as anything but a poetic dream,
the theory on which he founds it—is one of the most
nobly beautiful poems in our language :—

> "There was a time when meadow, grove, and stream,
> The earth, and every common sight,
> To me did seem
> Apparell'd in celestial light,
> The glory and the freshness of a dream.
> It is not now as it hath been of yore ;—
> Turn wheresoe'er I may,
> By night or day,
> The things which I have seen I now can see no more.
>
> "The rainbow comes and goes,
> And lovely is the rose ;
> The moon doth with delight
> Look round her when the heavens are bare ;
> Waters on a starry night
> Are beautiful and fair ;
> The sunshine is a glorious birth ;
> But yet I know, where'er I go,
> That there hath pass'd away a glory from the earth."

The summer, with all its gorgeous opulence of life,
possesses charms of its own ; nor is autumn destitute of an
idiosyncrasy which takes strong hold of our sympathies.
We cannot, indeed, divest ourselves of a certain feeling
of sadness, because we know that the season is in the
decrepitude of age, and is verging towards death. In
spring, hope is prominent ; in autumn, regret : in spring
we are anticipating life ; in autumn, death.

Yet a forest country in autumn presents a glorious spectacle, and nowhere more magnificent than in North America, where the decaying foliage of the hardwood forests puts on in October the most splendid colours. Every part of the woods is then glowing in an endless variety of shades; brilliant crimson, purple, scarlet, lake, orange, yellow, brown, and green : if we look from some cliff or mountain-top over a breadth of forest, the rich hues are seen to spread as far as the eye can reach ; the shadows of the passing clouds, playing over the vast surface, now dimming the tints, now suffering them to flash out in the full light of the sun ; here and there a large group of sombre evergreens,—hemlock or spruce, —giving the shadows of the picture, and acting as a foil to the brightness ;—the whole forest seems to have become a gigantic parterre of the richest flowers.*

> " Ere, in the northern gale,
> The summer tresses of the trees are gone,
> The woods of autumn, all around our vale,
> Have put their glory on.
>
> " The mountains that infold,
> In their wide sweep, the colour'd landscape round,
> Seem groups of giant kings, in purple and gold,
> That guard th' enchanted ground."—BRYANT.

---

* In examining the details of this mass of glowing colour, I have found that by far the greatest proportion is produced by the sugar-maple, and other species of the same genus. The leaves of these display all shades of red, from deepest crimson to bright orange; which generally occurring in large masses, not in individual detached leaves, prevents anything tawdry or little in the effect; on the contrary, when the full beams of the sun shine on them, the warm and glowing colours

It is observable that after all this short-lived splendour has passed away, and the trees have become leafless, in Canada and the Northern States, there always occur a few days of most lovely and balmy weather, which is called the Indian summer. It is characterised by a peculiar haziness in the atmosphere, like a light smoke, by a brilliant sun, only slightly dimmed by this haze, and by a general absence of wind. It follows a short season of wintry weather, so as to be isolated in its character. One circumstance I have remarked with interest,—the resuscitation of insect life in abundance. Beautiful butterflies swarm around the leafless trees; and moths in multitudes flit among the weeds and bushes, while minuter forms hop merrily about the heaps of decaying leaves at the edges of the woods. It is a charming relaxation of the icy chains of winter.

possess a great deal of grandeur. The poplar leaves often assume a crimson hue; the elm, a bright and golden yellow; birch and beech, a pale, sober, yellow-ochre; ash and basswood, different shades of brown; the tamarack, a buff-yellow. The beech, the ash, and the tamarack do not, in general, bear much part in this glittering pageant; the ash is mostly leafless at the time, and the glory has passed away before the other two have scarcely begun to fade. Indeed, the glossy green of the beech is perhaps more effective than if it partook of the general change; and even the gloomy blackness of the resinous trees, by relieving and throwing forward the gayer tints, is not without effect. This beauty is not shewn to equal advantage every year: in some seasons the trees fade with very little splendour, the colours all partaking more or less of dusky, sordid brown; early frosts seem to be unfavourable for its development: and even at its best it is a melancholy glory, a precursor of approaching dissolution, something like the ribbons and garlands with which the ancient pagan priests were accustomed to adorn the animals they destined for sacrifice.

Latrobe has depicted the aspect of the same season in the Alps, which may be compared with the American :—

" On. my arrival [at Neufchatel at the beginning of November], the vintage was over, and the vineyards, lately the scene of so much life and gaiety, now lay brown and unsightly upon the flanks of the mountain and border of the lake. The forest trees in the neighbourhood of the town, and the brushwood on the wide and steep acclivity of the Chaumont, were still decked in that splendid but transient livery which one frosty night's keen and motionless breath, or a few hours' tempest, must strew on the earth.

" There is something strangely moving in the few last short and tranquil days of autumn, as they often intervene between a period of tempestuous weather and the commencement of the frosts. The face of nature is still sunny, and bright and beautiful ; the forest still yields its shade, and the sun glistens warm and clear upon the flower and stained leaf.

" Then there is the gorgeous autumnal sunset closing the short day ; and in this land of the lake and mountain it is indeed a scene of enchantment. There is the rich tinge of the broad red sun stealing over and blending the thousand hues of the hill and forest, and the flood of glory upon the sky above and lake beneath, while the snows of the Alps are glowing like molten ore. I see it still, and it warms my heart's blood.

" A few more days, and then rises the blast, howling

through the pine forest and over the mountain-side, shaking from the tree its fair foliage, roughening the surface of the lake, and drawing over the sky a curtain of thick vapours that narrows the horizon by day, and shuts out the stars by night." *

The different divisions of the day—early morning, noon, evening, night—have each their peculiar phase of nature, each admirable. An early riser, I have always been in the habit of enjoying, with keen relish, the opening of day and the awakening of life. In my young days of natural history, when pursuing with much ardour an acquaintance with the insects of Newfoundland, I used frequently, in June and July, to rise at daybreak, and seek a wild but lovely spot a mile or two from the town. It was a small tarn or lake among the hills, known as Little Beaver Pond. Here I would arrive before the winds were up, for it is at that season generally calm till after sunrise. The scene, with all its quiet beauty, rises up to my memory now. There is the black, calm, glassy pond sleeping below me, reflecting from its unruffled surface every tree and bush of the dark towering hills above, as in a perfect mirror. Stretching away to the east are seen other ponds, embosomed in the frowning mountains, connected with this one and with each other in that chain-fashion which is so characteristic of Newfoundland; while, further on in the same direction, between two conical peaks, the ocean is perceived reposing under the mantle of the long dark clouds of morning.

* *Alpenstock*, p. 162.

There is little wood, except of the pine and fir tribe, sombre and still; a few birches grow on the hill-sides, and a wild cherry or two; but willows hang over the water, and many shrubs combine to constitute a tangled thicket redolent with perfume. Towards the margin of the lake, the ground is covered with spongy swamp-moss, and several species of *ledum* and *kalmia*, with the fragrant gale, give out aromatic odours. The low, unvarying, and somewhat mournful bleat of the snipes on the opposite hill, and the short, impatient flapping of wings as one occasionally flies across the water, seem rather to increase than to diminish the general tone of repose, which is aided, too, by yonder bittern that stands in the dark shadow of an overhanging bush as motionless as if he were carved in stone, reflected perfectly in the shallow water in which he is standing.

But presently the spell is broken; the almost oppressive silence and stillness are interrupted; the eastern clouds have been waxing more and more ruddy, and the sky has been bathed in golden light ever becoming more lustrous. Now the sea reflects in dazzling splendour the risen sun; nature awakes; lines of ruffling ripple run across the lake from the airs which are beginning to breathe down the glen; the solemn stillness which weighed upon the woods is dissipated; the lowing of cattle comes faintly from the distant settlements; crows fly cawing overhead; and scores of tiny throats combine, each in its measure, to make a sweet harmony, each warbling its song of unconscious praise to its beneficent Creator.

Then with what delight would I haste to the lake-side, where the margin was fringed with a broad belt of the yellow water-lily, whose oval leaves floating on the surface almost concealed the water, while here and there the golden globe itself protruded. Having pulled out my insect-net from a rocky crevice in which I was accustomed to hide it, I would then stretch myself on the mossy bank and peer in between the lily leaves, under whose shadow I could with ease discover the busy inhabitants of the pool, and watch their various movements in the crystalline water.

The merry little boatflies are frisking about, backs downwards, using their oar-like hind feet as paddles; the triple-tailed larvæ of dayflies creep in and out of holes in the bank, the finny appendages at their sides maintaining a constant waving motion; now and then a little water-beetle peeps out cautiously from the cresses, and scuttles across to a neighbouring weed; the unwieldy caddis-worms are lazily dragging about their curiously-built houses over the sogged leaves at the bottom, watching for some unlucky gnat-grub to swim within reach of their jaws; but, lo! one of them has just fallen a victim to the formidable calliper-compasses wherewith that beetle-larva seizes his prey, and is yielding his own life-blood to the ferocious slayer. There, too, is the awkward sprawling spider-like grub of the dragonfly; he crawls to and fro on the mud, now and then shooting along by means of his curious valvular pump; he approaches an unsuspecting blood-worm, and,—oh! I remember to this day the

enthusiasm with which I saw him suddenly throw out
from his face that extraordinary mask that Kirby has so
graphically described, and, seizing the worm with the
serrated folding-doors, close the whole apparatus up again
in a moment. I could not stand that: in goes the net; the
clearness is destroyed; the vermin fly hither and thither;
and our sprawling ill-favoured gentleman is dragged to
daylight, and clapped into the pocket-phial, to be fattened
at home, and reared " for the benefit of science."

Since then I have wooed fair nature in many lands,
and have always found a peculiar charm in the early
morning. When dwelling in the gorgeous and sunny
Jamaica, it was delightful to rise long before day and ride
up to a lonely mountain gorge overhung by the solemn
tropical forest, and there, amidst the dewy ferns arching
their feathery fronds by thousands from every rock and
fallen tree, and beneath the splendid wild-pines and orchids
that droop from every fork, await the first activity of some
crepuscular bird or insect. There was a particular species
of butterfly, remarkable for the extraordinary gem-like
splendour of its decoration, and peculiarly interesting to the
philosophic naturalist as being a connecting link between
the true butterflies and the moths. This lovely creature, I
discovered, was in the habit of appearing just as the sun
broke from the sea, and congregating by scores around
the summit of one tall forest-tree then in blossom, filling
the air with their lustrous and sparkling beauty, at a height
most tantalising for the collector, and after playing in giddy
flight for about an hour, retiring as suddenly as they came.

In these excursions I was interested in marking the successive awakening of the early birds. Passing through the wooded pastures and guinea-grass fields of the upland slopes, while the stars were twinkling overhead, while as yet no indication of day appeared over the dark mountain-peak, no ruddy tinge streamed along the east; while Venus was blazing like a lamp, and shedding as much light as a young moon, as she climbed up the clear, dark heaven among her fellow-stars;—the nightjars were unusually vociferous, uttering their singular note, "wittawittawit," with pertinacious iteration, as they careered in great numbers, flying low, as their voices clearly indicated, yet utterly indistinguishable to the sight from the darkness of the sky across which they flitted in their triangular traverses. Presently the flat-bill uttered his plaintive wail, occasionally relieved by a note somewhat less mournful. When the advancing light began to break over the black and frowning peaks, and Venus waned, the peadove from the neighbouring woods commenced her fivefold coo, hollow and moaning. Then the petchary, from the top of a tall cocoa-palm, cackled his three or four rapid notes, "OP, PP, P, Q;" and from a distant wooded hill, as yet shrouded in darkness, proceeded the rich, mellow, but broken song of the hopping-dick-thrush, closely resembling that of our own blackbird. Now the whole east was ruddy, and the rugged points and trees on the summit of the mountain-ridge, interrupting the flood of crimson light, produced the singularly beautiful phenomenon of a series of rose-coloured beams, diverging

B

from the eastern quarter, and spreading, like an expanded
fan, across the whole arch of heaven, each ray dilating as
it advanced. The harsh screams of the clucking-hen
came up from a gloomy gorge, and from the summit of
the mountain were faintly heard the lengthened flute-like
notes, in measured cadence, of the solitaire. Then mocking-birds all around broke into song, pouring forth their
rich gushes and powerful bursts of melody, with a profusion that filled the ear, and overpowered all the other
varied voices, which were by this time too numerous to
be separately distinguished, but which all helped to swell
the morning concert of woodland music.

A traveller in the mountain-regions of Venezuela has
described in the following words his own experience of a
similar scene :—

" That morning's moonlight ride along the summits of
the Sierra of Las Cocuyzas, was certainly one of the most
enjoyable I ever remember. It was almost like magic,
when, as the sun began to approach the horizon, the perfect stillness of the forests beneath was gradually broken
by the occasional note of some early riser of the winged
tribe, till, at length, as the day itself began to break, the
whole forest seemed to be suddenly warmed into life, sending forth choir after choir of gorgeous-plumaged songsters,
each after his own manner to swell the chorus of greeting
(a discordant one, I fear it must be owned) to the glorious
sun ; and when, as the increasing light enabled you to
see down into the misty valleys beneath, there were dis-

played to our enchanted gaze zones of fertility, embracing almost every species of tree and flower that flourishes between the Tierra Caliente and the regions of perpetual snow. It certainly was a view of almost unequalled magnificence. Riding amongst apple and peach-trees that might have belonged to an English orchard, and on whose branches we almost expected to see the blackbird and the chaffinch; while a few hundred yards below, parrots and macaws, monkeys and mocking-birds, were sporting among the palms and tree-ferns, and, in flights of two or three hundred yards, chasing each other from the climate of the torrid to that of the temperate zone, was not the least striking part of the scene." *

I cannot avoid quoting from Mr Atkinson a picture of day-break, as seen across the plains of Siberia from one of the peaks of the Oural; though its details scarcely bring it within the limits of natural history proper :—

"Day was rapidly dawning over these boundless forests of Siberia. Long lines of pale yellow clouds extended over the horizon; these became more luminous every few minutes, until at length they were like waves of golden light rolling and breaking on some celestial shore. I roused up my fellow-traveller that he might partake with me in my admiration of the scene, and a most splendid one it was. The sun was rising behind some very distant hills, and tipping all the mountain-tops with his glorious rays : even the dark pines assumed

* Sullivan's *Rambles in North and South America*, p. 395.

a golden hue. We sat silently watching the beautifully changing scene for an hour, until hill and valley were lighted up." *

Cowper has selected "The Winter Walk at Noon" for one of the books of his charming "Task;" and as *nihil quod tetigit non ornavit*, so he has sketched a beautiful picture :—

> " Upon the southern side of the slant hills,
> And where the woods fence off the northern blast,
> The season smiles, resigning all its rage,
> And has the warmth of May.   The vault is blue,
> Without a cloud, and white without a speck
> The dazzling splendour of the scene below.
>
> No noise is here, or none that hinders thought.
> The redbreast warbles still, but is content
> With slender notes, and more than half suppress'd :
> Pleased with his solitude, and flitting light
> From spray to spray, where'er he rests he shakes
> From many a twig the pendant drops of ice,
> That tinkle in the wither'd leaves below."

But how different from such a scene is a tropical noon —a noon in Guiana, or Brazil, for example ! There, too, an almost death-like quietude reigns, but it is a quietude induced by the furnace-like heat of the vertical sun, whose rays pour down with a direct fierceness, from which there is no shadow except actually beneath some thick tree, such as the mango, whose dense and dark foliage affords an absolutely impenetrable umbrella in the brightest glare. Such, too, is the smooth-barked manga-beira, a tree of vast bulk, with a wide-spreading head of

* Atkinson's *Siberia*, p. 59.

dense foliage, beneath which, when the sun strikes mercilessly on every other spot, all is coolness and repose. The birds are all silent, sitting with panting beaks in the thickest foliage ; no tramp or voice of beast is heard, for these are sleeping in their coverts. Ever and anon the seed-capsule of some forest-tree bursts with a report like that of a musket, and the scattered seeds are heard pattering among the leaves, and then all relapses into silence again. Great butterflies, with wings of refulgent azure, almost too dazzling to look upon, flap lazily athwart the glade, or alight on the glorious flowers. Little bright-eyed lizards, clad in panoply that glitters in the sun, creep about the parasites of the great trees, or rustle the herbage, and start at the sounds themselves have made. Hark! There is the toll of a distant bell. Two or three minutes pass,—another toll! a like interval, then another toll! Surely it is the passing bell of some convent, announcing the departure of a soul. No such thing; it is the note of a bird. It is the campanero or bell-bird of the Amazon, a gentle little creature, much like a snow-white pigeon, with a sort of soft fleshy horn on its fore-head, three inches high. This appendage is black, clothed with a few scattered white feathers, and being hollow and communicating with the palate, it can be inflated at will. The solemn clear bell-note, uttered at regular intervals by the bird, is believed to be connected with this structure. Be this as it may, the silvery sound, heard only in the depth of the forest, and scarcely ever except at midday, when other voices are mute, falls upon

the ear of the traveller with a thrilling and romantic
effect. The jealously recluse habits of the bird have
thrown an air of mystery over its economy, which
heightens the interest with which it is invested.

Before I speak of night, the most romantic of all seasons to the naturalist, I must quote two descriptions of
sunset in regions rarely visited by English travellers. The
first scene was witnessed from that rugged mountain-chain
which divides two quarters of the globe. We have just
looked at the *rising* sun from the same peaks, gazing
across the plains of Asia: we are now called to look
over Europe.

" I now turned towards the west, and walked to a high
crag overlooking the valley; here I seated myself to
watch the great and fiery orb descend below the horizon;
and a glorious sight it was! Pavda, with its snowy cap,
was lighted up, and sparkled like a ruby; the other
mountains were tinged with red, while in the deep
valleys all was gloom and mist. For a few minutes the
whole atmosphere appeared filled with powdered carmine,
giving a deep crimson tint to everything around. So
splendid was this effect, and so firm a hold had it taken
of my imagination, that I became insensible to the hundreds of mosquitoes that were feasting on my blood.
Excepting their painfully disagreeable *hum*, no sound,
not even the chirping of a bird, was to be heard: it was
truly solitude.

" Soon after the sun went down, a white vapour began
to rise in the valleys to a considerable height, giving to

the scene an appearance of innumerable lakes studded with islands, as all the mountain-tops looked dark and black. I was so rivetted to the spot by the scene before me, that I remained watching the changes until nearly eleven o'clock, when that peculiar twilight seen in these regions stole gently over mountain and forest. The effect I cannot well describe—it appeared to partake largely of the spiritual." *

The other sketch is by the same accomplished traveller, drawn in a mountain region still more majestically grand than the Oural,—the great Altaian chain of Central Asia.

" In the afternoon I rode to the westward ten or twelve versts, which afforded me a fine view of the beautiful scenery on and beyond the Bouchtaima river. The effect of this scene was magnificent; as the sun was sinking immediately behind one of the high conical mountains, I beheld the great fiery orb descend nearly over the centre of this mighty cone, presenting a singular appearance. Presently its long deep shadow crept over the lower hills, and soon extended far into the plain, till at length the place on which I stood received its cold gray tone. The mountains to the right and left were still shining in his golden light; the snowy peaks of the Cholsoum appearing like frosted silver cut out against the clear blue sky. Gradually the shades of evening crept up the mountain-sides; one bright spot after another vanished, until at length all was in shadowy gray,

* Atkinson's *Siberia*, p. 57.

except the snowy peaks.   As the sun sank lower, a pale
rose tint spread over their snowy mantles, deepening to a
light crimson, and then a darker tone when the highest
shone out, as sparkling as a ruby; and at last, for only a
few minutes, it appeared like a crimson star." *

We come back from scenes so gorgeous, to quiet, homely
England.   How pleasant to the schoolboy, just infected
with the entomological mania, is an evening hour in June
devoted to "mothing!"   An hour before sunset he had
been seen mysteriously to leave home, carrying a cup
filled with a mixture of beer and treacle.   With this he
had bent his steps to the edge of a wood, and with a
painter's brush had bedaubed the trunks of several large
trees, much to the bewilderment of the woodman and his
dog.   Now the sun is going down like a glowing coal
behind the hill, and the youthful savant again seeks the
scene of his labours, armed with insect-net, pill-boxes,
and a bull's-eye lantern.   He pauses in the high-hedged
lane, for the bats are evidently playing a successful game
here, and the tiny gray moths are fluttering in and out of
the hedge by scores.   Watchfully now he holds the net;
there is one whose hue betokens a prize.   Dash!—yes!
it is in the muslin bag; and, on holding it up against
the western sky, he sees he has got one of the most
beautiful of the small moths,—the "butterfly emerald."
Yonder is a white form dancing backward and forward
with regular oscillation in the space of a yard, close over
the herbage.   That must be the "ghost-moth," surely!—

* Atkinson's *Siberia*, p. 221.

the very same ; and this is secured. Presently there comes
rushing down the lane, with headlong speed, one far larger
than the common set, and visible from afar by its whiteness. Prepare! Now strike! This prize, too, is won—
the "swallow-tail moth," a cream-coloured species, the
noblest and most elegant of its tribe Britain can boast.

But now the west is fading to a ruddy brown, and the
stars are twinkling overhead. He forsakes the lane, and
with palpitating heart stands before one of the sugared
trees. The light of his lantern is flashed full on the
trunk ; there are at least a dozen flutterers playing
around the temptation, and two or three are comfortably
settled down and sucking away. Most of them are mean-
looking, gray affairs ; but stay ! what is this approaching,
with its ten patches of rosy white on its olive wings ?
The lovely "peach-blossom," certainly : and now a pill-
box is over it, and it is safely incarcerated. He moves
cautiously to another tree. That tiny little thing, sitting
so fearlessly, is the beautiful "yellow underwing," a sweet
little creature, and somewhat of a rarity ; this is secured.
And now comes a dazzling thing, the "burnished brass,"
its wings gleaming with metallic refulgence in the lamp-
light ; but (*O infortunate puer !*) a nimble bat is before-
hand with you, and snaps up the glittering prize before
your eyes, dropping the brilliant wings on the ground for
your especial tantalisation. Well, never mind ! the bat is
an entomologist, too, and he is out mothing as well as
you ; therefore allow him his chance. Here is the "copper
underwing," that seems so unsuspicious that nothing

appears easier than to box it; but, lo! just when the trap is over it, it glides slily to one side, and leaves you in the lurch. But what is this moth of commanding size and splendid beauty, its hind wings of the most glowing crimson, like a fiery coal, bordered with black? Ha! the lovely "bride!" If you can net her, you have a beauty. A steady hand! a sure eye! Yes!—fairly bagged! And now you may contentedly go home through the dewy lanes, inhaling the perfume of the thorn and clematis, watching the twinkle of the lowly glowworms, and listening to the melody of the wakeful nightingales.

It is always interesting to compare with our own experience pictures of parallel scenes and seasons in other and diverse lands, drawn by those who had an open eye for the poetical and beautiful in nature, though not in all cases strictly naturalists. Here is a night scene from the summit of the Niesen, a peak of the Central Alps, nearly 8000 feet above the sea level:—

"I would gladly give my reader an idea of the solemn scenery of these elevated regions, during the calm hours of a summer night. As to sounds they are but few; at least, when the air is still. The vicinity of man, productive in general of anything but repose, has caused almost profound silence to reign among these wilds, where once the cautious tread of the bear rustled nightly among the dry needles of the pine forest, and the howl of the wolf re-echoed from the waste. As I stood upon an elevated knoll wide of the châlet, through whose interstices gleamed the fire over which my companions were amusing themselves, my ear was struck from time to time by an abrupt and indistinct sound from the upper parts of the mountain ; probably caused by the crumbling rock, or the fall of rubbish brought down by the cascades. An equally dubious and sudden sound would occasionally rise from the deep valley beneath ; but else nothing fell upon the ear, but the monotonous murmur of the mountain torrent working its way over stock and rock in the depth of the ravine. The moon barely lighted up the wide pastures sufficiently to distinguish their extent or the objects sprinkled upon them. Here and there a tall bark-less pine stood conspicuously forward on the verge of the dark belt of forest, with its bleached trunk and fantastic branches glistening in the moonshine." *

I have noticed the peculiar silence of a mountain summit by night in the tropics, and this far more absolute and striking than that alluded to by Latrobe. I was spending a night in a lonely house on one of the Liguanea mountains in Jamaica, and was impressed with the very peculiar stillness ; such a total absence of sounds as 1 had never experienced before : no running water was near ; there was not a breath of wind ; no bird or reptile moved ; no insect hummed ; it was an oppressive stillness, as if the silence could be felt.

But at lower levels in tropical countries night is not characterised by silence. Strange and almost unearthly sounds strike the ear of one benighted in the forests of Jamaica. Some of these are the voices of nocturnal

* Latrobe's *Alpenstock*, p. 135.

birds, the rapid articulations of the nightjars, the monotonous hoot, or shriek, or wail of the owls, the loud
impatient screams of the *Aramus.* But besides these,
there are some which are produced by reptiles. The
gecko creeps stealthy and cat-like from his hollow tree, and
utters his harsh cackle; and other lizards are believed to
add to the concert of squeaks and cries. And then there
come from the depth of the forest-glooms sounds like the
snoring of an oppressed sleeper, but louder; or like the
groaning and working of a ship's timbers in a heavy gale
at sea. These are produced by great tree-frogs, of uncouth
form, which love to reside in the sheathing leaves of parasitic plants, always half full of cool water. These reptiles
are rarely seen; but the abundance and universality of the
sounds, in the lower mountain-woods, prove how numerous they must be. Occasionally I have heard other
strange sounds, as, in particular, one lovely night in June,
when lodging at a little lone cottage on a mountain-
side, in the midst of the woods. About midnight, as I
sat at the open window, there came up from every part of
the moonlit forest below, with incessant pertinacity, a clear
shrill note, so like the voice of a bird, and specially so like
that of the solemn solitaire, that it might easily be mistaken for it, but for the inappropriate hour, and the
locality. Like that charming bird-voice, it was beautifully trilled or shaken; and like it, the individual voices
were not in the same key. Listening to the mingled
sounds, I could distinguish two particularly prominent,
which seemed to answer each other in quick but regular

alternation; and between their notes, there was the difference of exactly a musical tone.

Darwin speaks of the nocturnal sounds at Rio Janeiro: —" After the hotter days, it was delicious to sit quietly in the garden, and watch the evening pass into night. Nature, in these climes, chooses her vocalists from more humble performers than in Europe. A small frog of the genus *Hyla* [*i. e.*, of the family *Hyladæ*, the tree-frogs already alluded to], sits on a blade of grass about an inch above the surface of the water, and sends forth a pleasing chirp; when several are together, they sing in harmony on different notes. . . . . Various cicadæ and crickets at the same time keep up a ceaseless shrill cry, but which, softened by the distance, is not unpleasant. Every evening, after dark, this great concert commenced; and often have I sat listening to it, until my attention has been drawn away by some curious passing insect." *

Edwards, in his very interesting voyage up the Amazon, heard one night a bell-like note, which he eagerly concluded to be the voice of the famed bell-bird. But on asking his Indian attendants what it was that was " gritando," he was told that it was a toad,—" everything that sings by night is a toad !"

I doubt much whether the voice first referred to in the following extract ought not to be referred to the same reptilian agency:—

" During our ride home, [in Tobago,] I was startled by hearing what I fully imagined was the whistle of a steam-

* *Naturalist's Voyage*, (ed. 1852,) p. 29.

engine; but I was informed it was a noise caused by a beetle that is peculiar to Tobago. It is nearly the size of a man's hand, and fixing itself against a tree, it commences a kind of drumming noise, which gradually quickens to a whistle, and at length increases in shrillness and intensity, till it almost equals a railroad-whistle. It was so loud that, when standing full twenty yards from the tree where it was in operation, the sound was so shrill, that you had to raise your voice considerably to address your neighbour. The entomological productions of the tropics struck me as being quite as astonishing in size and nature as the botanical or zoological wonders. There is another beetle, called the razor-grinder, that imitates the sound of a knife-grinding machine so exactly, that it is impossible to divest one's self of the belief that one is in reality listening to some 'needy knife-grinder,' who has wandered out to the tropical wilds on spec." *

This latter was pretty certainly not a beetle proper, but a *Cicada*,† an insect of another order; remarkable for its musical powers, even from the times of classical antiquity. These are doubtless sexual sounds; the serenades of the wooing cavaliers, who, as Mr Kirby humorously says,—

"Formosam resonare docent Amaryllida sylvas."

A friend who has resided in Burmah informs me that

---

* Sullivan's *Rambles in North and South America*, p. 307.

† Dr Hancock has made out the "razor-grinder" of Surinam to be the *Cicada clarisona.*

there at midnight the stranger is often startled by the
loud voice of a species of gecko, which is frequently
found in the houses. Its cry is exceedingly singular, and
resembles the word " tooktay," pronounced clearly and distinctly as if spoken by a human tongue. It is a source
of much alarm to the natives of India who accompany
Europeans to that country ; as they believe that the bite
of the little lizard is invariably fatal.

None of these sounds can compare in terrible effect
with the deafening howls that penetrate the forests of
Guiana after night has fallen,—the extraordinary vocal
performances of the alouattes or howling-monkeys. They
go in troops, and utter their piercing cries, which Humboldt affirms can be heard in a clear atmosphere at the
distance of two miles, in a strange concord, which seems
the result of discipline, and incomparably augments the
effect. The same traveller informs us that occasionally
the voices of other animals are added to the concert ; the
roarings of the jaguar and puma, and the shrill cries
of alarmed birds. "It is not always in a fine moonlight, but more particularly at the time of storms and
violent showers, that this tumult among the wild beasts
occurs."

I linger on these tropical pictures, where nature appears under aspects so different from those of our clime.
Here is another on the Amazon :—" No clouds obscured
the sky, and the millions of starry lights, that in this
clime render the moon's absence of little consequence,
were shining upon us in their calm, still beauty. The

stream where we were anchored was narrow; tall trees drooped over the water, or mangroves shot out their long finger-like branches into the mud below. Huge bats were skimming past; night-birds were calling in strange voices from the tree-tops; fire-flies darted their mimic lightnings; fishes leaped above the surface, flashing in the starlight; the deep, sonorous baying of frogs came up from distant marshes; and loud plashings inshore suggested all sorts of nocturnal monsters." *

Yet another, by the same pleasant writer, on the banks of the same mighty river:—" The flowers that bloomed by day have closed their petals, and, nestled in their leafy beds, are dreaming of their loves. A sister host now take their place, making the breezes to intoxicate with perfume, and exacting homage from bright, starry eyes. A murmur, as of gentle voices, floats upon the air. The moon darts down her glittering rays, till the flower-enamelled plain glistens like a shield; but in vain she strives to penetrate the denseness, except some fallen tree betrays a passage. Below, the tall tree-trunk rises dimly through the darkness. Huge moths, those fairest of the insect world, have taken the places of the butterflies, and myriads of fire-flies never weary in their torchlight dance. Far down the road comes on a blaze, steady, streaming like a meteor. It whizzes past, and for an instant the space is illumined, and dewy jewels from the leaves throw back the radiance. It is the lantern-fly, seeking what he himself knows best, by the fiery guide upon his head.

* Edwards's *Voyage up the Amazon,* p. 27.

The air of the night-bird's wing fans your cheek, or you are startled by his mournful note, ' wac-o-row, wac-o-row,' sounding dolefully—by no means so pleasantly as our whip-poor-will. The armadillo creeps carelessly from his hole, and, at slow place, makes for his feeding ground ; the opossum climbs stealthily up the tree, and the little ant-cater is out pitilessly marauding."[*]

Dr Livingstone has sketched the following pleasing picture of a midnight in the very heart of Africa; but romantic as the region is, it lacks the gorgeousness of the South American forest :—

" We were close to the reeds, and could listen to the strange sounds which we often heard there. By day I had seen water-snakes putting up their heads and swimming about. There were great numbers of others, which had made little spoors all over the plains in search of the fishes, among the tall grass of these flooded prairies ; curious birds, too, jerked and wriggled among these reedy masses, and we heard human-like voices and unearthly sounds, with splash, guggle, jupp, as if rare fun were going on in their uncouth haunts. At one time, something came near us, making a splashing like that of a canoe or hippopotamus : thinking it to be the Makololo, we got up, listened, and shouted ; then discharged a gun several times, but the noise continued without intermission for an hour."[†]

If the sounds of night possess a romantic interest for

---

[*] Edwards's *Voyage up the Amazon*, p. 30.
[†] Livingstone's *Africa*, p. 167.

C

the naturalist, so do those animal flames with which it is
illuminated,—

> "Stars of the earth, and diamonds of the night."

Mr Kirby, the most accomplished of entomologists,
speaks in rapturous terms of our own homely little glow-
worm. "If," says he, "living, like me, in a district where
it is rarely met with, the first time you saw this insect
chanced to be, as it was in my case, one of those delightful evenings which an English summer seldom yields,
when not a breeze disturbs the balmy air, and 'every
sense is joy,' and hundreds of these radiant worms, stud-
ding their mossy couch with wild effulgence, were presented to your wondering eye in the course of a quarter
of a mile,—you could not help associating with the name
of glow-worm the most pleasing recollections." *

It is, however, in America that these "diamonds of the
night" are observed to advantage. In Canada I have
seen the whole air, for a few yards above the surface of a
large field, completely filled with fire-flies on the wing,
thicker than stars on a winter's night. The light is
redder, more candle-like, than that of our glow-worm, and,
being in each individual alternately emitted and concealed,
and each of the million tiny flames performing its part in
mazy aerial dance, the spectacle was singularly beautiful.

A sight in every respect similar, though doubtless dependent on a different species, occurred to me in ascending the river Alabama from the Gulf of Mexico. As the
steamer passed booming along under the shadow of night,

---

* *Introduction to Entomology.* Letter xxv.

the broad belt of reeds which margined the river was
thronged with myriads of dancing gleams, and the air was
filled with what looked like thousands of shooting stars.

Beautiful, however, as these spectacles were, I had not
known what insects could effect in the way of illumi-
nation till I visited Jamaica. There, in the gorgeous
night of a tropical forest, I saw them in their glory. In
the glades and dells that open here and there from a
winding mountain-road cut through the tall woods, I have
delighted to linger and see the magnificent gloom lighted
up by multitudes of fire-flies of various species, peculiarities in whose luminosity—of colour, intensity, and inter-
mittence—enabled me to distinguish each from others. I
delighted to watch and study their habits in these lonely
spots, while the strange sounds, snorings, screeches, and
ringings of nocturnal reptiles and insects, already described, were coming up from every part of the deep forest
around, imparting to the scene a character which seemed
as if it would suit the weird hunter of German fable.

There are two kinds in particular, of larger size than
usual, which are very conspicuous. One of these * is
more vagrant than the other, shooting about with a
headlong flight, and rarely observed in repose. Its light
appears of a rich orange hue when seen abroad; but it
frequently flies in at open windows, and, when examined
under candle-light, its luminosity is yellow: when held
in the fingers, the light is seen to fill the hinder part of
the body with dazzling effulgence, which intermits its

* *Pygolampis xanthophotis.*

intensity. The other * is more commonly noticed resting on a twig or leaf, where it gradually increases the intensity of its light till it glows like a torch; then as gradually, it allows it to fade to a spark, and become extinct; in about a minute, however, it begins to appear again, and gradually increases to its former blaze; then fades again: strongly reminding the beholder of a revolving light at sea. The hue of this is a rich yellow-green; and sometimes a rover of the former species will arrest its course, and, approaching one of these on a leaf, will play around it, when the intermingling of the orange and green lights has a most charming effect.

In the lowland pastures of the same beauteous island, there is another insect † abundant, of much larger dimensions, which displays both red and green light. On the upper surface of the thorax, there are two oval tubercles, hard and transparent, like "bull's-eye" lights let into a ship's deck; these are windows out of which shines a vivid green luminousness, which appears to fill the interior of the chest. Then on the under surface of the body, at the base of the abdomen, there is a transverse orifice in the shelly skin, covered with a delicate membrane, which glows with a strong ruddy light, visible, however, only when the wing-cases are expanded. During the dark nights it is most interesting to mark these large beetles flying along over the herbage at the edges of the woods and in the pastures: the red glare, like that of a lamp, alternately flashing upon the beholder and concealed,

---

* *Photuris versicolor.*   † *Pyrophorus noctilucus.*

according as the insect turns its body in flight, but the ruddy reflection on the grass beneath being constantly visible, as the animal leisurely pursues its course. Now and then the green light from the upper "bull's-eye," which seems to be under the insect's control, is displayed, and then again the mingling of the two complementary colours, red and green, in the evolutions of flight, is indescribably beautiful.

I have gazed upon these changing lights, flitting here and there in the openings of the dense forest, during the stillness of the night, till I could scarcely divest myself of the persuasion that human intelligence and human will were concerned in their production. Thoughts of the once happy Indians, that enjoyed a simple life in these charming glades before Columbus discovered their retreats, would then crowd up ; and it required but little imagination to fancy myself surrounded by hundreds of the aborigines, holding their revels under the coolness of the night-season, as of old.

II

HARMONIES.

MODERN science has shewn that animals and plants are not scattered promiscuously over the world, but placed in spheres according to well-defined laws. A few kinds seem, indeed, cosmopolitan, but the great majority have a limited range, each inhabiting its own region, and each, in very many cases, replaced in other similar regions by species more or less closely allied and yet distinct. And more than this; that there are predominant forms of life in every region, so entirely governing the physiognomy of the landscape, that an accomplished naturalist, on being suddenly set down in any part of the earth's surface, would instantly tell in what region he was, by an examination of a few plants or animals.

The statistics on which this science of the geographical distribution of life is built up do not come within my present scope, which is to present the poetic side of nature ; but there is a collateral aspect of the same truths worthy of consideration, namely, the harmony which subsists between all the parts of a natural-history picture. If we look with interest on the lion, the jaguar, the zebra, the python, at the Zoological Gardens, or the palms, and bananas, and bamboos in the con-

servatories at Kew; how vastly more interesting would
it be to behold each in its own home; surrounded by all
the accessories of surface-form, of atmospheric phenomena, of vegetation, of animal life, which properly belong
to it, and without which it is merely an isolated object.
Let us select a few examples.

To see the ariel gazelle, accompany a troop of Bedouin
Arabs across the great Syrian desert. Grand and awe-
inspiring in its boundless immensity, unearthly and ocean-
like, the eye shrinks from contemplating the empty, cheer-
less solitude, and vainly wanders round for some object
which may relieve the sense of utter loneliness and desolation. Across the plain, far away towards the west, where
the fiery glow of the setting sun brings out their forms
in dark relief, a long interrupted line of columns is seen
stretching away below the horizon; while, as the troop
approaches, prostrate heaps of ruins appear, groups of
broken shafts and bases of columns, huge platforms of
stone, and fallen capitals, while here and there a solitary
monumental pillar rears itself above the rest in solemn
majesty. At the end of the sandy plain, the eye at
length rests upon the lofty colonnades of the Temple of
the Sun, encompassed by a dark elevated mass of ruined
buildings; but beyond, all around, right and left, as far
as the eye can reach, extends the vast level naked flat of
the great Desert, over which the eye runs in every direction, exploring the boundless horizon, without discovering
a human being, or a vestige that tells of existing human
life. Naked, solitary, unlimited space extends around,

where man never enjoys the refreshment of a shadow, or rests his limbs under cover of a dwelling. There is a deep blue aerial haze spread over the surface, but the distant horizon is nevertheless clear and sharply defined: not an eminence rises to break the monotonous flat, higher than the slight hillocks of sand sprinkled with a withered herbage, which are undiscerned except in their immediate proximity, while along the edge extends a large district covered with salt, distinguished from the rest by its peculiar colour.

Suddenly a herd of gazelles is seen playfully bounding over the sandy mounds, and displaying their elegant forms, and striking though simple colours, and the inimitable grace and beauty of all their actions. The Bedouins seize their lances, the travellers draw their pistols, and, distributing themselves into a wide circle, endeavour to encompass the herd. They seem heedless and unconscious for a time, and then, as the intruders approach, they hold up their beautiful heads, toss their curved and taper horns, and trot up into a closer group. Then, seeing their enemies spurring their steeds from behind the sandy hillocks all round them, they suddenly shoot away with the rapidity of the wind, easily dash through the loosely-formed circle, and, though lances are cast, and pistol-shots resound, unharmed they quickly distance the fleetest of their pursuers; turn and gaze, as if in mingled curiosity and contempt, and then away again, bounding over the tawny sand with an agility that seems rather that of flight than of running.

Or would you see the hyena, where he feels most at home, surrounded by scenes and circumstances most congenial to his habits? Then plod your weary way still further across the sands, and pause not till you encamp amid the gorgeous remains of that ancient City of the Wilderness,

> " Whose temples, palaces,—a wondrous dream,
> That passes not away,—for many a league
> Illumine yet the desert."

There sit down alone amid the ruined fanes lighted up by the setting sun, and watch the approach of night, just at the breaking up of the long dry season. Everywhere around are the remains of the glorious city; walls, and gateways, and columns of polished granite of rosy hue, or of marble that gleams like snow in the bright moonlight; many standing in their desolateness, but many more prostrate and half-buried in the drifted sand. Some of the pillars are but dimly seen in the gloomy shadow of the lofty walls, others stand out boldly and brightly in the soft moonbeams, while here and there a brilliant gleam slants down through the windows of a ruined edifice, and illumines the deep and delicate sculpture of a fallen capital, or spreads over a heap of disjointed stones. Under yon dark and gloomy portal the eye wanders over distant funereal towers crowning the eminences, the noble gateway of the grand avenue, and lines of columns gradually lost in the distance.

But while you gaze, there is a change. The breeze, which had lifted the sand in playful eddies, drops to perfect calmness. Black clouds are collecting over the mountain range that forms the distant horizon. The moon is obscured, and the whole heaven becomes black with tempest. A hurricane suddenly sweeps through the ruined palaces, and fills the whole air with a dense fog of blinding sand. Then a flash of forked lightning shoots between the columns, illuminating them for an instant, and is instantaneously followed by a bursting crash of thunder, which makes the tottering fanes tremble, and huge drops of warm rain, like blood-drops, are spattering the stones. The rain now comes down in one universal deluge, flooding the floors, and pouring off from the old marble platforms in cataracts. Flash follows flash in one continuous blaze of blinding light, bringing out the grim marble towers and pillars against the black clouds of midnight with an awfully sublime distinctness; and crash after crash, and peal after peal of thunder are blending into one uninterrupted roll.

But amidst the deep roar rises from the gaunt heaps of stone an unearthly sound, like the laugh of a demon. Again, the cackling mirth echoes along the ruined halls, as if exulting in the wild war of the elements, and in the desolation around. Lo! from out of yon low arch, in the Place of Tombs, gleam two fiery eyes, and forth stalks into the lightning the fell hyena. With bristling mane and grinning teeth, the obscene monster glares at you, and warns you to secure a timely retreat. Another appears, bearing in its jaws a loathsome human skull, which it has found in the caravan track. You

shudder as you hear the bones crack and grind between the powerful teeth, and gladly shrink away from the repulsive vicinity.

The home of the great Siberian stag is among the most magnificent scenery in the world. Search for him amidst the bold precipices of the Altaian chain, where enormous mountains of primeval formation are split and cleft into the wildest ravines, and where cascades fall in snowy foam down the terrible gorges bounded by sheer cliffs that almost meet far overhead, and shut out the light of heaven. Here is a little dell, embosomed in the mountains, as full of flowers as an English garden,—irises and columbines, primroses and peonies, of many rich hues and of kinds unfamiliar to us, and of a luxuriant growth which reaches up to a man's shoulders ;—then a tiny basin of clear water, intensely black from its unruffled stillness and its fathomless depth. Now the traveller crosses a sharp ridge, crowned with colossal needles of naked granite, where the furious gale, shrieking and howling through the crevices, threatens to hurl horse and man a thousand fathoms down ;—then he passes into a forest where not a breath waves the tops of the ancient cedars.

It is a region where animal life is not very abundant, but where the framework of the solid earth itself stands revealed in unrivalled gorgeousness. The cliffs are here of crimson or purple porphyry, as brilliant as the dyed products of the loom, there of dark-red granite seamed with thick veins of pure rose-coloured quartz, transparent

as glass. Here a vast, uncouth column of black basalt
rears its fused cylinders from the midst of a narrow
ravine; and here a vast precipice appears of white marble,
as pure as that of Paros. Rocks of all hues, bright red,
purple, yellow, green; of all combinations of colours,
white with purple spots, white with blue veins, brown
with pale green streaks, pale crimson with veins of black
and 'yellow, are scattered about in unheeded confusion;
while, above all, the rich and splendid jasper rises in
enormous masses, as if it were the vilest rock, yet glittering in gorgeous beauty,—mountains of gems. Here is
one of a dark sea-green, with cream-coloured veins; there
a mass of deep violet; and here a ribbon-stripe, marked
irregularly with alternate bands of red, brown, and green;
and yonder is a huge heap of shattered blocks of the
richest plum-purple, transmitting the light in sparkling
lustre through their translucent substance, as they lie
where they have been tumbled down from their beds by
the force of the torrent, and presenting the most agreeable contrasts between their own deep, rich, imperial hue,
and that of the yellow-green moss that springs in cushion-
like tufts from their angles and crevices.

You pursue the little mountain stream, through the
thick mass of tangled cedars and fallen rocks, slippery
and treacherous to the unwary foot, wading from stone
to stone through many a narrow gorge, till there bursts
before you a beautiful cascade, that comes bounding down
in three leaps from a height of sixty feet. The water is
white and sparkling as it plunges over the purple preci-

pice; the lowest fall spreading out like a fan of thin gauze, hanging over the rocky wall, and screening the black cavern behind.

With difficulty you climb through a ravine to the top of the waterfall, and follow the stream for a few hundred yards higher, till you find its origin in a little mountain tarn, deeply embosomed amidst perpendicular walls of rock, with no opening or outlet except the narrow cleft by which the tiny stream escapes. How beautiful is the little quiet lake, clear as crystal, but of great depth, and hence of a deep green hue, receiving and absorbing the sun's rays in its profundity, like a floor of polished beryl! And there on the opposite precipice, gazing down into the distant water, stand in antlered majesty three noble stags. Magnificent creatures! here they are at home, dwelling amidst this grandeur, the very presiding *genii loci*.*

We are familiar, by report, with that great bird of mighty wing, the lämmergeyer or bearded eagle, whose red eye is a fair index of its cruel ferocity, that preys not only on birds and quadrupeds, but even on children. We commonly associate this proud and savage bird with the crags of the Alps, but it is spread over the whole central line of Europe and Asia, wherever lofty and rugged mountain-chains arise. Mr Atkinson speaks of having shot one in a scene which for savage grandeur surpasses anything in the Alps. It was among the Alatou moun-

* Every feature in this picture is in Atkinson's *Siberia;* in the grouping only have I taken any liberty.

tains in Chinese Tartary, where the river Cora breaks out grandly into the plain, emerging from a rent in the lofty mountain-chain, where the rocks rise several thousand feet. "As I determined," says this intrepid traveller, "to explore this mighty gorge, and sketch the scenery, our horses were left at the mouth of the chasm, it being impossible to ride up the gorge; and track there was none. We had to climb over huge masses of rock; some we were obliged to creep under, they being much too high to climb over: in other plac_s, bushes and plants were growing in tropical luxuriance. A scramble of five hours brought me to a point I could not pass; here the rocks rose quite perpendicularly from the boiling flood, making ascent to the summit impossible. Nor can this be accomplished either in spring or summer; while in winter the chasm is so deep in snow—there being no *aoul* [hamlet] within several hundred versts—that it would be madness to attempt it at that time; thus these grand and wild scenes are closed to man, and the tiger remains undisturbed in his lair, the bear in his den, and the maral and wild deer range the wooded parts unmolested. A very large bearded eagle was found amongst these crags, which I shot. After making several sketches, I returned to the horses, and ascended towards the great plateau between the mountains, where I arrived in the evening, tired and hungry. The dark clouds which had obscured the mountains cleared off, and gave me a most splendid view of the Actou, which runs up towards the Ilia; the snowy peaks shining like rubies in the setting sun, while all

below them was blue and purple, with the shades of evening creeping over the lower range.   In the foreground
was my *yourt* [hut], with the Kirghis cooking the sheep
in a large cauldron, while the camels and horses were lying
and standing around.   Tired as I was, I could not resist
sketching the scene, which will ever be impressed upon
my memory, as well as the splendid sunset over the
Steppe." *

The describer, it must be remembered, is an artist in
search of the picturesque.   His eye was mainly on the
scenery; but surely the kingly eagle, seated in lone
majesty on that craggy throne of his, and surveying with
haughty eye his superb domain, was a very grand element
in the picture.

Again; let us look at Darwin and Captain Fitzroy
threading their perilous way from the Atlantic to the
Pacific through the Beagle Channel.   It is a straight
passage, not more than two miles wide, but a hundred
and twenty miles long, bounded on each side by mountains rising in unbroken sweep from the water's edge,
and terminating in sharp and jagged points three thousand feet high.   The mountain-sides for half their height
are clothed with a dense forest, almost wholly composed
of a single kind of tree, the sombre-leafed southern
beech.   The upper line of this forest is well defined, and
perfectly horizontal; below, the drooping twigs actually
dip into the sea.   Above the forest line the crags are
covered by a glittering mantle of perpetual snow, and

* *Siberia*, p. 574.

cascades are pouring their foaming waters through the woods into the Channel below. In some places magnificent glaciers extend from the mountain-side to the water's edge. " It is scarcely possible to imagine anything more beautiful than the beryl-like blue of these glaciers, and especially as contrasted with the dead-white of the upper expanse of snow." Heavy and sudden squalls come down from the ravines, raising the sea, and covering it with foam, like a dark plain studded with patches of drifted snow, which the furious wind is ever lifting in sheets of driving spray. The albatross with its wide-spread wings comes careering up the Channel against the wind, and screams as if it were the spirit of the storm. The surf breaks fearfully against the narrow shores, and mounts to an immense height against the rocks. Yonder is a promontory of blue ice, the sheer end of a glacier ; the wind and sea are telling upon it, and now down plunges a huge mass, which breaking into fragments, bespreads the angry sea with mimic icebergs.

In the midst of this war of the elements, appear a pair of sperm-whales. They swim within stone's-cast of the shore, spouting at intervals, and jumping in their unwieldy mirth clean out of the waters, falling back on their huge sides, and splashing the sea high on every hand, with a sound like the reverberation of a distant broadside.[*] How appropriate a place for these giants of the deep to appear ! and how immensely must their presence have enhanced the wild grandeur of that romantic scene !

* Darwin's *Voyage*, chap. x.

We turn from this inhospitable strait to a region if possible even more forbidding, more stern, more grandly awful; one of the passes of the mighty Andes, the Cordilleras of Peru.

"We now came," says a traveller, "to the Jaula, or Cage, from which the pass takes its name, where we took up our quarters for the night, under the lee of a solid mass of granite upwards of thirty feet square, with the clear, beautiful heavens for our canopy. Well may this place be called a cage. To give a just idea of it would be next to impossible, for I do not think a more wild or grander scene in nature could possibly exist; nevertheless I shall attempt a description. The foaming river, branching off into different channels formed by huge masses of granite lying in its course, ran between two gigantic mountains of about one thousand five hundred feet high, and not more than two hundred yards distant from each other; so that to look up at the summits of either, we had to lay our heads completely back on our shoulders. Behind us, these tremendous mountains met in a point, round which we had just passed, but now appeared as one mountain, closing our view in a distance of not more than four or five hundred yards; before was the mighty Cordillera, a mass of snow, appearing to block up further progress. Thus were we completely shut up in a den of mighty mountains; to look up either way— before, behind, right, or left—excited astonishment, awe, and admiration. Huge masses of granite, that had fallen from the awful heights above, lay scattered about, and

D

formed our various shelters for the night. The torrent, which now had become very formidable, rushed down with fury, bounding and leaping over the rugged rocks which lay in its course, keeping up a continued foam and roar close to our wild resting-place. The mules were straying about picking up the scanty shrubs; and our wild, uncouth-looking peons were assembled round a fire under the lee of a large rock, which altogether rendered it a scene most truly wild and surprising."*

Can animal life habitually exist in these awful solitudes? Is it possible that any creature can make its home amidst this waste of stark granite and everlasting ice? Yes; the guanaco, or Peruvian camel, delights to dwell here, and is as truly characteristic of the region as the Arabian camel is of the sandy desert. It snuffs the thin air in its wild freedom, and specially delights in those loftier ridges which the Peruvians term punas, where the elements appear to have concentrated all their sternness. It was the sudden appearance of a guanaco, on a lofty peak above the party, that gave occasion to the above description. The peons, with their dogs, had pursued it, and having overtaken it, had dragged down the carcase, and were now roasting its flesh over their camp-fire.

The wild reindeer, in his native snows, is seldom visited by civilised man; and it is a thing to be remembered during life to have seen him there. Climb the precipices of that rugged mountain-chain that forms the backbone of Norway; cross plain after plain, each more dreary than

* Brand's *Travels in Peru*, p. 102.

the last, as you reach a higher and a yet higher elevation, till you stand, in the sharp and thin air, catching your breath on the edge of the loftiest, the wildest, and most barren of those snowy fjelds. The highest hut you have left far below. You will spend the day and the night, (such night as an unsetting sun allows,) too, in traversing its lonely waste, and you will see neither habitation · nor human being, nor trace of human works; no tree, nor shrub, nor heath, nor even earth; nothing but hard, bare barren, lichen-clad rocks, or enormous fields and patches of snow. Here and there a little reindeer-moss fills the crevices of the shattered rocks, and this is all the verdure of this wilderness of rocks and snow. You must plunge through the soft snow above your knees for many a weary mile; this is very fatiguing: at other times, through bogs of moss and melted snow; and then, perhaps, through a wide torrent, whose waters reach to your middle. Now you have to cross a ridge of sharp rock, which stands like an island out of the snow, the sharp edges of the granite cutting into the leather of your shoes, now completely soft and sodden with the melted snow. Now you have to descend a steep snow-mountain; this is very difficult, and not without considerable danger if you are unaccustomed to it. As every one may not know what the descent of a Norwegian snow-mountain is, it may be well to explain it. Imagine a very steep mountain covered with deep, never-melting snow, perhaps five or six hundred feet in height, the side presenting a bank of snow as steep as the roof of a house. To try whether the descent is practicable, the guide places a large stone at the top, gives it a gentle push, and watches its progress. If the snow is soft enough to impede its pace, and allow it to form a furrow for itself and glide gradually down, the descent is pronounced feasible; if, on the contrary, the snow is not soft enough for this, but the stone descends in successive bounds, it is pronounced too dangerous to attempt. It is quite wonderful to see the rapidity and ease with which the guide will shoot down these snow-mountains, like an arrow from a bow. Placing both feet together, with nothing in his hands to steady him, but bearing your heavy provision-box and blankets at his back, down he goes, his pace accelerating every second till he reaches the bottom, and enveloped all the way down in a wreath of snow, which he casts off on both sides of his feet and legs as if it had been turned up by a plough, and marking his track by a deep furrow. You follow much more slowly, holding the barrel of your gun across you, while the butt end is plunged deep into the snow to steady you, and to slacken your pace. If you lean forward too much, you are in danger of going down head over heels; if you lean back too much, your feet will slip from under you, and the same result will inevitably follow, and you will have a roll of, perhaps, some hundred feet, without a chance of stopping till you reach the bottom; by no means pleasant even on snow, and especially when the snow-hill ends (as is not unfrequently the case) in a rocky precipice, to roll over which must be certain death.

Suddenly, rounding a rocky cliff, the guide makes a quick movement with his hand, and whispers the single word "reins!" pointing as he crouches down to three black specks on the white mountain-side full two miles off. Now all is excitement. The telescope distinctly makes them out,—an old buck above, as guard and watcher, a doe and her calf a little lower down. What caution now is necessary in stalking the noble game! There is a broad valley to cross full in their view; you must creep low, and in line, concealing your rifles, lest the flashing of the sun on the barrels betray you, and not speaking except in the gentlest whisper. The valley is securely crossed; there is a brawling torrent to be waded, and you will be among the rocks.

Has the buck winded you? He springs to his feet, shakes his spreading antlers, and sniffs the air, then walks leisurely up the hill-side, followed by his family, and all disappear over the rocky ridge.

Now is the time for speed! Up, up the hill, scramble under, over, through the great loose fragments, but noiselessly, silently, for the game are probably not far off. Now you are at the rock over which you saw them go. The guide peeps cautiously over, and beckons. You, too, peep, and there they are, all unsuspecting, a hundred yards off. The old guide now lies down on the snow, and wriggles along from rock to rock to get round, whence he may drive them toward you. The deer are still busy munching the moss, which they scrape from beneath the snow.

A few minutes of breathless excitement. The hunter shews himself on yonder peak. The noble buck trots majestically towards you, his head thrown up, and his fine horns spreading far on each side of his back. He stops—sniffs—starts; but too late! the rifle-ball has sped, and his hoofs are kicking up the blood-stained snow in dying convulsions.*

In our homely sheep, it must be confessed, the utilitarian element prevails over the poetic; but with the burrell, or wild sheep, of the Himalaya Peaks, the case is far otherwise. Twice the size of an English ram, with horns of such vastness, that into the cavity of those which lie bleaching on the frozen rocks, the fox sometimes creeps for shelter,† dwelling in the most inaccessible regions, the snow-covered ranges of the loftiest mountains in the world, or the mighty spurs that jut out from them, shy and jealous of the approach of man, whom it discerns at an immense distance,—the burrell is considered as the first of Himalayan game animals, and the killing of it the *ne plus ultra* of Himalayan shooting.

How grand are the regions in which it dwells! An enthusiastic and successful sportsman furnishes us with the following vivid picture of the wild sheep and its home :—

"We started early to reach the source of the mighty Ganges. The opposite bank being the best ground for burrell, we were in great hopes that we might find sufficient snow left to enable us to cross the river; but the

---

* See "Notes on Norway," by A. C. Smith. in the *Zoologist* for 1851.
† Hooker, *Himal. Jour.*, i. p. 243

snow that at times bridges over the stream was gone. The walking was bad, for in all the small tributary streams were stones and rocks incrusted with ice, which made them very difficult to cross. On the opposite side we saw immense flocks of burrell, but there was no getting at them.

" At last, the great glacier of the Ganges was reached, and never can I forget my first impressions when I beheld it before me in all its savage grandeur. The glacier, thickly studded with enormous loose rocks and earth, is about a mile in width, and extends upwards many miles, towards an immense mountain, covered with perpetual snow down to its base, and its glittering summit piercing the very skies, rising 21,000 feet above the level of the sea. The chasm in the glacier, through which the sacred stream rushes forth into the light of day, is named the Cow's Mouth, and is held in the deepest reverence by all the Hindoos ; and the regions of eternal frost in its vicinity are the scenes of many of their most sacred mysteries. The Ganges enters the world no puny stream, but bursts forth from its icy womb, a river thirty or forty yards in breadth, of great depth and very rapid. A burrell was killed by a lucky shot across the river just at the mouth ; it fell backwards into the torrent, and was no more seen. Extensive as my travels since this day have been through these beautiful mountains, and amidst all the splendid scenery I have looked on, I can recall none so strikingly magnificent as the glacier of the Ganges." *

* Markham, *Shooting in the Himal.*, p. 57.

Again; if we wish to see the vastest of terrestrial animals, it is not within the bars of a travelling menagerie that we should look for him, nor in the barbaric pomp or domestic bondage of India, but in the noble forest-glens of Africa.

. Mr Pringle has drawn a graphic sketch of such a valley, two or three miles in length, surrounded by a wild and bewildering region, broken into innumerable ravines, incumbered with rocks, precipices, and impenetrable woods and jungles, among lofty and sterile mountains. The valley itself is a beautiful scene; it suddenly bursts on the view of the traveller as he emerges from a wooded defile. The slopes and sides are clothed with the succulent spek-boom;* the bottom is an expanded grassy savanna or meadow, beautifully studded with mimosas, thorns, and tall evergreens, sometimes growing singly, sometimes in clumps and groves of varying magnitude.

Foot-tracks deeply impressed in the soft earth are everywhere visible; paths, wide and well trodden, like military roads, have been opened up through the dense thorny forest, apparently impenetrable. Through one of these a numerous herd of elephants suddenly appears on the scene; the great bull-elephant, the patriarch of the herd, marches in the van, bursting through the jungle, as a bullock would through a field of hops, treading down the thorny brushwood, and breaking off with his proboscis the larger branches that obstruct the passage; the females and younger males follow in his wake in single file.

* *Postulacaria afra.*

Other herds are seen scattered over the valley as the
prospect opens ; some browsing on the juicy trees, others
reposing, and others regaling on the fresh roots of huge
mimosas which have been torn up ; while one immense
monster is amusing himself, as if it were but play to him,
with tearing up these great trees for his expectant family.
He digs with his stout tusks beneath the roots, now on
this side, now on that, now using one tusk, now the other,
prizing, and forcing away, and loosening the earth all
around, till at length with a tremendous pull of his twisted
proboscis, he tears up the reluctant tree, and inverting the
trunk amidst a shower of earth and stones, exposes the
juicy and tender rootlets to his hungry progeny.   Well
may the traveller say that a herd of elephants browsing
in majestic tranquillity amidst the wild magnificence of
an African landscape is a very noble sight, and one, of
which he will never forget the impression.*

Who has ever gazed upon the lion under conditions so
fitted to augment his terrible majesty, as those in which
the mighty hunter of South Africa was accustomed to
encounter him ?   Who of us would have volunteered to
be his companion, when night after night he watched in
the pit that he had dug beside the Massouey fountain in
the remote Bamangwato country ?   There is the lonely
pool, situated in the open valley, silent and deserted by
day, but marked with well-beaten tracks converging to its
margins from every direction ; tracks in which the footprints of elephants, rhinoceroses, giraffes, zebras, and

* *African Sketches.*

antelopes, are crossed and recrossed by those of the great padding paws of huge lions. The hunter observes the paths, and selecting a spot, digs a hole in the earth just large enough to allow him and his Hottentot attendant to lie down in. He places his bedding in it, and prepares to spend his nights there. About sunset he repairs to his strange bed, and, with the sparkling stars above him, and silence deep as death around him, he keeps his watch.

Soon the stillness is broken by many sounds. The terrible roar of a lion is heard in the distance; jackals are heard snorting and snarling over a carcase; a herd of zebras gallops up toward the fountain, but hesitates to approach; then a pack of wild dogs is heard chattering around. By and by, a heavy clattering of hoofs comes up the valley, and on sweeps a vast herd of wildebeest; the leader approaches the water, when the hunter's rifle sends a ball through him, and he falls dead on the bank.

The herd disperses in terror; and presently a lion utters an appalling roar from a bushy ridge just opposite, which is succeeded by a breathless silence.

A quarter of an hour elapses. A peculiar sound causes the hunter to lift his head, when he sees, on the opposite edge of the pool, a huge and majestic male lion, with a black mane which nearly sweeps the ground, standing over the dead wildebeest. He seems suspicious; and stooping to seize the carcase, drags it up the slope. Again the intrepid watcher points his trusty rifle, and the tawny monarch sinks to the shot. At length with a deep growl he rises, and limps away to a bushy cover, where he roars mournfully, and dies.

Or take him a few nights afterwards, when from the same pit he sees six lions together approach to drink. Six lions at midnight there! two men here! nothing between the parties but a little pool, which a ten minutes' walk would encircle! One of the lions detects the intruder, and, with her eye fixed upon him, creeps round the head of the fountain. What a moment of suspense! But once more the fatal ball speeds; and the too curious lioness, mortally wounded, bounds away with a howl, followed by her five companions in a cloud of dust.

Very different from such a scene is the gorgeous gloom of a Brazilian forest, where the wiry-haired sloth hangs from the branches, the toothless ant-eater breaks up with its hoofs the great earthy nests of the termites, and the armadillo burrows in the soil; where the capybara and the tapir rush to the water; where painted toucans cry to each other, golden-plumaged trogons sit on the topmost boughs, and sparkling humming-birds flit over the flowers; where beetles, like precious stones, crawl up the huge trunks, and butterflies of all brilliant hues fan the still and loaded air. Not like the small and pale or sombre-hued species that we see in the fields and gardens of Britain are these: their numbers are prodigious; their variety bewildering; many of them are adorned with the most splendid colours, and some of the finest are of immense size. Very characteristic of this region are the species of the genus *Morpho;* great butterflies larger

than a man's open hand, with the lower surface of the
wings adorned with a pearly iridescence, and concentric
rings, while their upper face is of an uniform azure, so
intensely lustrous that the eye cannot gaze upon it in the
sun without pain.

Solemn are those primeval labyrinths of giant trees,
tangled with ten thousand creepers, and roofed with lofty
arches of light foliage, diversified with masses of glorious
blossom of all rich hues; while from the borders of the
igaripes, or narrow canals that permeate the lower levels,
spring most elegant ferns, lowly sensitive mimosas, great
and fantastic herbaceous plants, marbled and spotted
arums, closely compacted fan-palms with spreading crowns,
and multitudes of other strange forms of vegetation in
an almost inconceivable profusion. The gigantic scale of
life strongly excites astonishment in these forests. In
Europe we associate flowers with herbs or shrubs, but
here we see trees of colossal height, in all the splendour
of bloom, which clothes the whole crown with its colour.

The traveller sees with delight, trees covered with
magnificent, large lilac, orange, crimson, or white
blossoms, contrasting beautifully with the surrounding
varied tints of green. After enjoying, with a restless
glance, this display of colours, he turns to the deep
shades which lie disclosed, solemn and mournful, between the gigantic trees on the wayside. The flame-
coloured raceme of a *tillandsia*, resembling an immense
pine-apple, glows like fire among the dark foliage.
Again attention is attracted by the charming orchids,

with most fantastic flowers, climbing up the straight
trunks of the trees, or picturesquely covering their
branches, which seldom shoot out from the trunk at a
less height than fifty to eighty feet from the ground.
From the fertility of the soil, the trees spring up so
densely, that, when young, their branches, not having
room to expand freely, strive to overtop one another.
The tillandsias nestle at the ramification of the smaller
branches, or upon excrescences, where they often grow to
an immense size, and have the appearance of an aloe, the
length of a man, hanging down gracefully from a giddy
height over the head of the passer-by.

Among the various plants which spring from the
branches or cling to the stems of the trees, are gray, moss-
like plants hanging down, not unlike horses' tails, from
the branches which support the orchids and tillandsias ;
or one might fancy them the long beards of these venerable giants of the forest, that have stood unbent beneath
the weight of a thousand years. Myriads of lianes hang
down to the ground, or are suspended in the air, several
inches thick, and not unfrequently the size of a man's
body, coated with bark like the branches of the trees.
But it is impossible for any one to conceive the fantastic
forms they assume, all interlaced and entangled : sometimes they depend like straight poles to the ground,
where striking root, they might, from their thickness, be
taken for trees ; at other times they resemble large loops
or rings, from ten to twenty feet in diameter, or are so
twisted that they look like cables. Sometimes they lace

the tree regularly from distance to distance; often they
embrace it so closely as to choke it, and cause the leaves
to fall off, so that it stretches out its dead gigantic arms
like branches of white coral, among the fresh verdure of
the forest,—a picture of death, surprising us in the
midst of the most blooming life: frequently they give
the old trunk a new covering of leaves, so that the
same tree appears clothed in several different kinds of
foliage.*

So, if space permitted, we might depict the brown
bear emerging from his winter retreat in the dark pine
forests of Scandinavia; or the white bear seated on a
solitary iceberg in the Polar Sea; or the whale spouting
in the same frost-bound waters, and pursued by the har-
poon of his relentless persecutors; or the moose imprisoned in the "yard" which he has himself formed by
treading down the successive snows in the lofty woods of
America; or the chamois upon the peaks of the Alps, with
the eagle sweeping over him as he gazes contemptuously
down on the jäger far below; or the patient camel toiling
along the unbounded waste of tawny sand; or the kangaroo
bounding over the Australian scrub; or the seal basking
in his rocky cavern, while the surf is dashing high on the
cliffs around; or the wild-duck reposing at the margin of
a smooth river, when the red light of evening is reflected
in the line left by the tall and almost meeting trees overhead; or a group of snow-white egrets standing motionless in the shallows of a reedy lake at dawn of day; or

* *Travels of Prince Adalbert in Brazil*, p. 15, *et seq.*

the petrel careering over the long waves in the midst of the wide ocean ; or the tiny cyprides and cyclopes disporting in the umbrageous groves of their world,—a tiny tide-pool hollowed out of a limestone rock by the action of the waves. These and many more combinations might be suggested ; and we shall surely see how incomparably is the interest which attaches to each form enhanced, by associating with it those accompaniments and conditions of being, in which alone it is at home.

III.

DISCREPANCIES.

I USE the term at the head of this chapter for lack of a better. There are no real discrepancies in nature, but I may conveniently employ the word to distinguish a class of phenomena not without interest. We occasionally meet with animal or vegetable life existing under conditions, not which are not as truly proper to them as the jungle to the tiger or the river to the crocodile, but which appear to us strange and incongruous; which create in us *surprise*, as the most prominent emotion of the mind,— surprise at finding life, or any particular phase of it, in circumstances where we should not *a priori* have at all expected to find it. Examples will best explain what I mean.

Take, then, the existence of animal life at great depths of ocean. The researches of Sars, MacAndrew, and others, in the Norwegian seas, and those of Edward Forbes in the Ægean, have shewn that mollusca exist under two hundred fathoms of water. *Dead* shells, indeed, are continually dredged from far greater depths; but these may have been voided by the many fishes which feed on mollusca, and would, of course, fall to the bottom, whatever the depth of the sea in which the fish might happen to be swimming. *Dentalium entale, Leda pygmœa,* and *Cryptodon flexuosus* have been taken alive in the northern seas at two hundred fathoms' depth : in the Ægean Sea, *Kellia abyssicola* and *Neœra cuspidata,* two little bivalves, were dredged, the former in one hundred and eighty, the latter in one hundred and eighty-five fathoms; and *Arca imbricata* in two hundred and thirty fathoms.

Nor is the power of sustaining life at such immense depths confined to the molluscan tribes; zoophytes rival them in this respect. Great tree-like corals, *Primnoa* and *Oculina,* spring from the bottom-rocks, to which they are affixed, at a depth of a hundred fathoms and upwards : the magnificent *Ulocyathus arcticus,* a free coral, recently discovered by Sars, lives on the mud at two hundred fathoms; *Bolocera Tuediœ, Tealia digitata,* and *Peachia Bőeckii,* soft-bodied sea-anemones, reach to the same depth, while other species of the same race,—*Capnea sanguinea* and *Actinopsis flava* live at the amazing depth of from two hundred and fifty to three hundred fathoms.

It has been observed that the shells of *mollusca* which inhabit very deep water are almost entirely devoid of positive colour, and this has been supposed to be the inevitable result of the darkness in which they live ; for it is assumed that all or nearly all the sun's light must be absorbed by so vast a mass of water. But yet most of these zoophytes are highly-coloured animals, — the *Actinopsis* being of a fine yellow, the *Bolocera, Tealia,* and *Capnea* of a red more or less intense, and the *Ulocyathus* of the most refulgent scarlet. The pressure

E

of a column of sea-water, from twelve to eighteen hundred feet in height, must be quite inconceivable to us; and we are at a loss to imagine how the corporeal tissues can sustain it, and how the vital functions can be carried on. Yet the presence of these creatures implies the presence of others. The mollusca are mostly feeders on *infusoria* and *diatomaceæ;* therefore these minute animalcules and plants must habitually live there. The zoophytes are all carnivorous, and being all stationary, or nearly so, the prey on which they feed must be abundant there in proportion to their requirements. Perhaps this may partly consist of the mollusca; but it is highly probable that *crustacea* and *annelida* likewise abound.* One species of the former class has, indeed, been discovered in the profound sea. A small kind of lobster, named *Calocaris Macandreæ*, about as large as a small prawn, was dredged by Mr MacAndrew, (after whom it has been named,) in the Scottish seas, at a depth of one hundred and eighty fathoms.†

Who would expect to find the expanse of everlasting snow in the Arctic regions, and at the summits of the Alps, the seat of abundant life, whether vegetable or animal? Yet such is the fact. Ross observed, in Baffin's Bay, a range of cliffs covered with snow which was tinged with a brilliant crimson colour for an extent of eight miles, the hue penetrating from the surface down to the

---

* See, for the facts, Woodward's *Mollusca*, p. 441; and *Fauna Litt. Norveg.*, ii. pp., 73, 87.

† Bell's *Brit. Crust*, p. 233.

very rock, a depth of twelve feet. The same phenomenon has been observed in other parts of the Polar regions, on the glaciers of the Alps, and in other similar circumstances. Scientific investigation has proved this colour to be caused by the excessive abundance of minute organisms, mostly vegetable, of a very simple character, in the form, according to Dr Greville, of a gelatinous layer, on which rest a vast number of minute globules, resembling, in brilliance and colour, fine garnets.* Professor Agassiz, however, maintains that these globules are not vegetables, but the eggs of a minute though highly-organised animal, one of the *Rotifera,* named *Philodina roseola,* which animal he found in abundance, with the globules, in the glacier of the Aar.† Other minute animals were also found in the snow.

In Canada I have found, in the depth of winter, living and active insects on the surface of the snow, which are seen nowhere else, and at no other season. Little hopping atoms, of singular structure, adapted to a mode of progression peculiarly their own, dance about on the unsullied bosom of the new-fallen snow. They belong to the genus *Podura,* and are distinguished by having at the extremity of their body two long, stiff bristles, ordinarily bent up under the belly, but which, at the pleasure of the insect, fly out straight with great force, and thus jerk it into the air, on the principle of a child's toy-frog. Other curious species,—two in particular, both belonging to winged families, yet both without wings, the one a sort

* See *Cryptog. Flora,* p. 231.   † *Rep. Br. Assoc.,* 1840.

of wingless gnat,[*] the other something like a flea, but
really one of the *Panorpadæ*,[†]—I have found numerous
in similar circumstances, and *in no other*.

As a curious incident, not altogether out of place in
this connexion, though the parallelism of the cases is
more apparent than real, we may notice the trees which
Mr Atkinson found growing, under very unusual circumstances, in the valley of the Black Irkout, in Eastern
Siberia, a romantic gorge, whose precipitous sides are
formed of different marbles—one white, with deep purple
spots and small veins, another a rich yellow kind, equal,
if not superior, to the best Sienna, but wholly untouched
by man. "We reached," he says, "a part of the ravine
filled with snow and ice, where large poplars were growing, with only their tops above the icy mass; the
branches were in full leaf, although the trunks were
imbedded in the snow and ice to a depth of twenty-five
feet. I dismounted, examined several, and found that
there was a space around the stem, nine inches wide, filled
with water, the only parts that appeared to be thawing.
I have often seen flowers penetrating a thin bed of snow,
but this was the first time I had found trees growing
under such circumstances."[‡]

The burning, sandy deserts of Arabia and Africa seem
at first sight to be utterly without organic life, and doubtless they are the most barren of all regions. But even
there both animals and vegetables do exist. Several sorts

---

[*] *Chionea araneoides.*   [†] *Boreus hyemalis.*
[‡] Atkinson's *Siberia*, p. 595.

of hard, thorny shrubs are scattered over the dreary waste, the chief of which is the *Hedysarum* of the Sahara, a plant about eighteen inches high, which is green throughout the year; it grows absolutely out of the arid sand, and is eagerly cropped by the camels of the caravans. There are also beetles, which burrow in the sand; and nimble lizards which shine, as they bask in the burning sun, like burnished brass, and bury themselves on being alarmed. The lizards probably live upon the beetles; but what the beetles live upon is not so clear.

The enormous plains of South Africa, called karroos, though not so absolutely barren wastes as the Sahara, are still great wildernesses of sand, exposed to periodical droughts of long duration. These regions are occupied by a most singular type of vegetation; fleshy, distorted, shapeless, and often leafless, tribes of euphorbias, stapelias, mesembryanthemums, crassulas, aloes, and similar succulent plants, maintain their hold of the sandy soil by the weak support of a single wiry root, and are fed rather by the dews of heaven 'than by the moisture of the soil. During the rainless months of the dry seasons, these plains are scarcely less arid than the sandy deserts of the north; yet even then there are reservoirs beneath the surface. Livingstone speaks of a certain plant, named *leroshua*, which is a blessing to the inhabitants of this desert. " We see a small plant with linear leaves, and a stalk not thicker than a crow's quill; on digging down a foot or eighteen inches beneath, we come to a tuber, often as large as the head of a young child; when the rind is removed, we find it to be a mass of cellular tissue, filled with fluid much like that in a young turnip. Owing to the depth beneath the soil at which it is found, it is generally deliciously cool and refreshing. Another kind, named *mokuri*, is seen in other parts of the country, where long-continued heat parches the soil. This plant is a herbaceous creeper, and deposits underground a number of tubers, some as large as a man's head, at spots in a circle a yard or more, horizontally, from the stem. The natives strike the ground on the circumference of the circle with stones, till, by hearing a difference of sound, they know the water-bearing tuber to be beneath. They then dig down a foot or so, and find it." [*]

There are deserts on the Pacific coast of South America as horribly barren as any in Africa or Asia, if not so extensive. One of these is described by Mr Darwin, who was all day riding across it, as a " a complete and utter desert."

" The road," he says, " was strewed with the bones and dried skins of the many beasts of burden which had perished on it from fatigue. Excepting the *Vultur aura*, which preys on the carcases, I saw neither bird, quadruped, reptile, nor insect. On the coast-mountains, at the height of about 2000 feet, where during this season the clouds generally hang, a very few *Cacti* were growing in the clefts of rock, and the loose sand was strewed over with a lichen, which lies on the surface quite unattached. This plant belongs to the genus *Cladonia*, and somewhat resembles the reindeer lichen. In some parts it was in sufficient quantity to tinge the sand, as seen from a distance,

[*] Livingstone's *Travels*, p. 47.

of a pale yellowish colour. Further inland, during the whole ride of fourteen leagues, I saw only one other vegetable production ; and that was a most minute yellow lichen, growing on the bones of the dead mules."[*]

The rugged desolation which characterises the interior of the crater of a volcano, even though the fiery torrent which formed it be at the time dormant, seems ill-suited for the smiling beauty of flowers ; yet such occasionally exist there.

Sir Thomas Acland, who ascended to the summit of Schneehätten, the lofty volcano of Norway, describes the crater to be broken down on the northern side, surrounded on the others by perpendicular masses of black rock, rising out of, and high above, beds of snow that enveloped their bases. The interior sides of the crater descended in one vast sheet of snow to the bottom, where an icy lake closed the view, at the depth of 1500 feet from the highest ridge. "Almost at the top," he says, "and close to the snow, which had probably but a few days before covered them, were some very delicate and beautiful flowers, in their highest bloom, of the *Ranunculus glacialis*, growing most profusely; nor were they the only inhabitants : mosses, lichens, and a variety of small herbaceous plants were in the same neighbourhood ; and, lower down, dwarf-birch, and a species of osier, formed a pretty kind of thicket. The traces of reindeer appeared on the very topmost snow." [†]

The very dust of the air is found to be peopled with living plants and animals, and that where we should least have expected to find it so stocked; nay, where we should scarcely have looked for clouds of dust at all,—far out on the lone ocean, hundreds of miles from land. In Mr Darwin's voyage, he noticed, as he approached the Cape Verd Islands, this curious phenomenon:—"Generally the atmosphere is hazy; and this is caused by the falling of impalpably fine dust, which was found to have slightly injured the astronomical instruments. The morning before we anchored at Porto Praya, I collected a little packet of this brown-coloured fine dust, which appeared to have been filtered from the wind by the gauze of the vane at the masthead. Mr Lyell has also given me four packets of dust which fell on a vessel a few hundred miles northward of these islands. Professor Ehrenberg finds that this dust consists, in great part, of *infusoria** with siliceous shields, and of the siliceous tissue of plants. In five little packets which I sent him, he has ascertained no less than sixty-seven different organic forms! The *infusoria*, with the exception of two marine species, are all inhabitants of fresh water. I have found no less than fifteen different accounts of dust having fallen on vessels when far out in the Atlantic. From the direction of the wind whenever it has fallen, and from its having always fallen during those months when the harmattan is known to raise clouds of dust high into the atmosphere, we may feel sure that it all comes from Africa. It is, however, a

* Constituting the *Diatomaceæ* of modern science.

very singular fact, that, although Professor Ehrenberg knows many species of *infusoria* peculiar to Africa, he finds none of these in the dust which I sent him; on the other hand, he finds in it two species which hitherto he knows as living only in South America. This dust falls in such quantities as to dirty everything on board, and to hurt people's eyes; vessels even have run on shore owing to the obscurity of the atmosphere. It has often fallen on ships when several hundred, and even more than a thousand miles from the coast of Africa, and at points sixteen hundred miles distant in a north and south direction. In some dust which was collected on a vessel three hundred miles from the land, I was much surprised to find particles of stone, about the thousandth of an inch square, mixed with finer matter. After this fact, one need not be surprised at the diffusion of the far lighter and smaller sporules of cryptogamic plants."*

In all these situations, in which we have seen organic existence maintained, we must admit that there is nothing actually hostile to life. The snow, the hot sand, the calcined lava, the dust, seem ungenial spheres for living beings, offer but little encouragement to them, as we should have supposed, but are not actually destructive. What shall we say, however, to animals disporting themselves, by myriads, in brine so strong as to contain two pounds of salt to the gallon? A solution so concentrated is sufficient in general to destroy all life.† Yet, in the

* *Naturalist's Voyage*, chap. i.

† Goadby's preservative fluid contains but three-quarters of a pound of salts to a gallon of water.

salt-works at Lymington, in Hampshire, the reservoirs of
concentrated brine are always peopled by immense numbers of an elegant little animal, quite peculiar to such
situations, which sport about in all the enjoyment of
existence. The little creature is a sort of shrimp, and is
commonly known as the brine shrimp.[*] It is nearly
half an inch in length, and is furnished with eleven pairs
of leaf-shaped limbs. "There is nothing," says M. Joly,
"more elegant than the form of this little crustacean;
nothing more graceful than its movements. It swims
almost always on its back, and moves rapidly through
the element. The feet are in constant motion, and their
undulations have a softness difficult to describe." Besides
these animals, the brine is inhabited by incalculable multitudes of a microscopic animalcule of a crimson hue, on
which the brine-shrimp feeds, and which impart to its
translucent body their own roseate colour.

A similar creature, but of another species,[†] distinguished by a broad crescent-shaped shield over the head,
inhabits lakes, highly charged with nitre and common
salt, in North Africa. The animals are so numerous that
they are caught with muslin nets, and dried in the sun in
the form of a red paste or cake, which is highly esteemed
as an article of food, having the flavour of red herring.

Mr Darwin found, near Buenos Ayres, a shallow lake
of brine, which in summer is converted into a field of
snow-white salt. The border of the lake is a fetid, black

---

[*] *Artemia salina.*

[†] *A. Oudneyi.* See *Excelsior*, i., 229, for figures of both species.

mud, in which are imbedded large crystals of gypsum,
three inches long, and of sulphate of soda. "The mud,
in many places, was thrown up by numbers of some kind
of worm. How surprising is it that any creatures should
be able to exist in brine, and that they should be crawling among crystals of sulphate of soda and lime! And
what becomes of these worms when, during the long
summer, the surface is hardened into a solid layer of
salt?"* Exactly similar lakes, similarly peopled, occur
in Siberia also.†

Perhaps even stranger still is the circumstance that
fishes—vertebrate animals far higher in the organic scale
than shrimps or worms—can subsist, apparently in health,
in water sufficiently heated to boil them if dead. Brous-
sonet found, by experiments, that several species of fresh-
water fishes lived many days in water so hot that the
human hand could not be held in it for a single minute.
Saussure found living eels in the hot springs of Aix, in
Savoy, in which the temperature is pretty regularly 113
deg. of Fahrenheit. But still more extraordinary are
the facts recorded by Humboldt and Bonpland, who saw
living fishes, apparently in health and vigour, thrown up
from the crater of a volcano in South America, with
water and hot vapour that raised the thermometer to 210
deg. Fahrenheit, a heat less, by only two degrees, than
that of boiling water.

The same accomplished travellers visited hot springs in

---

* *Naturalist's Voyage*, chap. iv.
† Pallas's *Travels*, 1793 to 1794, pp. 129-134.

Venezuela, the temperature of which was above 194 deg., and which boiled eggs in less than four minutes. The vegetation around seemed to rejoice in the heat, being unusually luxuriant, the mimosas and fig-trees spreading their branches far over the hot water, and actually pushing their roots into it.

One of the most interesting discoveries of modern science is that of a subterranean fauna, all the members of which are blind. The transition from the illuminated tenants of this upper world to those darkened subjects of Pluto is indeed facilitated by certain intermediate conditions. Such is the guacharo, or fruit-eating nightjar, found by Humboldt inhabiting, in immense hosts, a deep, sepulchral cavern in South America, shut out far from the remotest ray of light, coming forth under the cover of night, and invested with superstitious terrors by the natives. Such, too, is the aspalax, or mole of eastern Europe, which habitually lives under ground; and such is the proteus, a strange sort of salamander found in the lakes of immense caverns in Illyria. They are believed to come from some great central, inaccessible reservoir, where no ray of light has ever penetrated, and whence occasional floods may have forced the individuals that have been discovered.*

I know not what the condition of the eye may be in the guacharo, but in the mammal and reptile, it exists only in the most rudimentary condition, completely covered by the integuments.

* See Davy's *Consolations in Travel.*

Very recently, however, investigations in various parts of the world have revealed the curious circumstance of somewhat extensive series of animals inhabiting vast and gloomy caves and deep wells, and perfectly deprived even of the vestiges of eyes. Enormous caves in North America, some of which are ten miles in length, and other vast and ramified grottoes in Central Europe, have yielded the chief of these; but even in this country we possess at least four species of minute shrimps,[*] three of which are absolutely blind, and the fourth (though it has a yellow speck in the place of an eye) probably so. All these have been obtained from pumps and wells in the southern counties of England, at a depth of thirty or forty feet from the surface of the earth.

The crustacean *Calocaris*, already mentioned as inhabiting the amazing depth of one hundred and eighty fathoms, appears to be blind, for though eyes are present, their surface is perfectly smooth and destitute of facetted corneæ, and white, shewing the absence of colouring pigment. Vision can scarcely exist with such a structure, and this is in keeping with the habits of the animal; for not only would the vast superincumbent body of water absorb all the rays of light, and make its sphere of being totally dark, but, in addition to this, it is of fossorial habits, burrowing into the sandy mud at the bottom.[†]

The Mammoth Cave in Kentucky consists of innumer-

---

[*] Belonging to the genera *Niphargus* and *Crangonyx*. (See *Nat. Hist Review*, 1859; *Pr. Soc.*, p. 164).

[†] Bell's *Brit. Crust.*, p. 236.

able subterranean galleries in the limestone formation, some of which are of great extent. The temperature is constant throughout the year—59 deg. Fahr. A darkness, unrelieved by the least glimmer of light, prevails. Animals of various races inhabit these caves, all completely blind; for though some have rudimentary eyes, they appear useless for purposes of vision. Among these are two kinds of bats, two rats, (one found at a distance of seven miles from the entrance,) moles, fishes, spiders, beetles, crustacea, and several kinds of infusoria [*]

In 1845, three caves near Adelsburg and one near Trieste were examined by Professor Schiödte. Koch, Schmidt, and others had already announced the existence in these caves of a blind fauna, besides the proteus. An *Oniscus*, a beetle of the family *Staphylinidæ*, and two belonging to the *Carabidæ*, were found to be either totally destitute of eyes, or to have these organs reduced to rudimentary specks. Schiödte added to these two new species of *Silphadæ*, a species of spring-tail, two remarkable spiders, each constituting a new genus, and a crustacean.[†] Still later, Schmidt has discovered two more beetles in these caves, inhabiting the deepest recesses, and described as perfectly eyeless, yet retreating quickly from the light of the explorers' torches into clefts of the rock; a curious circumstance, which would seem to indicate a certain sensibility to the stimulus of light.[‡] Indeed, in several

---

[*] *Trans. Roy. Soc. Edinb.*, Dec. 1853.
[†] Schiödte's *Spec. Faun. Subterr.*
[‡] *Laibacher Zeitung*, August 1852.

of the vertebrate creatures of the Kentucky cave, the optic nerve is found to exist, though the eyes are wanting.

Of the true relations of these remarkable beings with those which inhabit the sunny world without, there are various opinions. Some have thought it possible that they are the descendants of unfortunate individuals that, in unknown ages past, wandered into the caves, and were unable to find their way out again; the total absence of light, and the consequent disuse of the visual organs, inducing an obliteration of the organs themselves, or at least of the function. Others suppose that the animals were at the first assigned to such situations, and fitted for them at their creation. Others again, among whom may be reckoned the late Mr Kirby, in his "Bridgewater Treatise," contend that they form no portion of the fauna now in existence on the surface of the earth, but belong to a creation as distinct as we may suppose that of Venus or Jupiter to be. The data, however, scarcely warrant such a conclusion as this.

Mr Charles Darwin has lately alluded to these singular facts in confirmation of his theory of the origin of species by means of natural selection, or the preservation of favoured races in the struggle for life. He takes the first-named view, that in the subterranean animals the organs of sight have become (more or less completely) absorbed, in successive generations, by disuse of the function. " In some of the crabs the foot-stalk remains, though the eye is gone; the stand for the telescope is there, though the

telescope with its glasses has been lost. As it is difficult
to imagine that eyes, though useless, could be in any way
injurious to animals living in darkness, I attribute their
loss wholly to disuse. In one of the blind animals,
namely, the cave-rat, the eyes are of immense size; and
Professor Silliman thought that it regained, after living
some days in the light, some slight power of vision. In
the same manner as, in Madeira, the wings of some of
the insects have been enlarged, and the wings of others
have been reduced, by natural selection aided by use and
disuse, so in the case of the cave-rat, natural selection
seems to have struggled with the loss of light and to have
increased the size of the eyes; whereas, with all the other
inhabitants of the caves, disuse by itself seems to have
done its work.

".... On my view, we must suppose that American
animals, having ordinary powers of vision, slowly migrated
by successive generations from the outer world into the
deeper and deeper recesses of the Kentucky caves, as did
European animals into the caves of Europe. We have
some evidence of this gradation of habit; for, as Schiödte
remarks, 'animals not far remote from ordinary forms,
prepare the transition from light to darkness. Next
follow those that are constructed for twilight; and, last
of all, those destined for total darkness. By the time
that an animal has reached, after numberless generations,
the deepest recesses, disuse will on this view have more
or less perfectly obliterated its eyes, and natural selection
will often have effected other changes, such as an increase

in the length of the antennæ or palpi, as a compensation for blindness.

" . . . . Far from feeling any surprise that some of the cave-animals should be very anomalous, as Agassiz has remarked in regard to the blind fish, the *Amblyopsis*, and as is the case with the blind Proteus with reference to the reptiles of Europe, I am only surprised that more wrecks of ancient life have not been preserved, owing to the less severe competition to which the inhabitants of these dark abodes will probably have been exposed."*

Lone and barren rocks rising abruptly out of the solitary ocean often teem with animal life to an amazing extent, where the navigator might reasonably have looked for utter silence and desolation. For these are the resort of millions of oceanic birds, affording to these, whose proper home is on the wide and shoreless sea, the spots of solid matter which they require for the laying of their eggs and the hatching of their young. This brief occupation, lasting only for a few weeks in the year, appears to be the only link which connects these pelagic freebooters with the earth. Pelicans, gannets, boobies, cormorants, frigate-birds, tropic-birds, albatrosses, fulmars, skuas, petrels, gulls, terns, puffins, and multitudes of other tribes throng to such bare rocks in the season, in countless hosts, making the desolation horridly alive. Such a

---

* *Op. cit.*, p. 137. I am very far, indeed, from accepting Mr Darwin's theory to the extent to which he pushes it, completely trampling on Revelation as it does; but I think there is a *measure* of truth in it.

F

scene as ensues when man intrudes on it has been vividly depicted by Le Vaillant. "All of a sudden, there arose from the whole surface of the island an impenetrable cloud, which formed, at the distance of forty feet above our heads, an immense canopy, or rather a sky, composed of birds of every species, and of all colours: cormorants, sea-gulls, sea-swallows, pelicans, and I believe, the whole winged tribe of that part of Africa, were here assembled. All their voices, mingled together, and modified according to their different kinds, formed such a horrid music, that I was every moment obliged to cover my head to give a little relief to my ears. The alarm which we spread was so much the more general among those innumerable legions of birds, as we principally disturbed the females which were then sitting. They had nests, eggs, and young to defend. They were like furious harpies let loose against us, and their cries rendered us almost deaf. They often flew so near us, that they flapped their wings in our faces, and though we fired our pieces repeatedly, we were not able to frighten them: it seemed almost impossible to disperse this cloud."

How utterly desolate such insular rocks are is well illustrated by what Mr Darwin says of St Paul's cluster, situated in the midst of the Atlantic, under the equator. At a distance these rocks appear of a brilliant white colour, partly owing to the dung of the innumerable sea-fowl, and partly to a coating of a hard, glossy substance with a pearly lustre, which is intimately united to the surface of the stone. It seems to be a sort of inflores-

cence of the phosphate of lime, obtained by the solution of the bird-ordure in the elements, which takes on foliated forms imitative of lichens or nullipores.

There is not a vestige of vegetable life here, but of animals there are not a few. The booby and the noddy sit on the bare rock in startling tameness, apparently having less intellect than the far inferior races around them. "By the side of many of the nests a small flying-fish was placed, which, I suppose, had been brought by the male bird for its partner. It was amusing to watch how quickly a large and active crab, (*Grapsus*,) which inhabits the crevices of the rock, stole the fish from the side of the nest, as soon as we had disturbed the parent birds. Sir W. Symonds, one of the few persons who have landed here, informs me that he saw the crabs dragging even the young birds out of their nests, and devouring them. Not a single plant, not even a lichen, grows on this islet; yet it is inhabited by several insects and spiders. The following·list completes, I believe, the terrestrial fauna :—A fly (*Olfersia*) living on the booby, and a tick which must have come here as a parasite on the birds; a small brown moth, belonging to a genus that feeds on feathers; a beetle, (*Quedius*,) and a wood-louse from beneath the dung; and, lastly, numerous spiders, which I suppose prey on these small attendants and scavengers of the waterfowl. The often-repeated description of the stately palm, and other noble tropical plants, then birds, and lastly man, taking possession of the coral islets as soon as formed, in the Pacific, is pro bably not quite correct; I fear it destroys the poetry of this story, that feather- and dirt-feeding, and parasitic insects and spiders should be the first inhabitants of newly-formed oceanic land." *

The occurrence, far out on the boundless sea, of creatures which we habitually associate with the land, is a phenomenon which interests even those who are little observant of natural history. Visits of land-birds to ships have often been noticed by voyagers, and that not of those species only which are known to make long transmarine migrations, but of small and feeble-winged races, such as finches and warblers. It is much more remarkable, however, to see insects under such circumstances; yet examples of this are not wanting. Mr Darwin expresses his surprise at finding a considerable number of beetles, alive and apparently little injured, swimming in the open sea, seventeen miles off Cape Corrientes, at the mouth of the La Plata. These may have been carried down by a river, especially as several of them were water-beetles; but this will not account for aërial insects taking a sea voyage. The same naturalist was surrounded by flocks of butterflies of several kinds, (chiefly of the genus *Colias*,) ten miles off the same coast. They were in countless myriads, so that the seamen cried that it was "snowing butterflies," extending as far as the eye could range; and, even with a telescope, it was not possible to see a space free from butterflies. The day had been fine and calm, and so had the day before; so that

* *Naturalist's Voy.*, chap. i.

the supposition that the insects had been involuntarily, blown off the land was inadmissible.*

But in these cases the land was not beyond the range of moderate flight. What shall we say to jaunts of five hundred or a thousand miles performed by these filmy-winged and delicate creatures? Mr Davis has recorded † that a large dragon-fly, of the genus *Æshna*, flew on board the ship in which he was sailing, on the 11th of December 1837, when out at sea, the nearest land being the coast of Africa, which was distant five hundred miles.

The late Mr Newport, in his Presidential Address to the Entomological Society of London, for the year 1845, thus alluded to two other instances of the same interesting phenomenon :—" Mr Saunders exhibited, at our December meeting, a specimen of *Æshna*, that was taken at sea by our corresponding member, Mr Stephenson, in his voyage from this country to New Zealand, last year. This insect is a recognised African species, and was captured on the Atlantic, more than six hundred miles in a direct line from land. In all probability it had been driven across the ocean by the trade winds, which blow continuously at that season of the year in a direction oblique to the course of the ship that was conveying Mr Stephenson outwards. The other instance that has just come to my knowledge is mentioned in a letter from Mr Dyson to Mr Cuming. Mr Dyson states, that while at sea, in October last, when about six hundred miles from the

* *Nat. Voy.*, chap. viii.   † *Entom. Mag.*, v. p. 251.

Cape de Verd Islands, and twelve hundred from Guada-
loupe, he observed a large butterfly, apparently of the
genus *Morpho*, (?)* flying round the ship, but he could not
succeed in capturing it. These are facts related by entomologists who could not have mistaken the objects observed,
and consequently they are entitled to full credit. They
are full of interest in relation to a subject of physiological
discussion, the power of flight supposed to be possessed
by these, our little favourites, and the speed with which
they are conveyed across the ocean, whether by an actual
expenditure of muscular energy, or whether carried by the
force of the wind alone. My own opinion certainly is,
that the amount of muscular power exerted during flight
is trifling, compared with what we have usually supposed
it to be, and that in these instances the insects have been
greatly aided in their progress by the wind. The speed
at which they must have traversed the ocean seems to
confirm this view; as it is well known that the *Æshna*
will not live more than a few days, if unable to obtain its
living food."

The Atlantic being the great highway of nations, we
have more abundant observations on this than on other
oceans, but similar phenomena exist elsewhere. Humboldt mentions having seen, in the Pacific, at a vast dis-

---

* If the butterfly was indeed a *Morpho*,—and Mr Dyson, who was an
experienced lepidopterist, could scarcely have been deceived about so
remarkable a butterfly,—it could have come neither from the Cape de
Verd Isles nor the Antilles, but from the continent of South America,
to which the genus *Morpho* is limited. The nearest part of that continent is not less than one thousand five hundred miles from the position of the observer.

tance from the coast, large-winged *Lepidoptera* (butter-flies) fall on the deck of the ship.

Equally striking is the presence of winged insects at very lofty elevations. Saussure found butterflies at the summit of Mont Blanc, and Ramond observed them in the solitudes around that of Mont Perdu. Captain Fremont saw honey-bees at the top of the loftiest peak of the Rocky Mountains in North America, the height of which is 13,568 feet. Dr Hooker, in the Himalaya range, found insects plentiful at 17,000 feet; butterflies of the genera *Colias, Hipparchia, Melitæa,* and *Polyommatus,* besides beetles, and great flies. Humboldt saw butterflies among perpetual snow at yet loftier elevations in the Andes of Peru, but conjectured that they had been carried thither involuntarily by ascending currents of air. And the same great philosopher, when ascending Chimborazo, in June 1802, with Bonpland and Montufar, found winged flies (*Diptera*) buzzing around him at the height of 18,225 feet; while a little below this elevation Bonpland saw yellow butterflies flying over the ground.

I shall close this category with two examples of animal life in unwonted situations, less scientifically curious it may be than those already adduced, but more amusing. That fishes should fly in the air is strange enough, but we should scarcely expect that they would verify their generic name * by going to bed out of water. Yet Kotzebue was favoured with such an unexpected bedfellow :—

" The nights being warm," observes the voyager, " we

* *Exocætus,* the name of the flying-fish, from ἔξω, out, and κοιτάω, to sleep. The Greeks fancied that the fish left the water to sleep.

always sleep on deck, to recover ourselves from the heat of the day, a circumstance which occasioned me one night a very unexpected visit. I was awakened by the constant motion of a very cold animal at my side, which, when it writhed in my hand, I first took to be a lizard. This, I thought, might perhaps have been brought on board at Chili, with the wood. But, on examining, I found that it was a flying-fish that I had in my hands, and I am probably the first that has caught such a one in bed." *

The other incident occurred nearer home.

In the tremendous gale of the 25th October, 1859, which did so much damage on the coast of South Devon, a curious incident occurred to a gentleman whose house was situated close to the water-side. He was sitting with his parlour window open, when an enormous green wave came curling towards the house, and discharged its force full against the window. There was no time to shut the window; but, retreating as fast as he could, he pulled the door of the room after him, in order to keep the sea as far as practicable from the rest of the house. After some time he returned to see what amount of mischief was done, and, entering the room, found the floor covered with flapping and jumping fishes. The wave had brought forward a shoal of whiting, and had deposited them on the good man's carpet; where they tossed, much to his amusement and their own chagrin—fish out of water.

* *Voyage*, i. p. 145.

IV

MULTUM E PARVO.

NATURAL history affords not a few instructive examples of

"What great effects from little causes flow;"

and these are well worthy of our study, as presenting to us one peculiar aspect of the wisdom of God, with whom nothing is great, nothing small. Some of the mightiest operations in nature are the results of processes, and the works of agents, apparently feeble and wholly inadequate to produce them; and our wonder is excited when we are able intelligently to trace them to their causes. I propose, therefore, to devote this chapter to the consideration of a few of these, which come more immediately within the province of the naturalist. They may be classed, according to the nature of their operations, as either constructive or destructive.

How many a poetic dream is associated with the sunny isles of the Pacific! What a halo of romance encircles all our ideas of those mirror-like lagoons in the midst of the great ocean-waves, those long, low reefs just emerging from the sea, on which the cocoa-nut palm is springing from the very water's edge! Beautiful they are in our imagination, as we have realised the pictures drawn by

Cook, and Kotzebue, and Beechey, by Stewart and Ellis, Darwin and Cheever. But, when we know that these thousand isles, these endless reefs, these huge barriers that curb the furious ocean, are produced by tiny, soft-bodied sea-anemones, by atoms of pulp, sluggish and seemingly helpless morsels of animated jelly, individually no bigger than the smallest flower that nestles in the hedge-bank—our wonder, instead of being dispersed by our philosophy, is deepened and incomparably augmented by it. " We feel surprise when travellers tell us of the vast dimensions of the Pyramids, but how utterly insignificant are the greatest of these when compared to these mountains of stone accumulated by the agency of various minute and tender animals! This is a wonder which does not at first strike the eye of the body, but, after reflection, the eye of reason." *

The researches of the eminent naturalist whose words I have just quoted, have shewn us that the coral polype does not build from the fathomless depths of sea which immediately surround these reefs and islands. He seems to imply, indeed, that the coral animals cannot exist at a greater depth than thirty fathoms ; but, whatever may be the case in tropical seas, we have already seen that living corals exist and build compound polypidoms at far greater depths in our northern latitudes. Assuming, however, that no reef is commenced deeper than thirty fathoms, and that below that depth the building instinct is not carried on, the only hypothesis which meets all the exigencies presented by the actual phenomena of fring-

* Darwin, *Nat. Voy.*, chap. **xx.**

ing reefs, encircling or barrier reefs, and atolls or ring reefs, is that propounded and ably maintained by Darwin, that the whole area of the Pacific is slowly sinking; that all the reefs and islands are the summits of former mountains; that all the coral structures were originally attached to the land at a shallow depth, and that, to whatever depth below they now extend, it is only in a dead condition, and has been effected by the subsidence of the supporting land carrying the coral with it; while the successive generations of the living polypes, ever working upwards on the old dead foundation, have maintained a living coral structure near the surface, and that nearly in the same outline and form as the original foundation.

It does not accord with my purpose to enter into the details of this beautiful theory, but rather to present my readers with some vivid pictures of the wonderful structures themselves, as sketched by those who have seen them. In coasting along a tropical reef, the extreme clearness of the water permits the coral shrubs and groves to be distinctly seen, which rise from the blue transparent depths. They take various forms—some massive, with meandering channels over the rounded surface; some forming honey-combed blocks formed by the union of thin plates at various angles; many growing like trees or shrubs with leafless branches, more or less ramified, and with the twigs more or less slender and pointed, or thick and rounded. Under water, the whole surface is covered with a layer of jelly-like flesh, of many brilliant colours, formed by the crowding together of the myriad tiny polypes, which protrude their slender tentacles and expanding disks from the individual cells. Even when severed, the branches are exquisitely beautiful so long as they retain the faint purple halo that plays around their ivory tips, but which soon vanishes. A rude touch beneath the water will cause the lovely tints—brilliant crimson, orange, and emerald green—to disappear, by the withdrawal of the alarmed polypes; but they soon protrude again, and expand in their original loveliness.

The interest with which these gardens are contemplated is enhanced by the multitude of strange creatures which crawl over and through the shrubs. Fishes of the most gorgeous hues, elegant shells, with clouded and spotted animals carrying them, nimble prawns of crimson and yellow, long gliding green worms, and purple sea-urchins, with enormous spines, here find their home and live at ease beneath the unclouded sun.

The dimensions attained by the labours of the minute workmen are the most astonishing part of the spectacle. "Some individual specimens of *Porites*, in the rock of the inner reef of Tongatabu, are twenty-five feet in diameter; and *Astreas* and *Meandrinas*, both there and in the Fejees, measure twelve to fifteen feet. The platform resembles a Cyclopean pavement, except that the cementing material between the huge masses is more solid than any work of art could be.

"Sometimes the barrier reef recedes from the shore, and forms wide channels or inland seas, where ships find ample room and depth of water, exposed, however, to the danger of hidden reefs. The reef on the north-east coast of New Holland and New Caledonia extends four hundred miles, at a distance varying from thirty to sixty miles from shore, and having as many fathoms of depth in the channel. West of the large Fejee Islands the channel is in some parts twenty-five miles wide, and twelve to forty fathoms in depth. The sloop-of-war *Peacock* sailed along the west coast of both Viti Lebu and Vanua Lebu, within the inner reefs, a distance exceeding two hundred miles.

"A barrier reef, inclosing a lagoon, is the general formation of the coral islands, though there are some of small size in which the lagoon is wanting. These are found in all stages of development : in some the reef is narrow and broken, forming a succession of narrow islets with openings into the lagoon ; in others there only remains a depression of surface in the centre to indicate where the lagoon originally was.* The most beautiful are those where the lagoon is completely inclosed, and rests within, a quiet lake. Maraki, one of the Kingsmill group, is one of the prettiest coral islands of the Pacific. The line of vegetation is unbroken, and, seen from the mast-head, it lies like a garland thrown upon the waters.

"When first seen from the deck of a vessel, only a series of dark points is descried, just above the horizon. Shortly after, the points enlarge into the plumed tops of cocoa-nut trees, and a line of green, interrupted at intervals, is traced along the water's surface. Approaching still nearer, the lake and its belt of verdure are spread out before the eye, and a scene of more interest can scarcely

* This does not agree with Darwin's theory of subsidence.

be imagined. The surf, beating loud and heavy along the margin of the reef, presents a strange contrast to the prospect beyond—the white coral beach, the massy foliage of the grove, and the embosomed lake, with its tiny islets. The colour of the lagoon water is often as blue as the ocean, although but fifteen or twenty fathoms deep; yet shades of green and yellow are intermingled, where patches of sand or coral knolls are near the surface, and the green is a delicate apple shade, quite unlike the usual muddy tint of shallow waters.

" These garlands of verdure seem to stand on the brims of cups, whose bases root in unfathomable depth. Seven miles east of Clermont Tonnere, the lead ran out to eleven hundred and forty-five fathoms, (six thousand eight hundred and seventy feet) without reaching bottom. Within three-quarters of a mile of the southern point of this island, the lead had another throw, and, after running out for a while, brought up for an instant at three hundred and fifty fathoms, and then dropped off again and descended to six hundred fathoms without reaching bottom. The lagoons are generally shallow, though in the larger islands soundings gave twenty to thirty-five, and even fifty and sixty fathoms." *

The rate at which coral structures are formed is an interesting subject of inquiry, and various opinions have been formed on the point, some affirming that no perceptible increase takes place in several years, others that the process is so rapid, that the Pacific is fast filling up. Darwin's theory of subsidence negatives this conclusion,

* Cheever's *Sandwich Islands*, p. 152.

independently of the ratio of growth. There are facts on record, however, which imply that, in certain circumstances, the process is rapid. A channel that had been dug through the reef of Keeling Atoll for the passage of a schooner, that had been built on the island, from the lagoon into the sea, was found ten years afterwards to be almost choked up with living coral. An interesting experiment was tried at Madagascar, by securing several masses of living coral by stakes three feet below the surface. Seven months afterwards they were found nearly reaching to the surface, firmly cemented to the rock, and extended laterally several feet ; a remarkably rapid growth !

An ingenious inquiry has been started, whether the coral polypes may not yet be employed by man for the construction of sea-walls and reefs, in places within or near the tropics, where they are needed. Professor Agassiz has shewn that it is not difficult to obtain living specimens of the zoophyte, and to preserve them, so as to study at leisure their habits and motions. Why, then, it has been asked, as we employ the silk-worm, and furnish it with food and material to spin for us our silks, and as we plant and form beds of oysters in favourable locations, where we please, may we not also employ the agency of the coral lithophyte, to lay the foundations, for instance, of a lighthouse, or to form a breakwater where one is needed? Such a practical result is by no means improbable, from the minute and scientific observations now making upon these busy little builders of the deep.*

* Cheever's *Sandwich Islands*, Appx., p. 310.

Let us look now at another class of labourers by whom mighty deeds are performed, though the performers themselves are so inconceivably minute, that to say they bear the same relation to the coral polype that a mouse does to an elephant, would be greatly to overrate their dimensions. They are, in fact, invisible to the sharpest sight, except when aggregated together. I refer to the *Diatomaceæ*.

Of late years the attention of microscopic observers has been largely and increasingly occupied by a tribe of organic beings which are found to exist in all parts of the world, in fresh and salt waters chiefly, and present a great variety of species as well as of form and markings. They consist of a glassy shell, formed of flint, inclosing a soft coloured substance, generally of a golden yellow or brown hue. This is called the *endochrome*, and the shell is called the *frustule*. The latter has a determinate form, which often assumes extraordinary elegance, and is usually marked with series of specks, which are either knobs or pits, arranged in the most varied and exquisite patterns. They may exist either as isolated forms, or, more commonly, as united into long chains, or other connected figures. These are called Diatoms. They have spontaneous movements, and hence they were considered, when first discovered, to be animals; but the opinion now generally prevails, that they are plants of a very low grade.

The influence of these tiny atoms upon this world in which we live is almost beyond belief. " The whole bottom of the ocean," observes Dr Barclay Montgomery, " seems to be in a great measure made up of these bodies.

Sir John Ross and other Arctic explorers speak of a large bank called the Victoria Barrier, 400 miles long, and 120 miles wide, composed almost entirely of *infusoria*. During the last week I was engaged in examining a sounding from the bottom of the ocean at the depth of 2000 fathoms, on the exact spot where the Atlantic telegraph unfortunately gave way; although the quantity was minute, still I discovered a great number of interesting forms. What is known as Tripoli powder in the arts consists almost entirely of fossil deposits of the siliceous coats of *diatoms*, which from their hardness form an excellent means of polishing metals; these fossil deposits are very numerous and in great quantity in different parts of the world. The town of Richmond, in the United States, is built upon a stratum of these bodies twenty feet in thickness; in California and America generally, in Bohemia, throughout Europe and Africa, and even in our own country, we find similar deposits, varying of course in the different species present. . . . . . I have been enabled to examine some of the curious raised fossil beach near Copiapo in Chili, which is gradually forming into stone. Though this beach is one mile from the present shore, and 180 feet above the level of the sea, yet I have found in it *diatoms* of the same species as those that occur on the shore at the present day; the *diatoms* are also found in a fossil state in peat, coal, bog iron-ore, flint, and the chalk formation. Thus, in a geological view, though individually invisible, yet numerically they perform a most important part in the crust of the earth—

a part more important than all the mighty monsters that
lived in ages past. . . . . What purpose do these bodies
serve?   It is highly possible that they form, in a great
measure, the food.of all the minor aquatic animals more
highly organised than themselves ; I have often found, on
examining shrimps, that their stomachs, which are situated
behind the eyes, are entirely filled with *diatoms.*   That
the siliceous shell passes through nearly intact, there can
be no doubt, but it is certain that the internal structure,
the endochrome, may be digested and form the nutritive
portion ; in this view I am borne out by referring to
guano—a most prolific source of fossil *diatoms.*   Here
we find abundance of siliceous shells, in fact their presence
or absence is now the test of the genuineness of the
article ;—these, in past ages, must have been consumed
by small marine animals, these again consumed by fish,
and these in their turn by birds : in guano I have noticed
the proportion of *diatoms* to be in some specimens nearly
1 in 500 parts.   A correspondent from Callao, writing to
the *Illustrated London News,* on the Cincha guano
islands, says the export of guano from the islands has
increased considerably during the last ten years ; between
300,000 tons and 400,000 tons are the annual amount at
present : here, in a very moderate calculation, from one
spot alone, we have the annual removal of 500 tons of
diatoms." *

   The agency of these mighty but minute forms has been
still further developed in some researches of great interest

* *Report of Cornwall Polyt. Soc. for* 1857.

which have been very recently published by Dr Wallich. He has ascertained that they exist in a free, swimming condition, in various regions of the ocean, and at various depths from the surface downward; that their multitude is incalculable; and that they afford sustenance to immense numbers of molluscous and crustaceous animals, which in their turn constitute the food of the most gigantic creatures of the deep. Dr Joseph D. Hooker had noticed the vast profusion of *Diatomaceæ* in the Antarctic Sea; and he was struck by the conspicuous appearance presented by their masses imbedded in the substance of the ice, or washed up on its surface by the action of the billows.

Dr Wallich found the surface of the Bay of Bengal and the Indian Ocean to be crowded with masses of minute life, forming yellow streaks, flakes, and tufts, intermixed with glistening points, which, when examined, proved to be recognisable forms of the organisms in question. The mighty scale on which the *Diatomaceæ* really exist, did not become manifest, however, until he reached the Atlantic, between the Cape and St Helena.*

" It was here that, for many degrees, and in bright, breezy weather, the ship passed through vast layers of sea-water so thronged with the bodies of a species of *Salpa* (*S. mucronata*) as to present the consistence of a jelly. What their vertical limits were, it was impossible to discover, owing to the speed at which the ship was

* *See Annals Nat. Hist. for January* 1860; and *Quarterly Journ. Micr. Sci. for January* 1860.

moving. They appeared to extend deep, however, and in all probability, were of a similar character to the aggregations of what is called whale-food in the higher latitudes. Each of these *Salpæ* measured about half an inch in length ; but so close was their aggregation, that, by a sudden plunge of an iron-rimmed towing-net, half the cubic contents, from which all water had percolated, generally consisted of nothing but one thick gelatinous pulp. Each individual presented a minute yellow digestive cavity, of the size of a millet-seed, which contained Diatomaceæ, Foraminifera, and other organic particles.

"If we take into account the numbers of Diatomaceæ and Foraminifera that must exist in order to afford even a small integral proportion of the diet of these creatures, the vast renewal of supply that must be perpetually going on, and the equally vast multitude of these Diatom-consumers that yield, in their turn, a source of food to the gigantic Cetaceans and other large creatures of the sea,— it becomes possible, in some measure, at least, to form an estimate of the manner in which the deep-sea deposits become accumulated."

The same observer has, with great ingenuity, applied these facts to the solution of that much-vexed question, the origin of the masses of flint that are found in the chalk. Diatoms are found in great numbers in these nodules, but the difficulty was, how to account for their aggregation in these irregular masses. This is solved by the hypothesis that they are the excrement of whales,— the insoluble remains of the Diatoms, originally devoured by the Molluscs, which in their turn found a grave in the stomach of the Cetacean. "We find that the siliceous particles of the *Diatomaceæ, Polycistina, Acanthometræ,* and *Sponges,* exist not only in a state of the utmost purity, but that they occur precisely in that state of minute subdivision which favours the solvent or aggregative process in an eminent degree. We see that they are gathered together by the Salpæ, in the first instance, from the element in which they live, and that they are freed of all, or nearly all, their soft portions, by the action of the digestive cavities of these creatures. We find that the Salpæ again, in inconceivably vast numbers, afford almost the entire food of the largest orders of Cetaceans ; and I therefore think we are able to infer, with certainty, that, in the complex stomachs and intestines of the latter, the further process of aggregation of siliceous particles goes on upon a gigantic scale, aided by the presence of the alkalies, and that the aggregated masses being voided at intervals, slowly subside, without interruption, to the bed of the ocean."

Darwin records having seen clustered objects in the sea near Keeling Atoll, which he does not name, but which from the figures he has given must have been Diatoms. But all the streaks and bands of colour seen on the ocean are not attributable to plants : some of them are certainly of an animal nature. The following phenomenon was noticed by the observer last named on the coast of Chili. The vessel passed through broad bands of reddish water, which when examined microscopically swarmed

with minute active animalcules, darting about, and often
exploding. They swam by the aid of a ring of vibratory
cilia, which suggests the thought of the larvæ of some
Annelid. They were exceedingly minute, so as to be quite
invisible to the naked eye, being not more than one thousandth of an inch in length. Their numbers were infinite,
for the smallest drop of water which could be removed
contained very many. Yet in one day, they passed
through two spaces of water thus stained, one of which
alone must have extended over several square miles.
How utterly inconceivable, then, must have been the multitude of these minute creatures!

Other navigators have noticed broad expanses of the
ocean tinged with colour, well defined; as the red water
seen by M. Lesson off Lima, and that which in the vicinity
of California has been called the "Vermilion Sea;" to
which Sir E. Tennent has recently added the sea around
Ceylon, which is of a similar hue, and which he has
ascertained to be owing to the presence of infusorial
animalcules.[*]

Off the coast of Brazil, Kotzebue observed on the
surface of the sea, a dark brown streak, about twelve feet
wide, and extending in length as far as the eye could
reach. It was found to consist of an innumerable multitude of minute crabs, and the seeds [or air-vessels?] of a
submarine alga.

In certain parts of the Arctic Ocean the water, instead
of being colourless and transparent, is opaque, and of a ·

* *Ceylon,* i, p. 53.

deep green hue. Scoresby found that this was owing to
the presence of excessively numerous microscopic *Medusæ*.
He computes that within the compass of two square
miles, supposing these creatures to extend to the depth of
two hundred and fifty fathoms, (which, however, is scarcely
probable,) there would be congregated together a number
which eighty thousand persons, counting incessantly from
the creation till now, would not have enumerated,
though they worked at the rate of a million a-week! yet
it is calculated that the area occupied by this "green
water" in the Greenland Sea is not less than 20,000
square miles. What a union of the small and the great
is here!

It is little suspected by many how largely small seed-
eating animals, and especially birds, contribute to the
clothing of the earth with its varied vegetable riches.
Peculiar provision is made in many cases for the dissemi-
nation of seeds, in their own structure, of which the
pappus of the dandelion and the adhesive hooks of the
burdock are examples; but this is largely effected also in
the stomachs of birds, the seed being often discharged
not only uninjured, but made more ready to germinate
by the heat and maceration to which it has been subjected. "From trivial causes spring mighty effects:"
and the motto has been illustrated by a close observer
from this same subject. "Doubtless many of our most
richly wooded landscapes owe much of their timber to the
agency of quadrupeds and birds. Linnets, goldfinches,
thrushes, goldcrests, &c., feed on the seeds of elms, firs,

and ashes, and carry them away to hedge-rows, where, fostered and protected by bush and bramble, they spring up and become luxuriant trees. Many noble oaks have been planted by the squirrel, who unconsciously yields no inconsiderable boon to the domain he infests. Towards autumn this provident little animal mounts the branches of oak-trees, strips off the acorns and buries them in the earth, as a supply of food against the severities of winter. He is most probably not gifted with a memory of sufficient retention to enable him to find every one he secretes, which are thus left in the ground, and springing up the following year, finally grow into magnificent trees. Pheasants devour numbers of acorns in the autumn, some of which having passed through the stomach, probably germinate. The nuthatch in an indirect manner also frequently becomes a planter. Having twisted off their boughs a cluster of beechnuts, this curious bird resorts to some favourite tree, whose bole is uneven, and endeavours, by a series of manœuvres, to peg it into one of the crevices of the bark. During the operation it oftentimes fall to the ground, and is caused to germinate by the moisture of winter. Many small beeches are found growing near the haunts of the nuthatch, which have evidently been planted in the manner described." *

Not less important, perhaps, are the results of the destructive than those of the constructive propensities and powers of minute creatures. Of the charming *Introduction to Entomology*, by Messrs Kirby and Spence, no less

* *Zoologi.t*, p. 442.

than five entire epistles are occupied with the injuries which we sustain from insects, while two are devoted to the benefits they yield us. The former is almost an appalling array; the injuries done to us in our field-crops, in our gardens, in our orchards, in our woods and forests, not to mention those which attack our living stock or our persons, by these most minute of creatures, are indeed well calculated to impress on us the truth of that Oriental proverb, which tells us that the smallest enemy is not to be despised.

The locust has been celebrated in all ages as one of the scourges of God; and the Holy Scriptures bear testimony how often in ancient times, and with what effect, it was let loose upon the guilty nations. To outward appearance it is a mere grasshopper, in nowise more formidable than one of those crinking merry-voiced denizens of our summer-fields that children chase and capture; yet with what terror is it beheld by the inhabitants of the East! The speech which Mohammed attributed to a locust graphically represents the popular estimate of its powers: —" We are the army of the great God; we produce ninety-nine eggs; if the hundred were complete, we should consume the whole earth and all that is in it."

It is only a short time since the public papers were occupied with articles expressing the most gloomy fears for the noble oak and pine forests of Germany. It was stated that millions of fine trees had already fallen under the insidious attacks of a beetle, a species of extreme minuteness, which lays its eggs in the bark, whence the larvæ penetrate between the bark and the wood, and destroy the vital connexion between these parts, interrupting the course of the descending sap, and inducing rapid decay and speedy death.

In the north of France, the public promenades are almost everywhere shaded by avenues of noble elms. In very many cases these trees are fast disappearing before the assaults of a similar foe. And the grand old elms of our own metropolitan parks and gardens are becoming so thinned, that great alarm has been felt, and the resources of science employed for the checking of the mischief. Fifty thousand trees, chiefly oaks, have also been destroyed in the Bois de Vincennes, near Paris. In all these cases the minute but mighty agent has been some species or other of the genus *Scolytus.*

Fortunately in this clime we know only by report the consumptive energy of the termites, or white-ants ; " *calamitas Indiarum.*" Wood, timber of all kinds, with one or two exceptions, is the object of their attacks ; and so unrelenting is their perseverance, so incredible are their numbers, that all the wood-work of a house disappears before them in the course of a night or two ; though individually they are about the size of the common red ant of our woods. They have an aversion to the light, and invariably work under cover: hence, in attacking a tree, a post, a rafter, or a table, they eat out the interior, leaving the thinnest possible layer of the outer wood remaining. It frequently happens that, after their depredations have been committed, no indication of the work appears to the eye, but the least touch suffices to bring down the apparently solid structure, like a house of cards, amidst a cloud of blinding dust. If, however, as in the case of the supporting posts of a house, any incumbent weight has to be sustained, they have the instinct to guard against the crash which would involve themselves in ruin, by gradually filling up the hollowed posts with a sort of mortar, leaving only a slender way for their own travel; thus the posts are changed from wood to stone, and retain their solidity.

Forbes in his *Oriental Memoirs* * has recorded a curious, but by no means unusual example of the ravages of the termites. Having had occasion to shut up an apartment, he observed, on returning after a few weeks, a number of the well-known covered ways leading across the room to certain engravings hung in frames. The glasses appeared to be uncommonly dull, and the frames covered with dust. " On attempting," says he, " to wipe it off, I was astonished to find the glasses fixed to the wall, not suspended in frames as I left them, but completely surrounded by an incrustation cemented by the white ants, who had actually eaten up the deal frames and backboards, and the greater part of the paper, and left the glasses upheld by the incrustation or covered way, which they had formed during their depredations."

Smeathman tells of a pipe of old Madeira wine having been tapped and entirely lost by a band of these insects, who had taken a fancy to the oak staves of the

* Vol. i., p. 362.

cask. And Sir E. Tennent appears to have fared no
better; for he complains that, in Ceylon, he had a case of
wine filled, in the course of two days, with almost solid
clay, and only discovered the presence of the white ants
by the bursting of the corks.

They find their way into bureaux and cabinets, and
greedily devour all papers and parchments therein. and
"a shelf of books will be tunnelled into a gallery, if it
happen to be in their line of march." Hence, as Humboldt observes, throughout the equinoctial regions of
America,—and the same is true in similar climates of the
Old World, indeed, in all, where very special precautions
are not taken against it,—it is infinitely rare to find any
records much more than half a century old.

But though the exercise of their instinct brings these
little insects into collision with man, and so far they act
as his enemies, abundantly making up in pertinacity and
consociation what they lack in individual force,—we shall
greatly misunderstand their mission if we look at it only
in this aspect. As an example of mean agents performing great deeds, we must see them far from the haunts of
man, engaged as the scavengers of the forest-wilds of the
tropics; the removers of fallen trees, of huge giants of the
woods, commissioned to get rid of those enormous bulks
of timber, which, having stood in stately grandeur and
rich life for a thousand years, have at length yielded to
death. Not long does the vast mass lie cumbering the
soil beneath: the termites attack it, enter its substance
from the ground, and in the course of a few weeks suc-

ceed in so emptying it, as to leave it a mere deceptive shell, on which if you step, to use the comparison of Smeathman, "you might as well tread upon a cloud."

We presume that, in the following description of a scene in Brazil, we may understand the insects of which we are now speaking, though the traveller calls them "ants :"—

"A number of tall, prostrate trees were lying about, upon which large columns of ants of all kinds moved busily to and fro. In penetrating into the depths of the primeval forest, one sees evidence at every step that these minute creatures are the destroyers of the colossal trees, whose strength braves all the attacks of storm and wind. A striking instance is this of how small are often the means which the Creator employs to produce the mightiest results; for what greater disproportion can be imagined than between an ant and one of these giants of the forest? No sooner is a tree attacked by them than it is doomed; its size and strength are of no avail; and frequently these little insects will destroy it in such a manner that the bark alone remains, and all the woody fibres crumble away, until the tall tree falls at length to the ground with a tremendous crash, a prey to the united and persevering attacks of millions and millions of the ants. Besides these proofs of the destructive power of these insects, the forests along the Estrada exhibit evidence of their skill in the pyramidical ant-hills, similar to those we had seen on the coast of the province of Rio de Janeiro. We also observed large trunks of trees pierced with deep holes, having the appearance of filigree on a grand scale. This, too, was probably the work of these destructive insects."[*]

In Africa, there are flies which are the actual lords of certain extensive districts, ruling with so absolute a sway, that not only man and his cattle are fain to submit to them, but even the most gigantic animals, the elephants and rhinoceroses, cannot stand before them. There is the *zimb* of Abyssinia, the very sound of whose dreaded hum sends the herds from their pastures, and makes them run wildly about, till they drop with fatigue, fright, and hunger. There is no resource for the pastoral inhabitants but instantly to vacate the country, and retire with their herds to their nearest sands, where they will not be molested. This they would do, though they knew that hostile bands of robbers were waylaying them. Such is the terror of a fly.[†]

Quite as formidable in the southern portion of the same continent is the dreaded *tsetse*, like the *zimb* one of the *Tabanidæ*, though a different species. This insect, which is scarcely larger than our house-fly, reigns over certain districts, attacking the domestic animals. Its bite is certain death to the ox, horse, and dog; yet, strange to say, it produces no serious inconvenience to the human body, nor apparently to the wild game of the country—the buffaloes, giraffes, antelopes, and zebras, which roam by millions over the same plains.

The effect on the smitten beast is not immediate, nor

[*] Adalbert's *Travels*, ii., p. 237.   [†] Bruce's *Travels*, ii., p. 315.

does the buzz produce the terror which that of the zimb does. It is not till after several days that the poison begins to manifest its effect: then the eyes and nose discharge freely, the animal swells, and becomes gradually emaciated, till at length violent purging supervenes, and the animal perishes, the whole blood and flesh being unnaturally altered in condition.*

Nor is Europe wholly free from such plagues. There is, in Servia and the Banat, a minute fly,† from whose destructive assaults on the cattle the inhabitants have suffered immense losses. A traveller, arriving at Golubacs, on the Danube, thus speaks of it:—

" Near this place we found a range of caverns, famous for producing the poisonous fly, too well known in Servia and Hungary under the name of the Golubacser fly. These singular and venomous insects, somewhat resembling musquitoes, generally make their appearance during the first great heat of the summer, in such numbers as to appear like vast volumes of smoke. Their attacks are always directed against every description of quadruped, and so potent is the poison they communicate, that even an ox is unable to withstand its influence, for he always expires in less than two hours. This results, not so much from the virulence of the poison, as that every vulnerable part is simultaneously covered with these most destructive insects ; when the wretched animals, frenzied with pain, rush wild through the fields till death puts a period to

* Livingstone's *Travels*, p. 80, *et seq.*
† *Simulium Columbaschense*, Köll.

their sufferings, or they accelerate dissolution by plunging headlong into the rivers." *

Perhaps worse, however, than these, or any of them, are the musquitoes; not that their virulence or fatality equals that of the tsetse or zimb, but because they are almost universally distributed. Those, terrible as they are, are limited to certain districts, but the musquito is ubiquitous, and everywhere is a pest and a torment. One needs to spend a night among musquitoes to understand what a true plague of flies is. Hundreds of travellers might be cited on the subject, and if I adduce the following testimony, it is not because it is the strongest I could find, but because it is one of the most recent, and therefore least known :—

That traveller of all travellers, Mr Atkinson, who has laid open to us the most magnificent scenery of the world, and the most inaccessible, to whom neither the most fearful chasms and precipices, nor boiling torrents and swift rivers, nor earthquakes and furious storms, nor eternal frost and snow, nor burning waterless steppes, nor robbers, nor wild beasts, presented any impediment,—fairly confesses his conqueror in the musquito. The gnat alone, of all creatures, elicits from him a word of dread ;—he could not brave the musquitoes. Over and over he tells us in his mountain scrambles, that the musquitoes were there "in millions,"—that they were "taking a most savage revenge on him for having sent his horses out of their reach," — that they were "devouring" him,—that he

* Spence's *Travels in Circassia.* i., p. 59.

" neither dared to sleep nor to look out;"—that " the hum-ming sound of the millions was something awful;"—that he found himself "in the very regions of torment," which " it was utterly impossible to endure ;"—that " the poor horses stood with their heads in the smoke, as a protection against the pests ;"—and that "to have remained on the spot would have subjected them to a degree of torment neither man nor beast could endure, so that they were obliged to retreat." " I wish I could say," he feelingly adds, "that we left the enemy in possession of the field. Not so ; they pursued us with blood-thirsty pertinacity, until we reached some open meadows, when they were driven back into their fenny region by a breeze,—I hope to prey on each other."

* Atkinson's *Siberia,* p. 75, *et passim.*

V.

THE VAST.

THOUGH great and small must always be comparative terms, the human mind does ordinarily set up some standard of dimensions, for this or that particular class of entities, and is affected with emotions of surprise and admiration, in proportion as some examples either exceed or fall short of it. In living creatures, probably, the human body is the tacitly recognised medium of size; for we call a horse or a buffalo a large animal, a cat or a weasel a small one; while, in such as pass beyond these limits in either direction, we are conscious that the dimension becomes a prominent element in the interest with which we regard them. The first exclamation of one who sees an elephant for the first time, would probably be, "How big he is!" and in like manner the first impression produced by a humming-bird, in most cases, would not be "How beautiful! How glittering!" but "How very small!"

I well remember the interest and almost awe with which, on my first voyage across the Atlantic, I saw suddenly emerge from the sea, the immense black oily back of a whale. It was almost close to the ship, and it rose like a

great smooth bank out of the water, gave a sort of wallow-
ing roll, and quietly sank from sight again. The excitement of the momentary sight prevented my attempting to
estimate its measurement, besides that the entire animal
was not exposed, but it seemed to me nearly as large as
the vessel in which I sailed. The species was no doubt
the great rorqual, since the whalebone whale is said never
to venture beyond the limits of the Arctic Seas. This is
the most enormous of all the animals known to inhabit
this globe, attaining a length of a hundred feet and even
more. The skeleton of one which was stranded near
Ostend in 1827, which was subsequenty exhibited in Paris
and London, measured ninety-five feet. Two specimens
have been measured of the length of a hundred and five
feet, and Sir Arthur de Capel Brooke asserts that it is
occasionally seen of the enormous dimensions of one hundred and twenty feet.*

The "right" or whalebone whale, the object of commer-
cial enterprise in the Polar Seas, is little more than half
as large as this last-named bulk. Eighty and a hundred
feet are mentioned, indeed, by the earlier writers, as occasional dimensions of this species, but these statements are
possibly exaggerations, or else the distinction between
this and the rorqual may have been overlooked. A tradition exists of one Ochter, a Norwegian, of King Alfred's

* The gigantic whales that inhabit the Indian Ocean are probably of
this genus. One was stranded on the Chittagong coast in August 1842,
which measured ninety feet in length and forty-two in diameter; and
another on the coast of Aracan in 1851, which was eighty-four feet
long. (See *Zoologist for December* 1859, p. 6778.)

day, who "was one of six that had killed sixty whales in two days, of which some were forty-eight, some fifty yards long." The discrimination here would seem to imply actual measurement, though perhaps it was not very precise. At present, nothing like such a length is attained. The late Dr Scoresby, who was personally engaged in the capture of three hundred and twenty-two whales, never found one of this species that exceeded sixty feet. There is, however, one caveat needful to be remembered; that an animal naturally long-lived, and which probably grows throughout life, is not likely to attain anything like its full dimensions when incessantly persecuted as the whale of the Arctic Seas has been for ages past. However, a whale of sixty feet is estimated to weigh seventy tons, or more than three hundred fat oxen.

The sperm-whale or cachalot, whose home is the vast Pacific, from north to south and from east to west, holds a place as to bulk between the whalebone whale and the rorqual. Mr Beale, who is the authority in all that concerns this animal, gives eighty-four feet as the length of a sperm whale of the largest size, and its diameter twelve or fourteen feet. Of this huge mass, the head occupies about one third of the entire length, with a thickness little inferior to that of the body; while, as this thickness is equal throughout, the front of the head terminating abruptly, as if an immense solid block had been sawn off, this part of the animal bears no small resemblance to an immense box. The appearance of a whale when disturbed, and going what seamen call "head-out," this vast bluff head projected every few seconds out of water, has a most extraordinary appearance.

Undoubtedly the largest of terrestrial animals is the elephant,

> " The huge earth-shaking beast;
> The beast on whom the castle
> With all its guards doth stand;
> The beast that hath between his eyes
> The serpent for a hand."

But the specimens with which we are familiar in our zoological gardens and menageries, are inadequate representatives of the race. It is in their native regions, of course, that we look for the most magnificent specimens. Some exaggeration, however, has prevailed respecting the dimensions attainable by the elephant. "Seventeen to twenty feet" have been given as its occasional height in the Madras presidency. The Emperor Baber, in his Memoirs, alludes to the report that in the islands the elephants attain ten gez, or about twenty feet; but he adds, " I have never seen one above four or five gez," (eight or ten feet.) The East India Company's standard was seven feet and upwards, measured at the shoulder. Mr Corse says the greatest height ever measured by him was ten feet six inches. As an example of the deceptiveness of a mere conjecture even by experienced persons, he mentions the case of an elephant belonging to the Nabob of Decca, which was said to be fourteen feet high. Mr Corse wished to measure particularly, as he himself judged him to be twelve feet. The driver assured him that the beast was from fifteen to eighteen feet;—yet when carefully measured, he did not exceed ten feet. The Ceylon specimens rarely exceed nine feet; yet Wolf says, he saw one taken near Jaffna, which measured twelve feet one inch, of course to the arch of the back.

The elephants of the farther peninsula much excel those of India and Ceylon, perhaps because they are less disturbed. The skeleton of one in the museum at St Petersburg, which was sent to Peter the Great by the Shah of Persia, measures sixteen feet and a half in height; and probably this is the highest authentic instance on record.

The African elephant is perhaps not inferior to that of Pegu. Mr Pringle, in a very graphic picture, has described an unexpected rencontre with an enormous elephant in an African valley. " We halted, and surveyed him for a few minutes in silent admiration and astonishment. He was, indeed, a mighty and magnificent creature. The two engineer officers, who were familiar with the appearance of the elephant in his wild state, agreed that the animal before us was at least fourteen feet in height." Major Denham in his expedition into Central Africa, met with some which he guessed to be sixteen feet high; but one which he saw killed, and which he characterises as " an immense fellow," measured twelve feet six to the back.* Fossil remains of an elephant have been discovered at Jubbalpore, which measure fifteen feet to the shoulder.

I need only advert to other colossal quadrupeds, the

---

* Sir E. Tennent, (*Ceylon*, ii., p. 291,) quoting this account, says " nine feet six inches ; " but this is a mis-reading. It was nine feet six inches *to the hip-bone ;* and three feet more to the back.

seven or eight species of rhinoceros, the hippopotamus, the giraffe, the camel, the gaur, the gayall, and other great wild oxen of India; the urus, the bison, the Cape buffalo, the eland. Most of these dwell in the poor and arid regions of South Africa; where the nakedness of the country permits them to be seen to advantage. Dr Andrew Smith, in one day's march with the bullock-waggons saw, without wandering to any great distance on either side, between one hundred and one hundred and fifty rhinoceroses, which belonged to three species; the same day he saw several herds of giraffes, amounting together to nearly a hundred; and, though no elephants were observed, yet they are found in this district. At the distance of little more than an hour's march from their place of encampment on the previous night, his party actually killed at one spot eight hippopotamuses, and saw many more. In this same river there were likewise crocodiles.

Among birds, the condor of the Andes has been the subject of greatly exaggerated reports of its dimensions. When it was first discovered by the Spanish conquerors of America, it was compared to the Rokh of Arabian fable, and by some even considered to be the identical bird, " which is able to trusse an elephant." Garcilasso states that some of those killed by the Spaniards measured fifteen *or* sixteen feet (the vagueness of the " or " in what professes to be actual measurement is suspicious) from tip to tip of the extended wings. He adds that two will attack a bull and devour it, and that single individuals will slay boys of twelve years old.

Desmarchais improves upon this; stretches the expansion of the wings to eighteen feet; a width so enormous that, as he says, the bird can never enter the forest; and he declares that a single one will attack a man, and carry off a stag.

A modern traveller, however, soars far beyond these puny flights of imagination, and gravely gives forty feet as the measurement, carefully noted, as he informs us, "with his own hand," from the actual specimen. It is only charitable to conclude that he really measured sixteen *feet*, and that he either wrote "spaces" by mistake, or, which is most likely, wrote simply "16," translating it afterwards when he compared his notes with what others had said before him. Here, however, is the veracious description, which the reader will see does not lack romance in its embellishment.

"It was so satiated with its repast on the carcass of a horse, as to suffer me to approach within pistol-shot before it extended its enormous wings to take flight, which was to me the signal to fire; and having loaded with an ample charge of pellets, my aim proved effectual and fatal. What a formidable monster did I behold, screaming and flapping in the last convulsive struggle of life! It may be difficult to believe that the most gigantic animal which inhabits the earth or the ocean, can be equalled in size by a tenant of the air; and those persons who have never seen a larger bird than our mountain eagle, will probably read with astonishment of a species of that same bird, in the southern hemisphere, being so large and strong as to seize an ox with its talons, and to lift it into the air, whence it lets it fall to the ground, in order to kill it and prey upon the carcass. But this astonishment must, in a great measure, subside when the dimensions of the bird are taken into consideration, and which, incredible as they may appear, I now insert from a note taken by my own hand. When the wings are spread they measure sixteen spaces, forty feet in extent from point to point. The feathers are eight spaces, twenty feet in length, and the quill part, two palms, eight feet in circumference. It is said to have strength enough to carry off a living rhinoceros." *

Humboldt dissipated these extravagances; though he confesses that it appeared to himself of colossal size, and it was only the actual admeasurement of a dead specimen that corrected the optical illusion. He met with no example that exceeded nine feet, and he was assured by many of the inhabitants of Quito that they had never shot any that exceeded eleven. This estimate, however, appears to be below the reality; for Tschudi, a most careful and reliable authority, and an accomplished zoologist, assigns to this bird in one place an expanse of "from twelve to thirteen feet," while in another he says: " I measured a very large male condor, and the width from the tip of one wing to the tip of the other was fourteen English feet and two inches, an enormous expanse of wing, not equalled by any other bird except the white albatross." † So far from his " trussing a rhinoceros," or

* Temple's *Travels in Peru.* † *Travels in Peru.*

even an ox, he cannot, according to Tschudi, raise even a
sheep from the ground. "He cannot, when flying, carry
a weight exceeding eight or ten pounds." The voracity
of the obscene bird is very great. The owner of some
captive specimens assured the naturalist that he had
given to one, in the course of a single day, by way of
experiment, eighteen pounds of meat, consisting of the
entrails of oxen; that the bird devoured the whole,
and ate his allowance the next day with the usual ap-
petite.

We have all been accustomed from childhood to regard
with awe the enormous serpents of the hot and damp
intertropical forests; though the specimens carried about
in travelling menageries have but little contributed to
nurture the sentiment. A couple of coils of variegated
mosaic, looking like a tesselated pavement, about as
thick as a lacquey's calf, wrapped up in the folds of a
blanket at the bottom of a deal box, we had difficulty in
accepting as the impersonation of the demon which hung
from the branches of an Indian tree, and, having pressed
the life out of a buffalo in his mighty folds and broken
his bones, swallowed the body entire, all but the horns.
Here again there is incertitude and disappointment; and
the colossal dragon, which looms so large in the distance
of time and space, grows "small by degrees and beautifully less" in the ratio of its approach to our own times
and our own eyes. Yet enough of size and power remains, even when all legitimate deductions are made, to
invest the great boa with a romantic interest, and to

make the inquiry into its real dimensions worthy of prosecution.

I may observe, that several species of these great serpents exist in the intertropical regions of America, Africa, and Asia; but all these, though assigned by zoologists to distinct genera (the American species belonging to the genus *Boa*, and those of Africa and Asia to *Python*) have so much in common, in habits, structure, and size, that I shall speak of them without distinguishing the species.

The old Roman historians report that the army of Attilius Regulus, while attacking Carthage, was assaulted by an enormous serpent, which was destroyed only by the aid of the military engines crushing it with huge stones. The skin of this monster, measuring 120 feet in length, was sent to Rome, and preserved as a trophy in a temple till the Numantine war. Several writers mention the fact, and Pliny speaks of its existence as well known.

Diodorus Siculus mentions a serpent which was captured, not without loss of human life, in Egypt, and which was taken to Alexandria; it measured thirty cubits, or about forty-five feet in length.

Suetonius records that one was exhibited in front of the Comitium at Rome, which was fifty cubits, or seventy-five feet in length.

It is probable that these measurements were all taken from the skin after having been detached from the body. I have had some experience in skinning serpents, and am therefore aware of the extent to which the skin, when dragged off by force, is capable of stretching : one-fourth of the entire length may not unfairly be deducted on this account.   But even with this allowance, we must admit, unless we reject the testimony of sober historians, who could hardly have been mistaken so grossly as to warrant such rejection, that serpents did exist in ancient times which far exceeded the limits that have fallen under the observation of modern naturalists.

There is a well-known picture by Daniell, representing an enormous serpent attacking a boat's crew in one of the creeks of the Ganges.   It is a graphic scene, said to have been commemorative of a fact.   The crew had moored their boat by the edge of the jungle, and, leaving one of the party in charge, had gone into the forest.   He lay down under the thwarts, and was soon asleep.   During his unconsciousness an enormous python emerged from the jungle, coiled itself round the sleeper, and was in the act of crushing him to death, when his comrades returned. They succeeded in killing the monster, "which was found to measure sixty-two feet and some inches in length." This seems precise enough ; but we should like to know whether the measurement was made by the Lascars themselves, or by any trustworthy European.

A correspondent of the *Edinburgh Literary Gazette* has told, with every appearance of life-truth, a thrilling story of an encounter which he had with an enormous boa on the banks of a river in Guiana.   Awaked, as he lay in his boat, by the cold touch of something at his feet, he found that the serpent's mouth was in contact with them, preparing, as he presumed, to swallow him feet foremost. In an instant he drew himself up, and, grasping his gun, discharged it full at the reptile's head, which reared into the air with a horrid hiss and terrible contortions, and then, with one stroke of his paddles, he shot up the stream beyond reach. On arriving at his friend's house, it was determined to seek the wounded serpent, and several armed negroes were added to the party.

They soon found the spot where the crushed and bloody reeds told of the recent adventure, and proceeded cautiously to reconnoitre. Advancing thus about thirty yards, alarm was given that the monster was visible. "We saw through the reeds part of its body coiled up, and part stretched out; but, from their density, the head was invisible. Disturbed, and apparently irritated, by our approach, it appeared, from its movements, about to attack us. Just as we caught a glimpse at its head we fired, both of us almost at the same moment. It fell, hissing and rolling in a variety of contortions." Here one of the negroes, taking a circuit, succeeded in hitting the creature a violent blow with a club, which stunned it, and a few more strokes decided the victory. "On measuring it, we found it to be nearly forty feet in length, and of proportional thickness."

I do not know how far this story is to be relied on; but if it is given in good faith, the serpent was the longest dependable example I know of in modern times. Still, "*nearly* forty feet" is somewhat indefinite.

In Mr Ellis's amusing account of his visit to Manilla,

he mentions specimens of enormous size; but there does not seem to have been any actual admeasurement.

"On one occasion," he says, "I was driven by an Indian, (coachman to the gentleman with whom I was stopping,) in company with a friend, to the house of a priest, who had some singularly large specimens of the boa-constrictor [*python*]; one, of two that were in a wooden pen together, could hardly have been less than fifty feet long, and the stoutest part as thick round as a very fat man's body."*

Bontius speaks of some which were upwards of thirty-six feet long; doubtless Oriental pythons. An American boa is mentioned by Bingley, of the same length, the skin of which was in the cabinet of the Prince of Orange; and Shaw mentions a skin in the British Museum which measured thirty-five feet. Probably in these last two cases we must allow something for stretching. .

In the *Bombay Courier*, of August 31, 1799, a dreadful story is narrated of a Malay sailor having been crushed to death by a python on the coast of Celebes. His comrades, hearing his shrieks, went to his assistance, but only in time to save the corpse from its living grave. They, however, killed the serpent. It had seized the poor man by the wrist, where the marks of the teeth were very distinct, and the body shewed evident signs of having been crushed by coils round the head, neck, breast, and thigh. The length of the monster was "about thirty feet, and its thickness that of a moderate-sized man."

* Ellis's *Manilla*, p. 237.

Mr M'Leod, in the *Voyage of H. M. S. Alceste,* has minutely described the feeding of a python from Borneo, which was sixteen feet long, and observes that, at Whydah, in Africa, he had seen serpents "*more than double* the size" of this specimen; but it does not seem that they were measured.

The *Penang Gazette* of a late date says—"A monster boa-constrictor [*python*] was killed one morning this week by the overseer of convicts at Bayam Lepas, on the road to Telo' Kumbar. His attention was attracted by the squealing of a pig, and on going to the place he found it in the coils of the snake. A few blows from the changkolf of the convicts served to despatch the reptile, and, on uncoiling him, he was found to be twenty-eight feet in length, and thirty-two inches in girth. This is one of the largest specimens we have heard of in Penang." *

Dr Andrew Smith, in his *Zoology of South Africa,* records having seen a specimen of *Python Natalensis,* which was twenty-five feet long, *though a portion of the tail was wanting.* This is the largest specimen I know of, actually measured in the flesh by a perfectly reliable authority; and even here the amount to be added to the twenty-five feet can only be conjectured.

It may be interesting to compare these statements by setting them in a tabular form, indicating each specimen by some name that shall serve to identify it, and adding a note of the degree of credit due to each.

* Quoted in *The Times, Nov.* 1, 1859.

				Feet.	
Regulus .	.	.	.	120	probably stretched.
Suetonius	.	.	.	75	ibid.
Diodorus	.	.	.	45	ibid.
Daniell .	.	.	.	62	not reliable.
Ellis	.	.	.	50	conjectural.
Guiana .	.	.	.	40	anonymous.
Bontius .	.	,	.	36	reliable.
Bingley .	.	.	.	36	perhaps stretched.
Shaw	.	.	.	85	ibid.
M'Leod .	.	.	.	32	conjectural.
Celebes .	.	.	.	30	vague.
Penang .	.	.	.	28	perhaps reliable.
Smith .	.	.	.	+ 25	certainly correct.

Turning from the animal to the vegetable world, we find giants and colossi there which excite our wonder. There is a sea-weed, the *Nereocystis*, which grows on the north-west shores of America, which has a stem no thicker than whipcord, but upwards of three hundred feet in length, bearing at its free extremity a huge hollow bladder, shaped like a barrel, six or seven feet long, and crowned with a tuft of more than fifty forked leaves, each from thirty to forty feet in length. The vesicle, being filled with air, buoys up this immense frond, which lies stretched along the surface of the sea: here the sea-otter has his favourite lair, resting himself upon the vesicle, or hiding among the leaves, while he pursues his fishing. The cord-like stem which anchors this floating tree must be of considerable strength; and, accordingly, we find it used as a· fishing-line by the natives of the coast. But great as is the length of this sea-weed, it is exceeded by the *Macrocystis*, though the leaves and air-vessels of that plant are of small dimensions. In the *Nereocystis*, the stem is unbranched ; in *Macrocystis*, it branches as it approaches the surface, and afterwards divides by repeated forkings, each division bearing a leaf, until there results a floating mass of foliage, some hundreds of square yards in superficial extent. It is said that the stem of this plant is sometimes fifteen hundred feet in length.[*]

Mr Darwin,[†] speaking of this colossal alga at the southern extremity of America, where it grows up from a depth of forty-five fathoms to the surface, at a very oblique angle, says, that its beds, even when of no great breadth, make excellent natural floating breakwaters. It is quite curious to mark how soon the great waves from the ocean, in passing through the straggling stems into an exposed harbour, sink in elevation, and become smooth.

Such an enormous length is not without parallel in terrestrial plants. Familiar to every one,—from the schoolboy, over whom it hangs *in terrorem*, upward,—as is the common cane, with its slenderness, its flexibility, and its flinty, polished surface,—how few are aware that it is only a small part of the stem of a palm-tree, which, in its native forest, reached a length of five hundred feet ! These ratans form a tribe of plants growing in the dense jungles of continental and insular India, which, though they resemble grasses or reeds in their appearance, are true trees of the palm kind. They are exceedingly slender, never increasing in thickness, though immensely in length ;

[*] Harvey's *Marine Algæ*, p. 28.　　　[†] *Nat. Voyage*, xi.

in the forest they trail along the ground, sending forth leaves at intervals, whose sheathing bases we may easily recognise at what we call joints, climb to the summits of trees, descend to the earth, climb and descend again, till some species attain the astonishing length of twelve hundred feet.*

We are accustomed to consider the various species of *Cactus* as petted plants for our green-house shelves and cottage-windows; yet, in our larger conservatories, there are specimens which astonish us by their size. A few years ago there were at the Royal Gardens at Kew, two examples of *Echinocactus*, like water-butts for bulk; one of which weighed upwards of seven hundred pounds, and the other about two thousand pounds.

The species of *Cereus* which with us appear as green, succulent, angular stems, and bear their elegant, scarlet blossoms, adorned with a bundle of white stamens, grow, in the arid plains of South America, to thick lofty pillars or massive branching candelabra. Travellers in Cumana have spoken with enthusiasm of the grandeur of these rows of columns, when the red glow of sunset illumines them, and casts their lengthening shadows across the plain.

A kindred species in the Rocky Mountains of the northern continent has been thus described by a recent traveller:—

"This day we saw, for the first time, the giant cactus (*Cereus giganteus*); specimens of which stood at first

* *Rumph.*, v., p. 100.

rather widely apart, like straight pillars ranged along the sides of the valley, but, afterwards, more closely together, and in a different form—namely, that of gigantic candelabra, of six-and-thirty feet high, which had taken root among stones and in clefts of the rocks, and rose in solitary state at various points.

" This *Cereus giganteus*, the queen of the cactus tribe, is known in California and New. Mexico under the name of Petahaya. The missionaries who visited the country between the Colorado and the Gila, more than a hundred years ago, speak of the fruit of the Petahaya, and of the natives of the country using it for food ; and they also mention a remarkable tree that had branches, but no leaves, though it reached the height of sixty feet, and was of considerable girth. . . . . The wildest and most inhospitable regions appear to be the peculiar home of this plant, and its fleshy shoots will strike root, and grow to a surprising size, in chasms in heaps of stones, where the closest examination can scarcely discover a particle of vegetable soil. Its form is various, and mostly dependent on its age ; the first shape it assumes is that of an immense club standing upright in the ground, and of double the circumference of the lower part at the top. This form is very striking, while the plant is still only from two to six feet high, but, as it grows taller, the thickness becomes more equal, and when it attains the height of twenty-five feet, it looks like a regular pillar ; after this it begins to throw out its branches. These come out at first in a globular shape, but turn upward as they elongate, and then grow parallel to the trunk, and at a certain distance from it, so that a cereus with many branches looks exactly like an immense candelabrum, especially as the branches are mostly symmetrically arranged round the trunk, of which the diameter is not usually more than a foot and a half, or, in some rare instances, a foot more. They vary much in height; the highest we ever saw, at Williams' Fork, measured from thirty-six to forty feet; but, south of the Gila, they are said to reach sixty; and when you see them rising from the extreme point of a rock, where a surface of a few inches square forms their sole support, you cannot help wondering that the first storm does not tear them from their airy elevation. . . . .

"If the smaller specimens of the *Cereus giganteus* that we had seen in the morning excited our astonishment, the feeling was greatly augmented, when, on our further journey, we beheld this stately plant in all its magnificence. The absence of every other vegetation enabled us to distinguish these cactus-columns from a great distance, as they stood symmetrically arranged on the heights and declivities of the mountains, to which they imparted a most peculiar aspect, though certainly not a beautiful one. Wonderful as each plant is, when regarded singly, as a grand specimen of vegetable life, these solemn, silent forms, which stand motionless, even in a hurricane, give a somewhat dreary character to the landscape. Some look like petrified giants, stretching out their arms in speechless pain, and others stand like lonely sentinels, keeping their dreary watch on the edge of precipices, and gazing into the abyss, or over into the pleasant valley of the Williams' Fork, at the flocks of birds that do not venture to rest on the thorny arms of the Petahaya; though the wasp and the gaily variegated woodpecker may be seen taking up their abode in the old wounds and scars of sickly or damaged specimens of this singular plant." [*]

In the island of Teneriffe there still exists a tree which is an object of scientific curiousity to every visitor, the Dragon-tree of Orotava. It has been celebrated from the discovery of the island, and even earlier, for it had been venerated by the Guanches as a sacred tree from immemorial time. Its height is about seventy feet, but its bulk is far more extraordinary. Le Dru found the circumference of the trunk, near the ground, to be seventy-nine feet. Humboldt, who, when he ascended the Peak in 1799, measured it some feet from the ground, found it forty-eight feet; and Sir G. Staunton gives thirty-six feet as the circumference at a height of ten feet.

The banyan, or sacred fig of India, acquires a prodigious size, not by the enlargement of its individual trunk, but by the multiplication of its trunks, in a peculiar manner of growth. As its horizontal limbs spread on all sides, shoots descend from them to the earth, in which they root, and become so many secondary stems, extending their own lateral branches, which in turn send down fresh rooting shoots, thus ever widening the area of this wondrous forest, composed of a single organic life. This is

[*] Möllhausen's *Journey to the Pacific*, ii., p. 218.

the tree which Milton makes afford to our guilty first
parents the "fig-leaves" with which they hoped to clothe
their new-found nakedness.

> " So counsell'd he, and both together went
>   Into the thickest wood; there soon they chose
>   The fig-tree; not that kind for fruit renown'd;
>   But such as at this day, to Indians known
>   In Malabar or Decan, spreads her arms,
>   Branching so broad and long, that in the ground
>   The bended twigs take root, and daughters grow
>   About the mother-tree, a pillar'd shade
>   High overarch'd, and echoing walks between:
>   There oft the Indian herdsman shunning heat,
>   Shelters in cool, and tends his pasturing herds
>   At loopholes cut through thickest shade: those leaves
>   They gather'd, broad as Amazonian targe;
>   And, with what skill they had, together sew'd,
>   To gird their waist." *

Banyans exist which are much older than the Christian
era. Dr Roxburgh mentions some whose area is more
than fifteen hundred feet in circumference, and one hundred in height, the principal trunk being twenty or thirty
feet to the horizontal boughs, and eight or nine feet in
diameter. But the most celebrated tree of this kind is
one growing on the banks of the Nerbudda, and covering
an almost incredible area, of which the circumference still
existing is nearly two thousand feet, though a considerable portion has been swept away by the floods of the
river. The overhanging branches which have not (or had
not at the time this description was made) yet thrown
down their perpendicular shoots, cover a far wider space.

* *Paradise Lost,* book ix.

Three hundred and twenty main trunks may be counted, while the smaller ones exceed three thousand; and each of these is constantly sending forth its branches and pendent root-shoots to form other trunks, and become the augmenters of the vast colony. Immense popular assemblies are sometimes convened beneath this patriarchal fig, and it has been known to shelter seven thousand men at one time beneath its ample shadow.*

The Baobab, a tree of tropical Africa, but now naturalised in other hot countries, is one which attains an immense bulk. Its growth is chiefly in the trunk. It is by no means uncommon for a bole of seventy-five or eighty feet in circumference to begin to send out its branches at twelve or fifteen feet from the ground; and the entire height is frequently little more than the circumference of the trunk. The lower branches, at first horizontal, attain a great length, and finally droop to the ground, completely hiding the trunk, and giving to the tree the appearance of a vast hillock of foliage.

Some examples of the dimensions of this immense, but soft-wooded and spongy tree, may be adduced. Adanson, in 1748, saw, at the mouth of the Senegal, baobabs which were from twenty-six to twenty-nine feet in diameter, with a height of little more than seventy feet, and a head of foliage a hundred and eighty feet across. He remarks, however, that other travellers had found specimens considerably larger. Peters measured trunks from twenty to twenty-five feet thick, which he says were the

* Forbes' *Oriental Memoirs.*

largest he saw. Perrottet, in his *Flora of Senegambia*, declares that he had seen some thirty-two feet in diameter, and seventy to eighty feet high. Golberry found specimens attaining thirty-six feet in diameter, yet but sixty-four feet in height. And Aloysius Cadamosto, who was the first to describe the tree, found specimens whose circumference he estimated at seventeen fathoms, which would give a diameter of thirty-four feet.*

A kind of cypress, growing in Oaxaca, in Mexico, has attained great celebrity among botanists, De Candolle having stated its diameter at sixty feet. Humboldt, who speaks from personal examination, an advantage which the great botanist did not possess, reduces it to forty feet six inches—a very enormous bulk, however, still.

A recent traveller in Venezuela, thus notices a tree of remarkable dimensions :—

"Soon after leaving Turmero, we caught sight of the far-famed Zamang del Guayre, and in about an hour's time arrived at the hamlet of El Guayre, from whence it takes its name. It is supposed to be the oldest tree in the world,† for so great was the reverence of the Indians for it on account of its age at the time of the Spanish Conquest, that the Government issued a decree for its protection from all injury, and it has ever since been public property. It shews no sign whatever of decay, but is as fresh and green as it was most probably a thousand years ago. The trunk of this magnificent tree is only

---

* See Humboldt's *Aspects of Nature*.
† This is probably the exaggeration of local prejudice.

sixty feet high, by thirty feet in circumference, so that it is not so much the enormous size of the Zamang del Guayre that constitutes its great attraction, as the wonderful spread of its magnificent branches, and the perfect dome-like shape of its head, which is so exact and regular that one could almost fancy some extinct race of giants had been exercising their topiarian art upon it. The circumference of this dome is said to be nearly six hundred feet, and the measure [arch?] of its semicircular head very nearly as great. The zamang is a species of mimosa, and what is curious and adds greatly to its beauty and softness is, that the leaves of this giant of nature are as small and delicate as those of the silver-willow, and are equally as sensitive to every passing breeze."*

Even in temperate climates, among the trees with which we are familiar, vast dimensions are not unknown. A yew in the churchyard of Grasford, North Wales, measures more than fifty feet in girth below the branches. In Lithuania, lime-trees have been measured of the circumference of eighty-seven feet.† And, near Saintes, in France, there is an oak, which is sixty-four feet in height, and measures nearly thirty feet in diameter close to the ground, and twenty-three feet at five feet high. A little room, twelve feet nine inches in width, has been made in the hollow of the trunk, and a semicircular bench within it has been carved out of the living wood. A window

* Sullivan's *Rambles in North and South America*, p. 400.
† Endlicher, *Grundz. der Bot.*, p. 399.

gives light to the interior, and a door closes it, while elegant ferns and lichens serve for hangings to the walls.*

But let us look at examples in which prodigious height and immense bulk are united. The *Macrocystis* and the ratan are enormously lengthened, but they are slender; the baobab and the cypress are very thick, but they are short. The colossal locust-trees of equinoctial America are pre-eminent for vastness in both aspects. Von Martius has depicted a scene in a Brazilian forest,† where some trees of this kind occurred of such enormous dimensions, that fifteen Indians with outstretched arms could only just embrace one of them. At the bottom they were eighty-four feet in circumference, and sixty feet where the boles became cylindrical. "They looked more like living rocks than trees; for it was only on the pinnacle of their bare and naked bark that foliage could be discovered, and that at such a distance from the eye that the forms of the leaves could not be made out.

The various species of gum-trees‡ of Australia and Tasmania are prodigious examples of vegetable life, occasionally attaining a height of two hundred and fifty feet, with a proportionate thickness. The following statement of Mr Backhouse will give the reader a vivid idea of a Tasmanian forest. He is speaking of the stringy-bark : §—

---

* *Ann. Soc. Agr., Rochelle*, 1843.
† It is copied in Lindley's *Vegetable Kingdom*, p. 551.
‡ They form the genus *Eucalyptus*.   § *Eucal. robusta.*

"Some of the specimens exceed two hundred feet, rising almost to the height of the monument in London before branching; their trunks also will bear comparison with that stately column, both for circumference and straightness. One of them was found to measure fifty-five feet and a half round its trunk at five feet from the ground; its height was computed at two hundred and fifty feet, and its circumference was seventy feet at the base! My companions spoke to one another, and called to me when on the opposite side of the tree, and their voices sounded so distant that I concluded they had inadvertently quitted me in search of some other object. I accordingly called to them, and they in answer remarked the distant sound of my voice, and inquired if I possibly were behind the tree. At the time when the road was forming through the forest, a man, who had only two hundred yards to go from one company of people to another, lost his way; he shouted, and was repeatedly answered; but, getting farther astray among the prodigious trunks, his voice became inaudible, and he perished. A prostrate tree of this kind was measured two hundred and thirteen feet long; we ascended the trunk on an inclined plane, formed by one of its huge limbs, and walked four of us abreast with ease upon the trunk. In its fall it had hurled down another, one hundred and sixty-eight feet long, which had brought up with its roots a wall of earth twenty feet across!"

But examples of even superior size have been described by the Rev. T. Ewing of Hobart Town. The species is probably the same, though called by another provincial name.

"Last week I went to see two of the largest trees in the world, if not the largest, that have ever been measured. They were both on a tributary rill to the North-west Bay River, at the back of Mount Wellington, and are what are here called Swamp Gums. One was growing, the other prostrate; the latter measured, to the first branch, two hundred and twenty feet; from thence to where the top was broken off and decayed, sixty-four feet, or two hundred and eighty-four feet in all, so that with the top it must have been considerably beyond three hundred feet. It is thirty feet in diameter at the base, and twelve at the first branch. We estimated it to weigh, with the first branch, four hundred and forty tons! The standing giant is still growing vigorously, without the least symptom of decay, and looks like a large church tower among the puny sassafras trees. It measures, at three feet from the ground, one hundred and two feet in circumfurence; at the ground, one hundred and thirty feet! We had no means of ascertaining its height (which, however, must be enormous) from the density of the forest. I measured another not forty yards from it, and at three feet from the ground it was sixty feet round; and at one hundred and thirty feet, where the first branch began, we judged it to be forty feet; this was a noble column indeed, and sound as a nut. I am sure that within a mile there are at least one hundred growing trees forty feet in circumference."

The public exhibition of the " Mammoth-Tree " in London has, however, familiarised us with the fact that greater trees exist than any yet noticed. Upper California is the home of the most gigantic of vegetable productions, which form two species of a sort of Cypress, named respectively *Sequoia sempervirens* and *Seq. Wellingtonia.* The latter has attained the most celebrity.

" About thirty miles from Sonora, in the district of Calaveras, you come to the Stanislas river ; and, following one of its tributaries that murmurs through a deep, wooded bed, you reach the Mammoth-tree Valley, which lies fifteen hundred feet above the level of the sea. In this valley you find yourself in the presence of the giants of the vegetable world ; and the astonishment with which you contemplate from a distance these tower-like Coniferæ, rising far above the lofty pine-woods, is increased when on a nearer approach you become aware of their prodigious dimensions. There is a family of them, consisting of ninety members, scattered over a space of about forty acres ; and the smallest and feeblest among them is not less than fifteen feet in diameter. You can scarcely believe your eyes as you look up to their crowns, which, in the most vigorous of the colossal stems, only begin at the height of a hundred and fifty or two hundred feet from the ground." *

Each member of this wonderful group has received a familiar name, in many cases indicating in its homely associations the rude mind of the backwoodsman. A

* Möllhausen's *Journey to the Pacific,* ii., p. 363.

hotel has been built close to the group, which has become a scene of attraction to visitors from all parts of the country.   An enumeration of a few of the more prominent trees, with their statistics, will enable us better to form an idea of the scene, particularly if we take the monument of London as a standard of comparison, whose total height is two hundred and two feet, and fifteen feet the diameter of the column at the plinth.

Leaving the hotel, and proceeding into the grove, the visitor presently comes to the "Miner's Cabin," a tree measuring eighty feet in circumference, and attaining three hundred feet in height.   The "cabin," or burnt cavity, measures seventeen feet across its entrance, and extends upwards of forty feet.   Continuing our ramble, admiring the luxuriant growth of underwood, consisting of firs, cedars, dog-wood, and hazel, we come to the "Three Graces."   These splendid trees appear to grow, and perhaps do grow, from one root, and form the most beautiful group in the forest, towering side by side to the height of two hundred and ninety feet, tapering symmetrically from their base upwards.   Their united circumference amounts to ninety-two feet; it is two hundred feet to the first limb on the middle tree.   The "Pioneer's Cabin" next arrests our attention, rising to the height of one hundred and fifty feet, (the top having been broken off,) and thirty-three feet in diameter.   Continuing our walk, we came to a forlorn-looking individual, having many rents in the bark, and, withal, the most shabby-looking in the forest.   This is the "Old Bachelor;" it is about three hundred feet high, and sixty feet in circumference. The next tree is the "Mother of the Forest," presently to be mentioned as having been stripped of its bark by speculators in 1854. We are now amidst the "Family Group," and standing near the uprooted base of the "Father of the Forest." This scene is grand and beautiful beyond description. The venerable "Father" has long since bowed his head in the dust; yet how stupendous even in his ruins! He measures one hundred and twelve feet in circumference at the base, and can be traced three hundred feet, where the trunk was broken by falling against another tree. A hollow chamber, or burnt cavity, extends through the trunk two hundred feet, large enough for a person to ride through. Near its base is a spring of water. Walking upon the trunk, and looking from its uprooted base, the mind can scarcely conceive its prodigious dimensions, while on either hand tower his giant sons and daughters. Passing onward, we meet with the "Husband and Wife," leaning affectionately towards one another; they are each sixty feet in circumference, and two hundred and fifty feet in height. "Hercules," one of the most gigantic specimens in the forest, stands leaning in our path. This tree, like many others, has been burnt at the base; it is three hundred and twenty-five feet high, and ninety-seven feet in circumference. The "Hermit," rising solitary and alone, is next observed. This tree, straight and well-proportioned, measures three hundred and twenty feet high, and sixty feet in circumference. Still returning towards the hotel by the lower trail, we

pass the "Mother and Son," which together measure
ninety-three feet in circumference; the "Mother" is
three hundred and twenty, the "Son" a hopeful youth
of three hundred feet. The "Siamese Twins and their
Guardian" form the next group: the "Twins" have one
trunk at the base, separating at the height of forty feet,
each measuring three hundred feet high; the "Guardian"
is eighty feet in circumference, and three hundred and
twenty-five feet high. Beyond stands the "Old Maid,"
slightly bowing in her lonely grief; she measures sixty feet
in circumference, and is two hundred and sixty feet high.
Two beautiful trees, called "Addie and Mary," are the
next to arrest our attention, measuring each sixty-five feet
in circumference, and nearly three hundred feet high.
We next reach the "Horse-back Ride," an old fallen
trunk of one hundred and fifty feet in length, hollowed
out by the fires which have, in days gone by, raged
through the forest. The cavity is twelve feet in the clear
and in the narrowest place, and a person can ride through
on horseback, a distance of seventy-five feet. "Uncle
Tom's Cabin" next claims our admiration, being three
hundred feet high, and seventy-five feet in circumference.
The "Cabin" has a burnt entrance of two and a half feet
in diameter; the cavity within is large enough to seat fifteen persons. Two other trees we must note; one of
which, named the "Pride of the Forest," remarkable for
the smoothness of its bark, measures two hundred and
eighty feet in height, and sixty feet in circumference.
The "Burnt Cave" is also remarkable; it measures forty

feet nine inches across its roots, while the cavity extends to the distance of forty feet—large enough for a horseman to ride in, and, turning round, return. We now reach the "Beauty of the Forest," a tree sixty-five feet in circumference, fully three hundred feet high, symmetrical in form, and adorned with a magnificent crest of foliage. Reaching the road, and returning to the house, we pass the "Two Guardsmen," which tower to the height of three hundred feet, and are sixty-five and seventy feet in circumference, forming an appropriate gateway to this wonderful forest.

Two of these trees have been used for the satisfaction of public curiosity at a distance from their home. One of the noblest, called the "Big Tree," was felled; a work of no small labour, since the trunk was ninety-six feet in circumference at the base, and solid throughout. It was effected by boring holes with augers, which were then connected by means of the axe, and occupied twenty-five men for five days. But even when this was done, so accurately perpendicular was the noble column that it would not fall, and it was only by applying a wedge and strong leverage, during a heavy breeze, that its overthrow was at last effected. In falling it seemed to shake the ground like an earthquake; and its immense weight forced it into the soft virgin soil, so that it lies imbedded in a trench, and the stones and earth were hurled upward by the shock with such force that these records of the fall may be seen on the surrounding trees to the height of nearly a hundred feet. The stump was smoothed,

K

and has been fitted up for theatrical performances and
balls, affording ample room for thirty-two dancers. The
bark was removed for a certain length, and being put
up symmetrically, as it originally subsisted, constituted
a large room, furnished with a carpet, a piano, and seats
for forty persons. In this state it was exhibited in various
cities of America and Europe.

So successful was this speculation, that another hero
of the Barnum tribe proceeded to separate the entire bark
from the "Mother of the Forest," to a height of one hundred and sixteen feet, removing it in sections, carefully
marked and numbered, for future reconstruction. It is
this trophy which has been exhibited in London, first in
Newman Street, and afterwards at the Adelaide Gallery.
These buildings, however, would not admit of the erection
of the whole, so that it was removed in 1856 to the Crystal Palace, where it now delights the eyes of thousands
daily.

Perhaps we can scarcely regret the removal and trans-
port of these relics, especially as it is said the "Mother"
has not been perceptibly injured in health by the abstrac-
tion of her outer garment. Yet it is a matter of congra-
tulation that pecuniary avidity will no further diminish
this noble grove, for the law has now prohibited the
injury of any more trees, on any pretence whatever.*

All these are the mighty works of an Almighty God;
not self-produced, as some would fain assure us, by the

* This account is chiefly condensed from a memoir by Dr Berthold
Seemann, F.L.S., in the *Annals and Mag. of Nat. Hist.* for March 1859.

operation of what are called eternal "laws," but designed by a Personal Intelligence, created by a Living Word, and upheld by an Active Power.

"Praise the Lord from the earth, ye dragons, and all deeps : . . . mountains, and all hills; fruitful trees, and all cedars ; beasts and all cattle ; creeping things, and flying fowl ! His glory is above the earth and heaven." (Ps. cxlviii.)

VI

THE MINUTE.

IF great bulk excites our admiration, so does great minuteness. He who of old wrote the Iliad within the compass of a nut-shell, might have copied the poem a hundred times over, without eliciting one puff of that gas which enabled him " hominum volitare per ora," if he had confined himself to the ordinary scale ; and the curious interest with which we gaze on a dozen spoons carved out of one cherry-stone, and enclosed in another, we should not think of bestowing on the same number of dessert spoons in the plate-basket. The excessive minuteness of the object in question is the point to be admired, and yet not *mere* minuteness ; we might see objects much smaller, atoms of dust for instance, and pass them by without a thought. There must be minuteness combined with a complexity, which, in our ordinary habit of thinking, we associate with far greater dimensions : in the one case, the number, form, and order of the letters that make up the poem ; in the other, the number, shape, and carving of the toy-spoons.

And thus, when we look on the tiny harvest mouse, two of which scarcely weigh a halfpenny, and which brings up its large little family of eight hopeful mouse-lings in a nest no bigger than a cricket-ball, or the still tinier Etruscan shrew, it greatly enhances our interest to know that every essential organ is there which is in the giant rorqual of a hundred feet. The humming-bird is constructed exactly on the same model as to essentials as the condor; the little sphærodactyle, which we might put into a quill-barrel, and carry home in the waistcoat pocket, as the mighty crocodile; the mackerel-midge, which never surpasses an inch and a quarter in length, as the huge basking-shark of six-and-thirty feet.

Complexity of structure, the multiplicity and variety of organs, do not depend upon actual dimensions, but rather upon the position in the great plan of organic existence which the creature in question occupies. The harvest mouse possesses a much more elaborate organisation than the vast shark or colossal snake. In general, the creatures of simple structure are minute,—the *most* simple, the *most* minute; but we need to limit this proposition by many conditions and exceptions, before we shall fully apprehend the true state of the case. Ignorant exhibitors of oxy-hydrogen microscopes will frequently, indeed, be heard to declare that all the specks that are seen shooting to and fro, or revolving, top-fashion, in their populous drops of water, are furnished with all the organs, tissues, and members, that constitute the human frame; and similar statements were not uncommon in cheap compilations of natural history a few years ago. This has been abund-antly shewn to be erroneous; but the tendency has been to run into an opposite extreme; and to assume that what are

called "low forms" of organic life are exceedingly simple
in their structure.   There is, I say, error here; the microscope is daily revealing the fact, that in such beings
the tissues that had been too hastily thought simple and
almost homogeneous are really complex, and that systems
of organs of the most elaborate character are present,
which had been altogether overlooked and unsuspected.

What is more interesting than an examination, by means
of a first-rate microscope, of a tiny atom, that inhabits
almost every clear ditch,—the *Melicerta?*   The smallest
point that you could make with the finest steel-pen would
be too coarse and large to represent its natural dimensions; yet it inhabits a snug little house of its own construction, which it has built up stone by stone, cementing
each with perfect symmetry, and with all the skill of an
accomplished mason, as it proceeded.   It collects the
material for its mortar, and mingles it; it collects the
material for its bricks, and moulds them; and this with a
precision only equalled by the skill with which it lays
them when they are made.   As might be supposed, with
such duties to perform, the little animal is furnished with
an apparatus quite unique, a set of machinery, to which,
if we searched through the whole range of beasts, birds,
reptiles, and fishes, and then, by way of supplement,
examined the five hundred thousand species of insects to
boot,—we should find no parallel.

The whole apparatus is exquisitely beautiful.   The
head of the pellucid and colourless animal unfolds into
a broad transparent disk, the edge of which is moulded

into four rounded segments, not unlike the flower of the
heart's-ease, supposing the fifth petal to be obsolete.   The
entire margin of this flower-like disk is set with fine
vibratile cilia, the current produced by which runs uniformly in one direction.   Thus there is a strong and
rapid set of water around the edge of the disk, following
all its irregularities of outline, and carrying with it the
floating particles of matter, which are drawn into the
stream.   At every circumvolution of this current, however,
as its particles arrive in succession at one particular point,
viz., the great depression between the two uppermost
petals, a portion of these escape from the revolving
direction, and pass off in a line along the summit of the
face towards the front, till they merge in a curious little
cup-shaped cavity, seated on what we may call the chin.

This tiny cup is the mould in which the bricks are
made, one by one as they are wanted for use.   The
hemispherical interior is ciliated, and hence the contents
are maintained in rapid rotation.   These contents are the
atoms of sedimentary and similar matter, which have
been gradually accumulated in the progress of the ciliary
current; and these, by the rotation within the cup becoming consolidated, probably also with the aid of a viscid
secretion elaborated for the purpose, form a globular
pellet, which as soon as made is deposited, by a sudden
inflexion of the animal, on the edge of the tube or case, at
the exact spot where it is wanted.   The entire process of
making and depositing a pellet occupies about three
minutes.

I say nothing about the other systems of organs contained in this living atom : the arrangements destined to
subserve the purposes of digestion, circulation, respiration,
reproduction, locomotion, sensation, &c., though these are
all more or less clearly distinguishable in the tissues of the
animal, which is as translucent as glass. For the moment
I ask attention only to the elaborate conformation of
organs, which I have briefly described, for the special
purpose of building a dwelling. No description that I
could draw up, however, could convey any idea approaching to that which would be evoked by one good sight of
the little creature actually at work ;—a most charming
spectacle, and one which, from the commonness of the
animal, and its ready performance of its functions under
the microscope, is very easy to be attained.

It is impossible to witness the constructive operations
of the melicerta without being convinced that it possesses
mental faculties, at least if we allow these to any animals
below man. If, when the chinpanzee weaves together the
branches of a tree to make himself a bed; when the beaver,
in concert with his fellows, gnaws down the birch sap-
lings, and collects clay to form a dam ; when the martin
brings together pellets of mud and arranges them under
our eaves into a hollow receptacle for her eggs and young,
—we do not hesitate to recognise *mind*—call it instinct,
or reason, or a combination of both,—how can we fail to
see that in the operations of the invisible animalcule there
are the workings of an immaterial principle ? There must
be a power to judge of the condition of its case, of the

height to which it must be carried, of the time when this must be done ; a will to commence and to go on, a will to leave off, (for the ciliary current is entirely under control); a consciousness of the readiness of the pellet ; an accurate estimate of the spot where it needs to be deposited ; (may I not say also, a memory where the previous ones had been laid, since the deposition does not go on in *regular* succession, but now and then, yet so as to keep the edge tolerably uniform in height?); and a will to determine that there it shall be put. But surely these are mental powers. Yet mind animating an atom so small that your eyes strained to the utmost can only just discern the speck in the most favourable circumstances, as when you hold the glass which contains it between your eye and the light, so that the ray shall illumine the tiny form while the background is dark behind it !

It is a startling thought that there exists a world of animated beings densely peopling the elements around us, of which our senses are altogether uncognisant. For six thousand years generation after generation of *Rotifera* and *Entomostraca*, of *Infusoria* and *Protozoa* have been living and dying, under the very eyes and in the very hands of man ; and, until this last century or so, he has no more suspected their existence than if "the scene of their sorrow" had been the ring of Saturn. Dr Mantell wrote a pretty book, the secondary title of which was "A Glimpse of the Invisible World." It was a book about the Animalcules, which are revealed only by the microscope ; and though it gave little original information, and some of that unsound, yet, for the time, when the microscope was in far fewer hands than it is now, it contained much to interest and much to instruct. The minutely invisible world has now become tolerably familiar to most persons of education; and thousands of eyes are almost constantly gazing on the surprising forms of animals and plants, which the microscope reveals.

The study of one particular class of these organisms, the Diatoms, has become quite a fashion, and the reunions of our microscopists are almost exclusively occupied with the names, the scientific arrangement, the forms and sculpturings of these singular objects. I have already had occasion to mention them in relation to the important part they play in the economy of creation; but it may not be amiss to devote a few words more to them, with the view to make the reader better acquainted with their general appearance.

A flat pill-box or cylindrical tin canister, which is much wider than it is deep, will give a good idea of many of the Diatoms, such as *Arachnodiscus*. The top and bottom of the box are formed by flat circular glassy plates, called valves, and the sides by a ring or hoop of similar material. Sometimes the outline of the valves (with which the hoop agrees) is oval, or oblong, or square, or triangular, instead of circular; and their surface is sometimes convex in various degrees, but the side is generally upright, or in other words, the surface of the hoop passes in a straight line from the edge of one valve, whatever its outline, to that of the other.

Here then is a box formed of pure transparent flint-glass, very thin and delicate, and very brittle. The valves are marked with minute dots, which appear to be either knobs or pits; or with lines, either depressed or raised. In the beautiful *Arachnodiscus*, both of these modes of sculpturing are present. Each valve is marked with a number of most delicate lines, which radiate from a central circle of dots to the circumference; these radii are connected by a multitude of cross lines, bearing the closest resemblance to the elegant webs spun by our common geometric spiders, whence the name given to the genus; while in the spaces marked out by these reticulations there are rows of minute round dots. Altogether, the effect of this complex pattern of sculpture is most charming, and is heightened by the brilliant translucent material in which it is wrought, which, as has already been observed, is like the purest glass.

During life there is, in every individual, a small round body in the centre of the enclosed cavity, called the *nucleus*, and this is surrounded by irregular masses of yellowish substance, called the *endochrome*, the nature of which is not very clearly ascertained. The single specimen, including the two valves and the hoop, with their contents, is called a *frustule*.

The manner in which these beautiful, but most minute atoms increase, is highly curious. The pill-box-like frustule becomes deeper by the widening of the hoop, thus pushing the valves further from each other; then across the middle two membranes form, which, by and by, from

the deposition of flinty matter, become glassy valves, corresponding to the two outer valves, and then the whole
frustule separates between these two new valves, and
forms two frustules. The old hoop (in some cases at
least) falls off, or allows the hoops of the new-made frustules to slip out of it, like the inner tubes out of a telescope.

Now, the separation of the frustules thus made is not
always so complete, but that they remain adherent to one
another, by some point of contact; and hence arises a
most singular and interesting appearance often presented
by these bodies. Let us suppose that the original frustule
was of the shape of a brick, and that by successive acts of
self-division, it has formed itself into a number, say a
dozen of bricks. These, of course, are laid one on another,
forming a pile; but all the individuals adhere to one
another by a minute point at one corner, and the matter
of adherence is sufficiently tenacious and sufficiently
yielding to allow of the brick-shaped frustules moving
freely apart in every point, except just the connecting
angle. It is not *the same* corner that adheres all up the
pile; more frequently opposite corners alternate with each
other, yet not very regularly, and thus an angularly jointed
chain of the little bodies is formed, which is very characteristic. In some species, in which the form is a lengthened
oblong, the frustules have the faculty of sliding partially
over each other, and thus the chain resembles a series of
long steps.

Sometimes the frustules, perhaps of a graceful wedge-like outline, are attached at the end of long slender threads, which grow from a common point, and radiate in a beautiful fan-like manner ; at other times, the frustule is of an irregular trapezoidal form, and is connected with its fellows by a short intervening band. Perhaps the most common form of all is that of an italic f without the terminal dots, each frustule being unconnected with others. These have the power of spontaneous motion ; and it is very interesting to mark them creeping along in a vagrant, jerking manner over the field of the microscope, making no inconsiderable progress.

There are, then, several circumstances which combine to make the economy of these creatures full of interest, and give them a strong hold on our imagination.

1. Their inconceivable multitudes, and their universal distribution, especially in the waters of our globe, from the equator to the poles, or at least as near to them as man has been able to investigate, the everlasting glaciers of the icy seas being conspicuously stained with them.

2. The vast part assigned to them in the economy of creation, since, as we have seen, they not only enter largely into the composition of the solid crust of the globe, but sustain (mediately) the life of its very hugest creatures.*

3. The very great variety of forms assumed by the different kinds.

4. Their marvellous elegance and beauty, consisting in their material, their shapes, and their sculpturing.

5. Their spontaneous movements, and the mystery

* *See supra*, p. 101.

which hangs over the manner in which these are performed, a mystery which all the perseverance of hundreds of the best microscopists has not yet been able to dissipate.

6. The power which their structure possesses of taking up the siliceous matter held in solution in the waters, and forming of it solid flint,—a process which excites our wonder and which is quite beyond our comprehension.

7. The uncertainty which attends our conclusions as to their true character. Are they animals? Are they plants? The question is still before the judges. Ehrenberg and other names of high eminence have set them down as animals, but the preponderance of modern opinion is in favour of their vegetable nature. And there are some who would fain make of them a fourth kingdom, neither animal, nor vegetable, nor mineral, but an independent group possessing affinities with all.

8. Their minute dimensions. The actual size varies exceedingly, according to the species, between one-fiftieth, and one six-thousandth of an inch, or even wider limits. Perhaps, however, we may set down as an average size for an oblong frustule, a length of one-thousandth of an inch, and a width of one-five-thousandth; that is, that if you could make a chain of them, set end to end, in contact, it would take a thousand specimens to measure an inch, while, if you made a row of them, side by side, five thousand would be required to fill the same extent.

Highly attractive to a young observer is the variety of life which meets his eye, as he examines, with a good microscope, a drop of water from some pool rich in

organisms. Suppose he has nipped off the growing terminal bud of some *Myriophyllum* or *Nitella*, and, having a
little broken it down with the point of a needle, has placed
it in the animalcule-box of the instrument, with a small
quantity of the water in which it grew, selected from the
sediment of the pool-bottom. The amount of life at first
is bewildering; motion is in every part of the field;
hundreds and thousands of pellucid bodies are darting
across, making a mazy confusion of lines. Some are mere
immensurable points without apparent form or diameter;
others are definable and of exceedingly various shapes.
Aggregations of little transparent pears,[*] clinging together
by their stalks so as to form balls, go revolving merrily
through their waste of waters. Presently one of the pears
severs its connexion with the family, and sets out on a
voyage on its own individual responsibility; then another
parts company; and you see that there are plenty more
of the same sort, roving singly as well as in clusters;
little tops of clear jelly with a few specks in the interior.
Here comes rolling by, with majestic slowness, a globe of
glass, with sixteen emeralds imbedded in its substance,
symmetrically arranged,[†] each emerald carrying a tiny
ruby at one end; a most charming group. Elegant
forms,[‡] resembling fishes, or battledores, or poplar-leaves,
for they are of many kinds, all of a rich opaque green
hue, with a large transparent orange-coloured spot, wriggle
sluggishly by, the leaves now and then rolling themselves
up spirally, and progressing in a cork-screw fashion.

[*] *Uvella.*   [†] *Eudorina.*   [‡] *Euglena.*

Disks of clear jelly* are seen, which are continually altering their outline, so that you soon come to the conclusion that they have no particular form, but every imaginable one in turn.   The mass, which seems a mere drop of thin glaire, almost or quite homogeneous, with only one or two bubbles in it, pushes out points and projections from its outline, excavates other parts, lengthens here, rounds off a point there, and this as long as we look at it, so that it never appears twice in the same shape.   Here a tiny atom† arrests the eye by its singular movements.   Its appearance is that of an irregular ball, with a bright spot near the circumference ; the whole surface set with bristles projecting obliquely from the periphery, not perpendicularly, much thicker and stronger in the vicinity of the bright spot.   It remains in one place spinning round and round upon its centre, sometimes so rapidly as to preclude any sight of its distinctive characters, at others more deliberately, displaying its bristles and surface. Sometimes it rolls over in all directions, as if to let us see that it is sub-spherical, not discoid.   And now and then it takes a sudden spring sideways, to a distance perhaps twenty times its diameter, when it spins as before, or else skips about several times in succession.   Altogether this is a very active little merry-andrew.

A great oblong purplish mass‡ comes rolling along, a very Triton among the minnows.   He suddenly arrests his headlong course, makes his hinder-end take hold of a fragment of leaf, and unfolds his other end into an elegant

---

* *Amœba.*   † Perhaps *Trichodina grandinella.*   ‡ *Stentor.*

trumpet, with one portion of the lip rolled-in with a sort
of volute, something like the beautiful African Arum or
Calla. The body now lengthens, and goes on lengthening, until the lower part, which is adherent, is drawn out
to a very slender foot. The open mouth, studded round
with a wreath of vigorous cilia in rapid rotatory motion,
strikes us with a pleased surprise. The cilia are seen,
like hooks, at those parts of the circle, which in perspec-
tive are brought in or near the line of vision, either
turned outward or inward according as their motion is
more or less rapid; the other parts of the wreath being
visible only as a thin film along the line of their points,
and like little teeth at their bases. The obscure semi-
transparency of the texture of the animal renders it very
difficult to discern the form of the trumpet-outline satis-
factorily; at one time it appears as if circular, but with
a large round piece cut out of one side; which yet has a
thin filmy edge, as if the hiatus were covered by a transparent membrane. Then perhaps the mouth is turned
slightly towards the eye, and this hiatus is no longer discernible anywhere, but one part of the margin is rolled
inwards spirally, but how the other part joins this it is
difficult to see. Then suddenly the orifice appears again,
but as a large round hole cut out of the side, with the
margin quite entire above it; then in a moment this
aperture is seen rapidly to contract, and close up to a
point. But all these appearances,—the mystery of which
so greatly heightens the interest of these creatures to a
young observer,—seem to depend on the presence of a

L

contractile bladder which alternately fills and empties it-self, and, when distended, frequently displaces the coloured parenchyma or flesh, to such a degree that only the thin-nest film of transparent skin bounds it externally.

The tuft of needle-like leaves, too, is full of life. To the outer ones are clinging multitudes of Diatoms in fans and fantastic chains; and multitudes more of single ones are sprawling about the field, contrasting, by their slow, jerking progress, with the rapid, headlong dash of the animalcules. On the plant-stem, as if on solid ground, is fixed a beautiful tree,* with many slender, divergent branches, springing from a straight trunk. The branches bear, instead of leaves, elegant transparent bells or wine-glass-like vases, which are scattered thickly over them; and each vase is furnished with a ring of cilia round the mouth, which rotates while it is open, but which at will can be withdrawn and quite concealed by the closing up of the mouth. Every moment one or other of the numer-ous branches contracts spirally, with force, like a wire-spring when weighted, and then deliberately straightens itself again. And, now and then, the main trunk itself contracts in the same manner, but less perfectly; and when it extends we may see a band running down through the middle of its pellucid substance, in which the contractile power manifestly resides, and which is probably of the nature of muscle. The elegant vases have several globules of yellowish matter in their clear substance, which seem to be stomachs, or more correctly

* *Carchesium.*

temporary cavities for the reception of food ; for if a little
indigo or carmine be mingled with the drop of water, the
ciliary rotation brings it to the mouth, and presently we
see globules of a faint blue or pink hue appear in the
colourless flesh, and these speedily augment the depth of
their tint, as more and more of the pigment is imbibed,
until they at length attain the richest deep blue, or full
crimson.

The observer may, perhaps, see also that most elegant
of animalcules the *Floscularia.* A tube of jelly stands up
from one of the leaves, so filmy and transparent, that one
perceives it only by the sedimentary matters that have
become entangled in its outer surface. It seems to be deposited progressively,—a mucus excreted and thrown off
by the skin of the tenant ; and hence the upper portion,
being the most recently formed, is destitute of such ex-
traneous substances, and can with the greatest difficulty
be traced to its termination. Within this tube resides
the beautiful constructor ; a very slender foot or pedicle,
capable of being drawn out to such a length as to equal
that of the tube, and of being suddenly contracted at the
pleasure of the animal, merges into an ovate body of
translucent flesh, in which all the organs are clearly visible. The upper portion expands into a most exquisite
disk or shallow cup of clear gelatinous membrane, having
five angles, each angle being terminated by a rounded
knob. Each of these five knobs is the seat of a pencil of
long straight bristles, of the most subtle tenuity, which
look as if they had been drawn out of the finest spun-glass.

There may be perhaps fifty hairs in each pencil, which
radiate from their common base in all directions, and, as
they are graduated in length, the effect of these hairs is
most charming.   Any little shock, such as a jar to the
table, or the shutting of a door, alarms the beautiful creature, and it suddenly closes up its elegant flower, and
retreats into its tube, the hairs forming a cylindrical
bundle as it goes down.   It presently emerges again, however, and unfolds its array as before.   The pencils of
hairs are carried quite motionless when expanded, but
when the united bundle is in the act of protrusion, a kind
of thrill, a quivering wave, is frequently seen to run
through it from end to end.   There is a wreath of rotat-
ing cilia on the face of the disk, the effect of which is to
draw floating bodies around into its vortex; and the
little giddy monads, that are whirling heedlessly along,
may be seen to be thus entrapped by the living whirl-
pool, one after another, and engulphed in the transparent
prison.   And there we may follow them with our eye, and
watch their fate.   Hurled round and round in the capacious crop, a pair of nipper-like jaws at length catches
hold of them, gives them a squeeze, lets them go round
again, presently seizes and nips them again, until, after
a few preliminary bruisings of this sort, the ill-fated
atom suddenly goes with a gulp down a kind of trap-door
into the true digestive stomach, and is presently dimmed
and lost in the mass.

Several tiny creatures are labouring with the most
praiseworthy industry among the close leaves of the plant,

Here is one which may remind us of a guinea-pig in its general outline, but you must suppose the two hind-feet to be changed into a divergent fork, and the fore-feet to be obliterated.* It is a most restless little rogue; ranging among the filamentous leaves of the *Myriophyllum* with incessant activity, he now pokes his way through some narrow aperture, using his curious forked foot as a point of resistance, now pauses to nibble among the decaying rind, and now scuttles off through the open water to some other part. We see his large eye, shining with the colour of a ruby, and set, like that of Polyphemus, right in the middle of his forehead, and his curious apparatus of jaws, the points of which are protruded from the front of his head, and vigorously worked, when he is grubbing among the decaying vegetable matter, adding continually morsel after morsel to the great mass of yellow-green food, which is already swelling out his abdomen to a pig-like plumpness. And when he swims away and gives a fair view of his back to us, we notice the evolution of a pair of hemispherical swellings, one on each side of the broad head, and which are evidently connected with his locomotion. The whole front is clothed with vibrating cilia, but they are more developed on these organs, which are only pushed out at the will of the little animal, when they form strong vortical currents.

In another part of the bunch of leaves possibly a group of *Salpinæ* may be feeding equally busily. These are something like the former, but their bodies are inclosed

* *Notommata lacinulata.*

in a sort of shell or transparent case, much arched along
the back, nearly straight along the belly, and hollowed
out at each extremity. This shell is a very beautiful
object, when we meet with it, as we often do, completely
cleaned of the softer parts, the animal having died. It is
hard, perfectly transparent, but marked all over with
minute pits. It is closed on all sides, except before and
behind, where, as I have said, it is cut away, as it were,
for the egress of the head, and the forked foot: along the
back it rises into two tall, longitudinal, sharp ridges with
a deep furrow between them, and the appearance of this
double ridge, from the perfect transparency of the material,
has a curious effect as the animal moves about. Both
before and behind, the ridges run out into projecting
points, those of the front arching over the head like curving horns. These little animals derive their nourishment
likewise from the soft vegetable tissues, or the half-dis-
solved matter that accumulates on the stems and leaves
of the aquatic plants. On this they feed greedily, and
nearly the whole of their time is spent in munching away
this with the mouth. To do this the foot, which consists
of two stiff unjointed styles, is brought into requisition.
These are capable of being opened or closed like the feet
of a pair of compasses, and of being brought round into
any position through the flexibility of the base, which
forms false or telescopic joints. The tips of these foot-
styles are used as a pivot on which the animal moves;
they are placed perpendicularly to the stem, or other substance, on which it means to crawl or feed, and the body

is brought down horizontally, so that the head can touch the same plane. Thus, without moving its points of support, the animal can reach a considerable extent of surface with its mouth, either stretching forward until the feet are nearly horizontal, or drawing backward until the points are under the belly.

When I used the term "greedily" in describing its eating, it was rather with reference to the activity and apparent eagerness with which the little creature labours, than to the quantity actually devoured. This indeed is not very perceptible, though the jaws are continually thrust forward, and are opened and closed with untiring perseverance and energy. Probably they are not capable of detaching more than the minutest particles, for the effect produced is not the visible admission of atoms into the stomach, as in the former example, but the gradual discoloration of the viscera, which become stained with a yellowish olive hue, that grows more and more intense.

The large oval eggs of this animalcule may also be seen adhering to the leaves here and there, so large as to be nearly half as long as the whole animal; they are beautifully symmetrical, are inclosed in a brittle transparent shell, and look like birds' eggs. If we watch an individual, we may easily see an egg laid; taking care to select one that is in the egg-producing condition; a selection which the perfect transparency of the tissues enables us to make readily. The ovary occupies the ventral region, and when an egg is in process of development, its mass gradually becomes more and more opaque, and larger and larger, until nearly half of the bulk of the body is filled up with it. Then suddenly it is discharged, a soft and shell-less mass, but immediately on exclusion it takes its regular oval figure, and the integument presently hardens into a shell.

Patience, moreover, for a few hours will be rewarded by a sight of a living well-formed animal hatched from this new-laid egg. At first it remains so turbid as to be almost opaque; but in the course of a couple of hours or so, it is perceptible that the contents are becoming pellucid flesh, and developing into organs and viscera, the integuments and membranes becoming more and more manifest in their overlying infoldings. Another hour passes; and now the action of the frontal cilia is discernible; at first as faint fitful waves, which, however, become momentarily more vigorous, until at length their lashings are distinct and incessant. Meanwhile the eye has been coming into view, visible first as a pale red tinge in a particular spot near the middle of the egg, and gradually acquiring a definite outline, and a ruby-like translucent brilliancy. After this a little working action is perceived behind the eye, which shews that there the jaws are already developed, and that their proper muscles are assuming form and contractile power. About four hours have now elapsed since the egg was laid; the movements of the embryo are now vigorous, sudden, and spasmodic, the folds of the body-integument change their places, and the cilia work more rapidly. Presently, the oval form of the egg undergoes a slight alteration; it becomes more elliptical, and then slightly constricted in the middle, apparently by the pushing outwards and inflating of the two extremities of the body. At this moment a white line flies round the anterior end of the egg : it is a crack, and the next instant the separated portion of the egg-shell is pushed off, and the head protrudes, the cilia waving nimbly in the water. A moment the new-born young sits in the shell as in a nest; but now it glides forth, and we see that in every point of form and structure it is the very counterpart of its parent, the shell, the foot, all the internal viscera, being perfect and *comme il faut.*

The shells in which these little creatures are enveloped are models of symmetry and elegance, and display great variety of form. Some of them are sculptured in curious and beautiful patterns, an elaboration which is truly surprising when we think of the invisible minuteness of the entire creature. One is clothed * with a shell of the usual glassy mail, nearly circular in outline, very flat, but a little arched on the back aspect, the chin hollowed out in a semicircle, and the brow armed with two horns curving downward ; the posterior extremity square, with two lateral spines. The entire surface of this shell is covered with minute elevated points, which extend even to the horns and spines ; and besides these, the dorsal surface is marked with elevated ridges, which form a regular raised pattern, impossible to describe by words, but of curious symmetry, forming three perfect pentagonal areas, and parts of eight others surrounding them.

This kind of sculpturing is most remarkable in a little

* *Noteus quadricornis.*

active genus,[*] which, being wholly without the foot common to this class of animals, is always found swimming,
being apparently incapable of resting, or, at least, of
crawling. The group contains many species, and most of
them have their shells ornamented with some symmetrical
variation of the surface. In one,[†] a ridge runs down the
middle of the back, dividing the shell into two equal
lateral portions, each of which is subdivided into about
ten polyhedral areas by intervening ridges, of which no
two are alike in form, though each corresponds accurately
with its fellow on the opposite side. The form of each
area is constant in every individual. In another,[‡] the
medial line is occupied by five areas, of which the first is an
imperfect hexagon, the second is square, and the posterior
three are hexagons; from the salient angles, other ridges
run off sidewise, and form other imperfect polygons. In
others,[§] the division is into many hexagonal tesselations,
varied with other forms in the outer or hinder areas
according to the species, and having the peculiarity that
the dividing ridges are well-defined narrow elevations
armed throughout with conical points in single row.

I may be accused of exaggeration in presuming all these
creatures to be seen in one drop of water. I do not pretend to be depicting them from one single actual observation; at the same time I may say that I have described
nothing but what I have personally observed; and I
have known many small pools and other collections of

---

[*] *Anuræa.*   [†] *A. tecta.*   [‡] *A. curvicornis.*
[§] *A. aculeata, serrulata,* &c.

water, sufficiently rich in organic life to afford examples of quite as many species as I have enumerated, aye, and many more, *in a single dip taken at random,* though all might not appear in the live-box at one time. However, the point is, these and hundreds of others are easily obtainable, and cannot fail to delight the observer. The variety is almost endless.

Scarcely anything more strikes the mind with wonder than, after having been occupied for hours, perhaps, in watching the movements and marking the forms of these and similar creatures, till one has become quite familiar with them, suddenly to remove the eye from the instrument, and taking the cell from the stage, look at it with the naked eye. Is this what we have been looking at? This quarter-inch of specks, is this the field full of busy life? are here the scores of active creatures feeding, watching, preying, escaping, swimming, creeping, dancing, revolving, breeding? Are they here? Where? Here is nothing, absolutely nothing, but two or three minutest dots which the straining sight but just catches now and then in one particular light.

Truly, the world which we are holding between our finger and thumb—this world in a globule of water—this world of rollicking, joyous, boisterous fellows, that a pin's point would take up, is even more wonderful than the shoals of whales that wallow in Baffin's Bay, or the herds of elephants that shake the earth in the forests of Ceylon. Truly, the great God who made them is *maximus in minimis !*

VII.

THE MEMORABLE.

EVERY naturalist can recall certain incidents in his communion with nature, which have impressed themselves upon his imagination with a vividness that the lapse of time in no wise effaces, and which he feels never will be effaced. They came upon him with a power which at the moment burnt-in the image of each in his remembrance; and there they remain, and must remain while memory endures, ever and anon starting up with a palpable clearness that is all the more observable from the ever increasing dimness and vagueness into which the contemporary impressions are fading. They form the great landmarks of his life: they stand out like the promontories of some long line of coast, bold and clear, though the intervening shore is lost to view.

Every close observer of natural phenomena is familiar with such *memorabilia*, and those know them best whose minds are most poetic in temperament, most disposed to receive pleasurable emotions from that which is new or strange, or noble, or beautiful. Each has his own; he will fail, perhaps, to communicate to another the same impressions when he communicates the facts, because the halo with which the particular object or incident is invested in his remembrance, depends very greatly on the idiosyncrasy of his own mind, or on some peculiar conditions of thought or feeling with which that particular object was associated. That which sent such a thrill of delight through your heart, is to him a mere fact, and perhaps a fact of very little value. For the thing may be a very little matter in itself; it is the time, the place, the association, the anticipation that makes it what it is. Let me adduce a few examples.

Living for years in Newfoundland and Canada, Wilson's *American Ornithology* had become almost as familiar to me as my alphabet, and when at length I travelled into the Southern States, many of the birds which do not extend their visits to the north had become objects of eager interest to me. Prominent among these was that nightjar* whose nocturnal utterances are thought to repeat the words, "chuck-will's widow." I know not what made this particular bird so interesting; perhaps the singularly true resemblance to the human voice of its cry; perhaps the solemn hour of its occurrence, for night-sounds have always an element of romance about them; perhaps the rarity of a sight of the bird; perhaps the superstitions with which it is invested; perhaps all of these combined; or perhaps none of them;—I cannot tell; but so it was: I ardently desired to hear the chuck-will's widow.

I went to the South, and arrived in the hill-country of Alabama as spring was merging into the early summer. I had not been domiciled many days, when one night I

* *Caprimulgus Carolinensis.*

remained sitting at the open window of my bedroom, long
after the household had retired to bed.   It was a lovely
night; a thunder-storm had just passed, which had cleared
and cooled the air; the moon was in the west, and the
stars were twinkling; the rain-drops still hung upon the
trees, sparkling as the beams fell on them; the large
white blossoms of a catalpa tree were conspicuous just
under my window, and gushes of rich fragrance came up
from a clematis which thickly covered the trellis-work of
the ladies' arbour.   The solemn forest, with its serried
ranks of primeval trees, girdled-in the little garden, and
lay dark and vague beyond.   It was too early for the
noisy cicadæ that in the later summer make the woods
ring with their pertinacious crinking, and not a sound
broke the profound silence.   Every element was poetry,
and my mind was in a state of quiet but high enjoyment.
It wanted but a few minutes of midnight, when suddenly
the clear and distinct voice of the chuck-will's widow rose
up from a pomegranate tree in the garden below the window where I was sitting, and only a few yards from me.
It was exactly as if a human being had spoken the words,
"chuck—widowwidow."   I had not been thinking of this
bird, but of course I recognised it in a moment, and a
gush of delight and surprise went through me.   I scarcely
dared to breathe, lest any sound should alarm and drive it
away, and my ears were strained to catch every intonation
uttered.   It continued to repeat its singular call at intervals of a few seconds for about half an hour, when another
from a little distance answered, and the two pursued their

occupation together, sometimes calling alternately, sometimes both at the same instant. By and by, a third further
off in the forest joined them, and the first flew away. The
spell was broken, and I went to bed; but even in sleep
the magic sounds seemed to be ringing in my ears.

A very vivid emotion of delight was produced in my
mind on my visit to Jamaica, by the sight of *Heliconia
Charitonia.* The appearance of this fine butterfly is so
totally different from that of any of the species with which
I had been familiar,—the form is so peculiarly intertropical,
so associated with the gorgeous glooms of South American
scenery,—that nothing like it had occurred to me either in
Europe, or in any part of the northern continent. I first
saw it fluttering, slowly and fearlessly, over a great thicket
of *Opuntia* in full flower, itself a memorable object to behold. The beauty and singularity of the form, the very
remarkable shape of the wings, so long and so narrow,
the brilliant contrasts of colour with which they are
adorned, lemon-yellow and velvety black in bands, and
the very peculiar flapping of these organs in flight, as if
their length rendered them somewhat unwieldy, altogether
took a strong hold on my imagination. I subsequently
saw it under circumstances which greatly heightened the
interest with which I had first beheld it.

Passing along a rocky footpath on a steep, wooded
mountain-side, my attention was attracted, just before
sunset, by a swarm of these butterflies in a sort of rocky
recess, overhung by trees and creepers. They were about
twenty in number, and were dancing to and fro exactly

in the manner of gnats, or as the ghost-moth in England plays at the side of a wood. After watching them awhile, I noticed that some of them were resting with closed wings at the extremities of one or two depending vines. One after another fluttered from the group of dancers to the reposing squadron, and alighted close to the others, so that, at length, when only about two or three of the fliers were left, the rest were collected in groups of half a dozen each, so close together that each group might have been grasped by the hand. When once one had alighted it did not in general fly again, but a new-comer, fluttering at the group, seeking to find a place, sometimes disturbed one recently settled, when the wings were thrown open, and one or two flew up again. As there were no leaves on the hanging stalks, the appearance presented by these butterflies, so crowded together, their long erect wings pointing in different directions, was not a little curious. I was told by persons residing near, that every evening they thus assembled, and that I had not seen a third part of the numbers often collected in that spot.

Another sight which I can never forget is the swarming of *Urania Sloanus* around a blossoming tree at sunrise. This is one of the most gorgeously beautiful of butterflies, its broad wings and body being arrayed in a dress of rich velvet black and emerald green, arranged in transverse bands, with a broad disk of ruddy gold, the whole sparkling with a peculiar radiance, like powdered gems. It is, besides, an insect of unusual interest to the philosophic entomologist, because it is one of those transitional forms by which great groups are linked together. Every one would say, on looking at it, that it is a butterfly, and yet it possesses the technical characters of a moth.

At a certain season, in Jamaica, viz., in the first week of April, with very accurate regularity, this magnificent insect suddenly appears in great numbers. The avoçada pear, a kind of *Laurus*, whose fruit is much esteemed, is then in blossom, and is the centre of attraction to these butterflies. As the approaching sun is casting a glow of gold over the eastern sky, one after another begins to come, and by the time the glorious orb emerges from the horizon, the lovely living gems are fluttering by scores, or even by hundreds, around some selected tree. The level sunbeams, glancing on their sparkling wings, give them a lustre which the eye can scarcely look upon ; and, as they dance in their joyousness over the fragrant bloom, engage in the evolutions of playful combats, or mount up on the wing to a height of several hundred feet above the tree, they constitute, in that brief hour of morning, a spectacle which has seemed to me worth years of toil to see.

If I may allude to one more memorable incident in my own natural-history experience, it shall be the interior of a forest in the mountains of Jamaica. From the almost insufferable glare of the vertical sunshine, a few steps took me into a scene where the gloom was so sombre,— heightened doubtless by the sudden contrast,—as to cast a kind of awe over the spirit. Yet it was a beauteous gloom,—rather a subdued and softened light, like that which prevails in some old pillared cathedral when the

M

sun's rays struggle through the many-stained glass of a painted window. Choice plants that I had been used to see fostered and tended in pots in our stove-houses at home, were there in wild and *riant* luxuriance. The very carpet was a dense *Lycopodium*, of most delicate tracery, cast thick over the prostrate tree-trunks, and the rugged masses of rock; and elegant ferns were arching out of the crevices. Enormous towering figs and Santa-Marias were seen here and there, venerable giants of a thousand years at least, whose vast trunks pierced through the general roof of quivering foliage, and expanded far above, while from the crevices of their rough bark, and from the forks of the lesser trees curious and elegant parasites, —wild pines, ferns, orchids, cactuses, pothoses,—were clustering in noble profusion of vegetable life. These trees, too, were connected and laced together by long leaves, just as the masts of a ship are laced with the various stays, braces, and halyards; some of them stout and cable-like, others mere slender cords, passing to and fro, hanging in loops, or loosely waving in the air.

Yet amidst all this magnificence of vegetation, there was nothing that took so strong a hold on my imagination as the arborescent ferns. To see these plants, whose elegant grace I had so often admired in our English lanes, so magnified that the crown of out-curving fronds shaded an area of twenty feet in diameter, and yet preserving all the voluptuous lightness and minute subdivision which are so characteristic of these plants, and this feathery diadem of leaves reared on the summit of a

stem as high as its own width ;—to stand under the beautiful arch and gaze upwards on the filigree-fretted fronds that formed a great umbrella of verdure,—this was most charming, and never to be forgotten.

The eloquent pen of Charles Darwin has revivified for us, with a peculiar charm, the impressions made on his refined and poetic mind by the strange scenes of other lands. His first experiences of the forests of South America he has thus recorded :—" The day has passed delightfully. Delight itself, however, is a weak term to express the feelings of a naturalist, who, for the first time, has wandered by himself in a Brazilian forest. The elegance of the grasses, the novelty of the parasitical plants, the beauty of the flowers, the glossy green of the foliage, but, above all, the general luxuriance of the vegetation, filled me with admiration. A most paradoxical mixture of sound and silence pervades the shady parts of the wood. The noise from the insects is so loud, that it may be heard even in a vessel anchored several hundred yards from the shore ; yet within the recesses of the forest a universal silence appears to reign. To a person fond of natural history, such a day as this brings with it a deeper pleasure than he can hope to experience again." *

Again, at the close of his eventful voyage, he thus reverts to the same scenes :—" Such are the elements of the scenery, but it is a hopeless attempt to paint the general effects. Learned naturalists describe these scenes of the tropics by naming a multitude of objects, and men-

* *Naturalist's Voyage*, ch. i.

tioning some characteristic feature of each. To a learned traveller this, possibly, may communicate some definite idea; but who else, from seeing a plant in a herbarium, can imagine its appearance when growing in its native soil? Who, from seeing choice plants in a hothouse, can magnify some into the dimensions of forest-trees, and crowd others into an entangled jungle? Who, when examining, in the cabinet of the entomologist, the gay, exotic butterflies, and singular cicadas, will associate with these lifeless objects, the ceaseless harsh music of the latter, and the lazy flight of the former,—the sure accompaniments of the still, glowing noonday of the tropics? It is when the sun has attained its greatest height, that such scenes should be viewed: then the dense, splendid foliage of the mango hides the ground with its darkest shade, whilst the upper branches are rendered, from the profusion of light, of the most brilliant green. In the temperate zones the case is different: the vegetation there is not so dark or so rich; and hence the rays of the declining sun, tinged of a red, purple, or bright yellow colour, add most to the beauties of those climes.

" When quietly walking along the shady pathways, and admiring each successive view, I wished to find language to express my ideas. Epithet after epithet was found too weak to convey to those who have not visited the intertropical regions the sensations of delight which the mind experiences. I have said that the plants in a hothouse fail to communicate a just idea of the vegetation, yet I must recur to it. The land is a great, wild, untidy, luxuriant hothouse, made by Nature for herself, but taken possession of by man, who has studded it with gay houses and formal gardens. How great would be the desire of every admirer of nature to behold, if such were possible, the scenery of another planet! yet to every person in Europe it may be truly said that, at the distance of only a few degrees from his native soil, the glories of another world are opened to him. In my last walk, I stopped again and again to gaze at these beauties, and endeavoured to fix in my mind for ever, an impression which at the time I knew sooner or later must fail. The form of the orange-tree, the cocoa-nut, the palm, the mango, the tree-fern, the banana, will remain clear and separate ; but the thousand beauties which unite these into one perfect scene must fade away ; yet they will leave, like a tale heard in childhood, a picture full of indistinct, but most beautiful figures." *

The late James Wilson made his first acquaintance with the storks of Holland under very impressive circumstances. One summer evening, of a beautifully calm and serene character, he had sauntered into a churchyard, and found himself, when the sun had set, and the dim twilight was fading into darkness, alone. All was solemnly still, as became the scene; not a sound being audible to disturb the perfect solitude and silence with which he was surrounded. Suddenly, a soft and winnowing sound in the air attracted his attention, and, looking up, with involuntary thoughts of angels and spiritual visitants, he saw

* Ibid., ch. xxi.

two white-winged beings hovering in the air, who presently descended and alighted close to his feet. They were storks ! attracted, doubtless, to the moist and rank herbage by the expectation of a plentiful repast on insects and slugs which the dews had drawn abroad. To have found a living man, where they had been accustomed to find only the dead, seemed to disturb them, however; for they presently spread their ample wings, and mounted to the spire, where, perched, they gave utterance to their wild and singularly plaintive cries, which added greatly to those impressions of loneliness and seclusion that the incident had already inspired. No wonder that the naturalist could never afterwards behold a stork without having presented to his imagination, in vivid force, that startling rencontre in the graveyard of Delft. *

Very few persons capable of appreciating the interest of the spectacle have ever beheld the gorgeous bird of paradise in his remote equatorial forests. The land in which it dwells is still a *terra incognita* to science. Nearly all the world has been laid open to the perseverance of modern explorers; but the sullen ferocity of the savages of New Guinea, and their hostility to strangers, keep us to this day in ignorance of the largest island of the world. A few glances at the coast, obtained by adventurous travellers, who, well armed, have penetrated a mile or two from the sea, have only served to whet curiosity, and to stimulate desire for an acquaintance with the productions in which it appears so rich.

* Hamilton's *Memoirs of Wilson*, p. 33.

Specimens of the birds of paradise had found their way to Europe, through the native traders of the Oriental Archipelago, and their surpassing gorgeousness of plumage had disposed the credulous to receive the fabulous narrations with which their history was invested.   Gradually these absurdities were exploded; but still no naturalist had ever beheld the birds in native freedom, till M. Lesson, the zoologist attached to one of the French exploring expeditions, touched at the island.   He diligently used the few days' stay he made on the coast, and obtained a score of the birds.   Thus he narrates his first observation of the living gem :—

" Soon after my arrival in this land of promise for the naturalist, I was on a shooting excursion.   Scarcely had I walked some hundred paces in those ancient forests, the daughters of time, whose sombre depth was perhaps the most magnificent and stately that I had ever seen, when a bird of paradise struck my view; it flew gracefully, and in undulations; the feathers of its sides formed an elegant and aerial plume, which, without exaggeration, bore no remote resemblance to a brilliant meteor.   Surprised, astounded, enjoying an inexpressible gratification, I devoured this splendid bird with my eyes; but my emotion was so great that I forgot to shoot at it, and did not recollect that I had a gun in my hand till it was far away." *

The bright spot in the memory of Audubon, the enthusiastic biographer of the birds of America, was the dis-

* *Voy. de la Coquille.*

covery of the fine eagle which he has named "the Bird of Washington." "It was on a winter's evening," he observes, "in the month of February 1841, that, for the first time in my life, I had an opportunity of seeing this rare and noble bird, and never shall I forget the delight it gave me. Not even Herschel, when he discovered the famous planet which bears his name, could have experienced more happy feelings; for to have something new to relate, to become yourself a contributor to science, must excite the proudest emotion of the human heart. We were on a trading voyage, ascending the upper Mississippi; the keen winter blasts whistled over our heads, and the cold from which I suffered had, in a great degree, extinguished the deep interest which, at other seasons, this river has been wont to awake in me. I lay stretched beside our patroon; the safety of the cargo was forgotten; and the only thing that called forth my attention was the multitude of ducks, of different species, accompanied by vast flocks of swans, which from time to time would pass us. My patroon, a Canadian, had been engaged many years in the fur-trade: he was a man of much intelligence, who, perceiving that these birds had engaged my curiosity, seemed only anxious to find some new object to divert me. The eagle flew over us. 'How fortunate!' he exclaimed; 'this is what I could have wished. Look, sir! the great eagle; and the only one I have seen since I left the lakes.' I was instantly on my feet; and having observed it attentively, concluded, as I lost it in the distance, that it was a species quite new to me."

It was not till some years afterwards that he had an opportunity of seeing this noble bird again. On the face of a precipice was the nest of what the country-people called the "brown eagle," and some peculiarities in the situation induced the ornithologist to hope that it might be the species of which he was in quest. He determined to see for himself. "In high expectation," he continues, "I seated myself about a hundred yards from the foot of the rock. Never did time pass more slowly. I could not help betraying the most impatient curiosity, for my hopes whispered it was the great eagle's nest. Two long hours had elapsed before the old bird made his appearance, which was announced to us by the loud hissings of the two young ones, who crawled to the extremity of the hole to receive a fine fish. I had a perfect view of this noble bird, as he held himself to the edging rock; his tail spread, and his wings partly so, and hanging something like a bank swallow. I trembled lest a word should escape from my companions—the slightest murmur had been treason from them; they entered into my feelings, and, although little interested, gazed with me. In a few minutes the other parent joined her mate, which, from the difference in size, (the female being much larger,) we knew to be the mother-bird. She also had brought a fish; but, more cautious than her mate, ere she alighted, she glanced her quick and piercing eye around, and instantly perceiving her procreant bed had been discovered, she dropped her prey, with a loud shriek communicated the alarm to the male, and, hovering with him over our heads, kept up a growling, threatening cry, to intimidate us from our suspected design."

Tempestuous weather prevented access to the nest for several days, at the end of which time it was found that the young had been removed by the parents. " I come at last to the day I had so often and so ardently desired. Two years had gone by since the discovery of the nest, but my wishes were no longer to remain ungratified. I saw one day one of these birds rise from a small inclosure, where some hogs had been slaughtered, and alight upon a low tree branching over the road. I prepared my double-barrelled piece, which I constantly carry, and went slowly and cautiously towards him; quite fearless, he awaited my approach, looking upon me with an undaunted eye. I fired, and he fell; before I reached him he was dead. With what delight I surveyed this magnificent bird! I ran and presented him to my friend, with a pride which those can only feel, who, like me, have devoted their earliest childhood to such pursuits, and have derived from them their first pleasures; to others, I must seem ' to prattle out of fashion.' " *

I have already mentioned my own first acquaintance with one of the nightjars; the reader may be pleased to have the particulars of a nocturnal interview with our native species, as sketched by a plain but trustworthy observer, a thorough out-of-door naturalist.† It occurred under somewhat romantic circumstances. The worthy

---

* Loudon's *Mag. Nat. Hist.*, i., p. 118.
† Mr Thomas, the Bird-keeper at the Surrey Zoological Gardens.

man had taken a holiday from his metropolitan occupations, and, to make the most of it, had determined to spend a summer night *sub dio*. By sunset he found himself many miles from London, in a field in which the new-made hay was ready for carrying. No human being was near, and so he threw two of the haycocks into one, at the edge of a wood, and "mole-like, burrowed into the middle of the hay," just leaving his head exposed for a little fresh air, and free for any observations he might make under the light of the unclouded moon. In such a soft, warm, and fragrant bed, sleep soon overcame him, till he awoke with a confused idea of elves, sprites, fairies and pixies, holding their midnight dances around him.

" I had not been long again settled," he says, " on my grassy couch, reflecting upon my wild, fantastic dream, with all its attendant revelry, when my attention was drawn to the singular, wild, ringing strain of the fern-owl. It resembled, at times, the whirring, rapid rotation of a wheel, now swelling, now diminishing, the sounds intermixed with curring and croaking notes, some of the sounds having a ventriloquial effect; there was now and then a sharp, unearthly kind of shriek; presently there were the same sounds issuing from other quarters of the wood, until the whole place was ringing with the wild nocturnal notes. As daybreak advanced, I could see the fern-owls (there were at least from four to six birds,) hawking for moths, chasing and pursuing each other, and sweeping along with surprisingly sudden turns and tumblings. As I sat motionless, with my head just above the surface of the haycock,

I had a good view of their proceedings; the birds were continually snapping at the numerous small moths which were hovering over the heaps of hay. The birds are not very shy when pursuing their prey, for they would glide along close by me; amidst the gloom one could see them looming in certain positions, as a ship at sea is sometimes to be seen in the night-time. At times the fern-owls would suddenly appear close to me, as if by magic, and then shoot off, like meteors passing through the air.

"The spectral and owl-like appearance, the noiseless, wheeling flight of the birds as they darted by, would almost persuade one that he was on enchanted ground. Spell-bound, whilst witnessing the grotesque gambols of this singular bird, there only wanted Puck, with his elfin crew, attendant fairies, &c., in connexion with the aerial flights of the fern-owl, to have made it, as it was to me, a tolerably complete 'Midsummer Night's Dream,' especially as the fever of my night-haunted imagination had not as yet vanished. As it was, I was delighted with this nocturnal and beautiful scene from nature, and I wished at the time that some of our museum naturalists had been with me, to have shared the pleasure that I felt." *

The entomological cabinets of Europe have long counted as one of their most prized treasures, a gorgeous butterfly named *Ornithoptera Priamus*. Linnæus named those butterflies which are included by modern naturalists under the family *Papilionidæ, Equites;* and he divided them into Greeks and Trojans, naming each individual species

* *Zoologist,* p. 3650.

after some one of the Homeric heroes, choosing a name
from the Trojan list, if black was a prominent colour, as if
mourning for a defeat, and from the Greeks if the prevailing hues were gay. The one I speak of was called after the
king of Ilium, because it was the finest species of the butterfly then known. It is found only in Amboyna; its elegant
wings expand fully eight inches, and they are splendidly
coloured with the richest emerald green and velvety black.

Other species of the same noble genus have recently
been discovered in the same Archipelago; but the Trojan
monarch remained without a rival. About a year ago,
however, Mr A. R. Wallace, an accomplished entomologist,
and one who has had a greater personal acquaintance
than any other man of science, with the Lepidoptera of
the very richest regions of the globe—Brazil, and the
Indian Isles,—announced by letter the discovery and
capture of a still more magnificent species.   Having
arrived at Batchian, one of the isles of the eastern part of
the Archipelago, on an entomological exploration, he presently caught sight of a grand new *Ornithoptera*, which,
though the specimen was a female, and escaped capture,
gave promise for the future. At last the expected capture
was made, and Mr Wallace thus records his emotions on
the occasion;—emotions, it must be remembered, of no
tyro, but of a veteran insect-hunter.

" I had determined to leave here about this time, but
two circumstances decided me to prolong my stay: *first,*
I succeeded at last in taking the magnificent new *Ornithoptera,* and, *secondly,* I obtained positive imformation

of the existence here of a second species of *Paradisea*, apparently more beautiful and curious than the one I have obtained. You may, perhaps, imagine my excitement when, after seeing only two or three times in three months, I at length took a male *Ornithoptera*. When I took it out of my net, and opened its gorgeous wings, I was nearer fainting with delight and excitement than I have ever been in my life; my breast beat violently, and the blood rushed to my head, leaving a headache for the rest of the day. The insect surpassed my expectations, being, though allied to *Priamus*, perfectly new, distinct, and of a most gorgeous and unique colour; it is a fiery, golden orange, changing, when viewed obliquely, to opaline-yellow and green. It is, I think, the finest of the *Ornithopteræ*, and, consequently, the *finest butterfly in the world!* Besides the colour, it differs much in markings from all the *Priamus* group. Soon after I first took it, I set one of my men to search for it daily, giving him a premium on every specimen, good or bad, he takes; he consequently works hard from early morn to dewy eve, and occasionally brings home one; unfortunately, several of them are in bad condition. I also occasionally take the lovely *Papilio Telemachus.*" *

The sight of so noble an aquatic plant as the gigantic *Victoria regia*, the rosy-white water-lily of South America, reposing on one of the glassy igaripès of the mightiest river in the world, must be an incident calculated to excite enthusiasm in any lover of the grand or

* *Zoologist*, p. 6621.

the beautiful in nature. Thus speaks Schomburgk, to whom we owe our knowledge of this magnificent plant, and its introduction to the aquaria of Europe. " It was on the 1st of January 1837, while contending with the difficulties which, in various forms, nature interposed to bar our progress up the Berbice River, that we reached a spot where the river expanded, and formed a currentless basin. Something on the other side of this basin attracted my attention ; I could not form an idea what it might be ; but, urging the crew to increase the speed of their paddling, we presently neared the object which had roused my curiosity, and lo ! a vegetable wonder ! All disasters were forgotten ; I was a botanist, and I felt myself rewarded." *

Mr Bridges, too, in the course of a botanical expedition in Bolivia, speaks of the delighted surprise with which he first gazed on the lovely queen of water-lilies. "During my stay in the Indian town of Santa Anna," observes this traveller, " in June and July 1845, I made daily shooting excursions in the vicinity, and on one occasion I had the good fortune, while riding along the wooded banks of the Yacuma, a tributary of the Mamoré, to arrive suddenly at a beautiful pond, or rather small lake, embosomed in the forest, where, to my delight and surprise, I descried for the first time the queen of aquatics, *Victoria regia !* There were at least fifty flowers in view ; and Belzoni could not have been more enraptured with his Egyptian discoveries, than was I, on beholding

* *Bot. Mag.,* 1847.

this beautiful and novel sight, which few Englishmen can have witnessed. Fain would I have plunged into the lake to obtain specimens of the splendid flowers and foliage; but the knowledge that these waters abounded with alligators, and the advice of my guide, deterred me."[*]

In the travels of Mungo Park in the interior of Africa, he is said to have been at one time so exhausted by fever, and so depressed with his forlorn and apparently hopeless condition, that he had lain down to die. His eye, however, chanced to light on a minute moss,[†] with which he had been familiar in his native Scotland. The effect on him was magical; the reflection instantly occurred, that the same Divine hand which made that little plant to grow beneath that burning clime was stretched out in loving care and protection over him; and, smiling amidst his tears, he cast himself on the love of his heavenly Father, and was comforted. We may well believe that the sight of the fork-moss would ever afterwards call up a vivid recollection of that desolate scene, and that he could never look on it without strong emotion.

If it should be thought that some of the incidents and objects which I have adduced as examples of the memorable, are mean and slight, and far less worthy of notice than multitudes of other things that might have been selected, I would suggest that what makes them worthy of remembrance is not their intrinsic value, but their connexion with the thoughts of the observer; a connexion

* *Lond. Journ. of Botany*, iv., p. 571.   † *Dicranum bryoides.*

which cannot be commanded nor controlled. Why one man should have a powerful longing to behold a certain sort of butterfly or to hear a particular bird, when he cares nothing about the lion or the elephant; why a fern should fill one mind with strong emotion, and a spray of moss another, while the magnificent palm leaves both unmoved, we can give no reason but those peculiarities of thought and feeling which constitute the individuality of minds. Yet, that such is the fact, every admirer of nature who has an element of poetry in his soul will admit. He well knows that the distinct and prominent points in memory, those which invariably start up in association with certain scenes, are by no means those — at least, not invariably or necessarily — which are of most intrinsic importance, but such as to another will often seem trivial and destitute of æsthetic power.

"The desire," says Humboldt, "which we feel to behold certain objects is not excited solely by their grandeur, their beauty, or their importance. In each individual this desire is interwoven with pleasing impressions of youth, with early predilections for particular pursuits, with the inclination for travelling, and the love of an active life. In proportion as the fulfilment of a wish may have appeared improbable, its realisation affords the greater pleasure. The traveller enjoys, in anticipation, the happy moment when he shall first behold the constellation of the Cross, and the Magellanic clouds circling over the South Pole; when he shall come in sight of

N

the snow of the Chimborazo, and of the column of smoke ascending from the Volcano of Quito; when, for the first time, he shall gaze on a grove of tree-ferns, or on the wide expanse of the Pacific Ocean. The days on which such wishes are fulfilled mark epochs in life, and create indelible impressions; exciting feelings which require not to be accounted for by a process of reasoning."*

* *Views of Nature*, p. 417.

VIII

THE RECLUSE.

THERE are regions where the presence of man is a thing so totally out of experience, that the wild animals manifest no sort of dread of him when he does by accident intrude on their solitude. In the Galapagos Islands, perhaps the most singular land in the world, all the animals appear quite devoid of the fear of man. Cowley, in 1684, observed that the doves there "were so tame that they would often alight on our hats and arms, so as that we could take them alive." Darwin saw a boy sitting by a well with a switch, with which he killed the doves and finches as they came to drink. He had already obtained a heap of them for his dinner, and he said he had been constantly in the habit of doing this. The naturalist himself says that a mocking-bird alighted on the edge of a pitcher which he held in his hand, and began quietly to sip the water;—that a gun is superfluous, for with the muzzle he actually pushed a hawk off the branch of a tree: in fact, all the birds of the islands will allow themselves to be killed with a switch, or even to be caught in a hat.

Other naturalists have noticed the extreme tameness of many kinds of birds at the Falkland Islands; where,

though they take precautions against the attacks of foxes,
they appear to have no dread of man. Formerly they were
more confiding than at present. When the Isle of Bourbon
was discovered, all the birds, except the flamingo and
goose, were so tame that they could be caught with the
hand; and on the lone islet of Tristan d'Acunha in the
Atlantic, the only two land-birds, a thrush and a bunting,
were so tame as to suffer themselves to be caught with a
hand-net. I have myself had large and beautiful butterflies come and suck at flowers in my hand, in the forest-
glades of North America.

Cowper has finely used this phenomenon to heighten
the desolation of a solitary island, when he makes Sel-
kirk, on Juan Fernandez, complain,—

> " The beasts that roam over the plain,
>   My form with indifference see;
> They are so unacquainted with man;
>   Their tameness is shocking to me."

But these facts are only local and partial exceptions to
a general rule. They can in nowise be allowed to set
aside the prevalence of that pristine law, by which God
covenanted to implant a terror of man in all the inferior
creatures, even those which are far stronger than he.
" And the fear of you and the dread of you shall be upon
every beast of the earth, and upon every fowl of the air,
upon all that moveth upon the earth, and upon all the
fishes of the sea."* Often have I seen, and marked with
wonder, the excessive vigilance and jealousy with which

---

* Gen. ix. 2.

fishes watch the least approach of man. Often have I stood on a rock in Jamaica, and seen the little shoals come playing and nibbling at my feet, apparently all unconscious of the monster that was watching them; but the least movement of the hand towards them was sufficient to send them like arrows in all directions. And how often have I been tantalised by the excessive prudence of some fine butterfly that I eagerly desired to capture, when, day after day, I might see the species numerous enough at a particular part of the forest, and by no means shy of being seen, playing in the air, and alighting continually on the leaves of the trees, and continuing there, opening and closing their beauteous wings in the sun, and rubbing them together with the most fearless unconcern, though I walked to and fro with upturned face below,—*yet invariably taking care to keep themselves just out of the reach of my net!*

This power of judging of actual danger, and the free-and-easy boldness which results from it, are by no means uncommon. Many birds seem to have a most correct notion of a gun's range, and, while scrupulously careful to keep beyond it, confine their care to this caution, though the most obvious resource would be to fly quite away out of sight and hearing, which they do not choose to do. And they sometimes appear to make even an ostentatious use of their power, fairly putting their wit and cleverness in antagonism to that of man, for the benefit of their fellows. I lately read an account, by a naturalist in Brazil, of an expedition he made to one of the islands of the Amazon to shoot spoonbills, ibises, and other of the magnificent grallatorial birds, which were most abundant there. His design was completely baffled, however, by a wretched little sandpiper, that preceded him, continually uttering its tell-tale cry, which at once aroused all the birds within hearing. Throughout the day did this individual bird continue its self-imposed duty of sentinel to others, effectually preventing the approach of the fowler to the game, and yet managing to keep out of the reach of his gun.

There is, however, in some animals, a tendency to seek safety in an entire avoidance of the presence of man; a jealous shyness which cannot bear to be even looked at, and which prompts the creature to haunt the most recluse and solitary places. This disposition invests them with a poetic interest. The loneliness of the situations which they choose for their retreats has in itself a charm, and the rarity with which we can obtain a glimpse of them in their solitudes makes the sight proportionally gratifying when we can obtain it.

The golden eagle seeks for its eyrie, the peak of some inaccessible rock, far from the haunts of man, whose domain it shuns. Here it forms its platform-nest, rearing its young in awful silence and solitude, unbroken even by the presence of bird or beast; for these it jealously drives from its neighbourhood. The bald eagle of North America achieves the same end by selecting the precipices of cataracts for its abode. Lewis and Clarke have described *

* *Expedition*, i., p. 264.

the picturesque locality of the nest of a pair of these birds amidst the grand scenery of the Falls of the Missouri. Just below the upper fall there is a little islet in the midst of the boiling river, well covered with wood. Here, on a lofty cotton-wood tree, a pair of bald eagles had built their nest, the undisputed lords of the spot, to contest whose dominion neither man nor beast would venture across the gulf which surrounds it, the awfulness of their throne being further defended by the encircling mists which perpetually arise from the falls.

Our own wild-duck or mallard is a shy bird, avoiding the haunts of man, and resorting to the reedy margins of some lonely lake, or broad reach of a river. The summer-duck of America has similar habits, but more delights in woods. I have often been charmed, when standing by the edge of some darkling stream, bordered with lofty trees that so overhang the water as nearly to meet, leaving only a narrow line of sky above the centre of the river, with the sight of the coy summer-duck. When the western sky is burning with golden flame, and its gleam, reflected from the middle of " the dark, the silent stream," throws into blacker shadow the placid margins, then, from out of the indistinct obscurity, a whirring of wings is heard, and the little duck shoots plashing along the surface into the centre, leaving a long V-shaped wake behind her, till, rising into the air, she sails away on rapid pinion till the eye loses her in the sunset glow.

On other occasions we trace the same bird far up in the solitudes of the sky, breaking into view out of the objectless expanse, and presently disappearing in the same blank. We wonder whence it came ; whither it is going. Bryant's beautiful stanzas, though well known, will bear repetition here :—

TO A WATER-FOWL.

Whither, 'midst falling dew,
While glow the heavens with the last steps of day,
Far through their rosy depths, dost thou pursue
    Thy solitary way?

Vainly the fowler's eye
Might mark thy distant flight to do thee wrong,
As, darkly painted on the crimson sky,
    Thy figure floats along.

Seek'st thou the plashy brink
Of weedy lake, or marge of river wide,
Or where the rocking billows rise and sink
    On the chafed ocean side?

There is a Power whose care
Teaches thy way along that pathless coast,—
The desert and illimitable air,—
    Lone wandering, but not lost.

Al' day thy wings have fann'd,
At that far height, the cold, thin atmosphere,
Yet stoop not, weary, to the welcome land,
    Though the dark night is near.

And soon that toil shall end.
Soon shalt thou find a summer home, and rest,
And scream among thy fellows; reeds shall bend,
    Soon, o'er thy shelter'd nest.

Thou'rt gone, the abyss of heaven
Hath swallow'd up thy form; yet, on my heart,
Deeply hath sunk the lesson thou hast given,
    And shall not soon depart.

> He who, from zone to zone,
> Guides through the boundless sky thy certain flight,
> In the long way that I must tread alone,
> Will lead my steps aright.

The ostrich is remarkably shy and wary. A native of wide sandy plains, its stature enables it to command a wide horizon, while its great fleetness makes the chase a most severe exercise. "When she lifteth herself on high, she scorneth the horse and his rider." The rheas, which are the representatives of the ostrich in South America, inhabit regions presenting many of the characteristics of the African plains, and have much the same habits. They are extraordinarily vigilant, and so swift of foot, that it is only by surrounding them from various quarters, and thus confusing the birds, who know not whither to run, that the Gauchos are able to entangle them with the bolas or weighted cord. Mr Darwin says that the bird takes alarm at the approach of man, when he is so far off as to be unable to discern the bird.

Ancient writers mention a species of ox as inhabiting the forests of Europe, which they call the urus. It is described as being of a most savage and untameable disposition, delighting in the most wild and recluse parts of the forest, of vast size and power. It is generally believed that this race is preserved in some semi-wild oxen of a pure white colour, which inhabit one or two extensive woodland parks in the northern parts of our own island. It is interesting to observe the effect which the presence of man produces upon these animals. On the appearance

of any person, the herd sets off at full gallop, and, at the
distance of two or three hundred yards, they make a wheel
round, and come boldly up again, tossing their heads in a
menacing manner; on a sudden they make a full stop, at
the distance of forty or fifty yards, looking wildly at the
object of their surprise; but, upon the least motion being
made, they all again turn round and fly off with equal
speed, but not to the same distance; forming a shorter
circle, and again returning with a bolder and more
threatening aspect than before, they approach much
nearer, probably within thirty yards, when they make
another stand, and again fly off; this they do several
times, shortening their distance, and advancing nearer,
till they come within ten yards; when most people think
it prudent to leave them, not choosing to provoke them
further; for there is little doubt but, in two or three turns
more, they would make an attack.

The cows and calves partake of this jealous seclusion.
When the former bring forth, it is in some sequestered
thicket, where the calf is carefully concealed until it is
able to accompany its dam, who, till that time, visits it
regularly twice or thrice a day.   Should accident bring a
person near the secret place, the calf immediately claps its
head upon the ground, and seeks concealment by lying
close like a hare in its form.   A hidden calf of only two
days old, on being disturbed, manifested its inborn wild-
ness in a remarkable manner.   On the stranger stroking
its head, it sprang to its feet, though very lean and very
weak, pawed two or three times like an old bull, bellowed

very loud, stepped back a few paces, and bolted at his legs with all its force; it then began to paw again, bellowed, stepped back and bolted as before. The observer, however, now knowing its intention, stepped aside, so that it missed its aim and fell, when it was so very weak that it could not rise, though it made several efforts to do so. But it had done enough ; the whole herd had taken the alarm, and, coming to its rescue, obliged the intruder to retire.

In the forests of Lithuania there yet linger a few herds of another enormous ox, which at one time roamed over the whole of Europe, including even the British Isles— the European bison. The great marshy forest of Bialowicza, in which it dwells, is believed to be the only example of genuine primeval or purely natural forest yet remaining in Europe, and the habits of the noble ox are in accordance with the prestige of his ancient domain.

A few years ago the Czar of Russia presented a pair of half-grown animals of this species to the Zoological Society of London ; and a very interesting memoir on their capture, by M. Dolmatoff, was published in their *Proceedings*. A few extracts from that paper will illustrate the seclusion of their haunts and manners. " The day was magnificent, the sky serene, there was not a breath of wind, and nothing interrupted that calm of nature which was so imposing under the majestic dome of the primitive forest. Three hundred trackers, supported by fifty hunters, had surrounded, in profound silence, the solitary valley where the herd of bisons were found. Myself, accompanied by thirty other hunters,.

the most resolute and skilful, had penetrated in Indian
file the circle, advancing with the utmost precaution, and
almost fearing to breathe.   Arrived at the margin of the
valley, a most interesting spectacle met our eyes.   The
herd of bisons were lying down on the slope of a hill,
ruminating in the most perfect security, while the calves
frolicked around the herd, amusing themselves by attacking one another, striking the ground with their agile
feet, and making the earth fly into the air; then they
would rush towards their respective dams, rub against
them, lick them, and return to their play.   But at the
first blast of the horn the picture changed in the twinkling of an eye.   The herd, as if touched with a magic
wand, bounded to their feet, and seemed to concentrate
all their faculties in two senses, those of sight and hearing.   The calves pressed timidly against their mothers.
Then, while the forest re-echoed with bellowings, the
bisons proceeded to assume the order which they always
take under such circumstances, putting the calves in
front to guard them from the attack of pursuing dogs,
and carrying them before.   When they reached the
line occupied by the trackers and hunters, they were received with loud shouts and discharges of guns.   Immediately the order of battle was changed; the old bulls
rushed furiously towards the side, burst through the line
of the hunters, and continued their victorious course,
bounding along, and disdaining to occupy themselves
with their enemies, who were lying close against the great
trees.   The hunters managed, however, to separate from

the herd two calves ; one of these, three months old, was taken at one effort, another of fifteen months, though seized by eight trackers, overturned them all, and fled." It was subsequently taken, as were five others, in another part of the forest, one of them only a few days old. The savage impatience of man manifested by these young sylvans, was in the ratio of their age and sex. The bull of fifteen months maintained for a long time its sullen and morose behaviour ; it became furious at the approach of man, tossing its head, lashing its tail, and presenting its horns. After a while, however, it became tolerant of its keeper, and was allowed a measure of liberty.*

All the kinds of deer are shy and timid, but that fine species the moose of North America is peculiarly jealous and suspicious. The Indians declare that he is more shy and difficult to take than any other animal ; more vigilant, more acute of sense, than the reindeer or bison ; fleeter than the wapiti, more sagacious and more cautious than the deer. In the most furious tempest, when the wind, and the thunder, and the groaning of the trees, and the crash of falling timber, are combining to fill the ear with an incessant roar, if a man, either with foot or hand, break the smallest dry twig in the forest, the Indians aver that the moose will take notice of it ; he may not instantly take to flight, but he ceases to eat, and concentrates his attention. If, in the course of an hour or so, the man neither moves nor makes the slightest noise, the animal may begin to feed again ; but he does not forget

* *Proc. Zool. Soc.*, 1848, p. 16.

what attracted his notice, and for many hours manifests an increased watchfulness. Hence, it requires the utmost patience of an Indian hunter to stalk moose successfully.

The Indians believe that this animal, when other resources fail, has the power of remaining under water for a long time. It may be an exaggeration growing out of their experience of the many marvellous devices which he occasionally practises for self-preservation, and in which they believe he is more accomplished than the fox, or any other animal. A curious story is told, which may serve to illustrate the reputation of the beast in the eyes of those children of the forest, if it be worth no more. If there is any truth in it, we must assume that the animal managed to bring his nostrils to the surface at intervals; but how he could do this so as to elude the observation of his hunters is the marvel. For it must be borne in mind that they were Red Indians, not white men.

Two credible Indians, after a long day's absence on a hunt, came in and stated that they had chased a moose into a small pond; that they had seen him go to the middle of it and disappear, and then, choosing positions from which they could see every part of the circumference of the pond, smoked and waited until evening; during all which time they could see no motion of the water, or other indication of the position of the moose.

At length, being discouraged, they had abandoned all hope of taking him, and returned home. Not long afterwards came a solitary hunter, loaded with meat, who related, that having followed the track of a moose for some distance, he had traced it to the pond before mentioned; but having also discovered the tracks of two men, made at the same time as those of the moose, he concluded they must have killed it. Nevertheless, approaching cautiously to the margin of the pond, he sat down to rest. Presently, he saw the moose rise slowly in the centre of the pond, which was not very deep, and wade towards the shore where he was sitting. When he came sufficiently near, he shot him in the water.

The manner of hunting moose in winter is also illustrative of his recluse disposition. Deer are taken extensively by a process called "crusting;" that is, pursuing them, after a night's rain followed by frost has formed a crust of ice upon the surface of the deep snow. This will easily bear the weight of a man furnished with *rackets*, or snow-shoes, but gives way at once under the hoof of a moose or deer; and the animal thus embarrassed is readily overtaken and killed.

The moose, though occasionally taken by "crusting," seems to understand his danger, and to take precautions against it.

The sagacious animal, so soon as a heavy storm sets in, begins to form what is called a "moose-yard," which is a large area, wherein he industriously tramples down the snow while it is falling, so as to have room to move about in and browse upon the branches of trees, without the necessity of wandering from place to place, struggling through the deep drifts, exposed to the wolves, who, being of lighter make, hold a carnival upon the deer in crusting

time.   No wolf, however, dares enter a moose-yard.   He
will troop round and' round upon the snow-bank which
walls it, and his howling will, perhaps, bring two or three of
his brethren to the spot, who will try to terrify the moose
from his vantage ground, but dare not descend into it.

The Indians occasionally find a moose-yard, and take
an easy advantage of the discovery, as he can no more
defend himself or escape than a cow in a village pound.
But, when at liberty, and under no special disadvantage,
the moose is one of the noblest objects of a sportsman's
ambition, at least among the herbivorous races.   His
habits are essentially solitary.   He moves about not like
the elk, in roving gangs, but stalks in lonely majesty
through his leafy domains ; and, when disturbed by the
hunter, instead of bounding away like his congeners, he
trots off at a gait which, though faster than that of the
fleetest horse, is so easy and careless in its motion that it
seems to cost him no exertion.   But, though retreating
thus when pursued, he is one of the most terrible beasts
of the forest when wounded and at bay ; and the Indians
of the north-west, among some tribes, celebrate the death
of a bull-moose, when they are so fortunate as to kill one,
with all the songs of triumph that they would raise over
a conquered warrior.*

Who has not read of the chamois of the Alps and the
Tyrol? and who does not know with what an unrelaxing
vigilance it maintains its inaccessible strongholds?   As
long as summer warms the mountain air, it seeks the

* Hoffmann's *Forest and Prairie*, i., p. 92.

loftiest ridges, ever mounting higher and higher, treading with sure-footed fearlessness the narrow shelves, with precipices above and below, leaping lightly across yawning chasms a thousand yards in depth, and climbing up the slippery and perilous peaks, to stand as sentry in the glittering sky. Excessively wary and suspicious, all its senses seem endowed with a wonderful acuteness, so that it becomes aware of the approach of the daring hunter when half-a-league distant. When alarmed, it bounds from ledge to ledge, seeking to gain a sight of every quarter, uttering all the while its peculiar hiss of impatience. At length it catches a glimpse, far below, of the enemy whose scent had come up upon the breeze. Away now it bounds, scaling the most terrible precipices, jumping across the fissures, and leaping from crag to crag with amazing energy. Even a perpendicular wall of rock thirty feet in depth does not balk its progress: with astonishing boldness it takes the leap, striking the face of the rock repeatedly with its feet as it descends, both to break the violence of the shock, and to direct its course more accurately. Every danger is subordinate to that of the proximity of man, and every faculty is in requisition to the indomitable love of liberty. Hence the chamois is dear to the Swiss: he is the very type of their nation ; and his unconquerable freedom is the reflection of their own.

The character of this interesting antelope, as well as that of the scenery in which it dwells, are so pleasantly touched in a little poem that I have lately met with, by Miss Crewdson, that I make no apology for quoting it at length :—

O

THE GEMZÉ FAWN.*

In a sunny Alpine valley
  'Neath the snowy Wetterhorn,
See a maiden, by a châlet,
  Playing with a Gemzé fawn.
How he pricks his ears to hear her,
  How his soft eyes flash with pride,
As she tells him he is dearer
  Than the whole wide world beside!
Dearer than the lambkins gentle,
  Dearer than the frisking kids,
Or the pigeon on the lintel,
  Coming—going—as she bids.
Dearer than the first spring lily,
  Peeping on the snowy fell;
Dearer than his little Willie
  To the heart of William Tell.

By a gushing glacier fountain,
  On the giant Wetterhorn,
'Midst the snow-fields of the mountain,
  Was the little Gemzé born:
And his mother, though the mildest
  And the gentlest of the herd,
Was the fleetest and the wildest,
  And as lightsome as a bird.
But the gazer watch'd her gliding
  In the silence of the dawn,
Seeking for a place of hiding,
  For her little, tender fawn;
So he mark'd her, all unheeding
  (Swift and sure the bolt of death);
And he bore her, dead and bleeding,
  To his Alpine home beneath.

---

* In all the German-Swiss cantons, and throughout the Tyrol, the Chamois is called the " Gemzé;" the other name, "Chamois," prevailing only in those cantons in which French is spoken.

And the orphan Gemzé follows,
　Calling her with plaintive bleat,
O'er the knolls and through the hollow,
　Trotting on with trembling feet.

See, the cabin latch is raised
　By a small and gentle hand,
And the face that upward gazed
　Had a smile serene and bland;
Bertha was the Switzer's daughter,
　And herself an orphan child;
But her sorrows all had taught her
　To be gentle, kind, and mild.
You might see a tear-drop quivering
　In her honest eye of blue,
As she took the stranger, shivering,
　To her heart so warm and true.
"*I* will be thy mother, sweetest,"
　To the fawn she whisper'd low;
"I will heed thee when thou bleatest,
　And will solace all thy woe."
Then the tottering Gemzé, stealing
　Towards her, seem'd to understand,
Gazing on her face, and kneeling,
　Placed his nose within her hand!

Every day the Switzer maiden
　Shared with him her milk and bread;
Every night the fawn is laid on
　Moss and ling beside her bed.
Blue as mountain periwinkle
　Is the ribbon round his throat,
Where a little bell doth tinkle
　With a shrill and silvery note.
When the morning light is flushing
　Wetterhorn so cold and pale,
Or when evening shades are hushing
　All the voices of the vale,
You might hear the maiden singing
　To her happy Gemzé fawn,

While the kids and lambs she's bringing
  Up or down the thymy lawn.

Spring is come, and little Bertha,
  With her chamois at her side,
Up the mountain wander'd further
  Than the narrow pathway guide.
Every step is paved with flowers :—
  Here the bright mezereon glows;
Here the tiger-lily towers,
  And the mountain cistus blows;
Here the royal eagle rushes
  From his eyrie overhead;
There the roaring torrent gushes
  Madly o'er its craggy bed.
Hark !—from whence that distant bleating,
  Like a whistle clear and shrill?
Gemzé! Ah, thy heart is beating,
  With a wild and sudden thrill!
Voices of thy brothers, scouring
  Over sparkling fields of ice,
Where the snow-white peaks are towering
  O'er the shaggy precipice.

Bertha smiled to see him listening,
  (Arching neck, and quivering ear,
Panting chest, and bright eyes glistening,)
  To that whistle wild and clear.
Little knew she that it sever'd
  All that bound him to the glen,
That her gentle bands are shiver'd,
  And the tame one—*wild again!*
To the next wild bleat that soundeth,
  Makes he answer strong and shrill;
Wild as wildest, off he boundeth
  Fleet as fleetest o'er the hill.
"Gemzé! Gemzé! Kommt, mein lieber!"
  Echoes faint, from height to height:

* Come, my darling!

Dry thy tears, sweet Bertha! never
  Will he glance again in sight.
But, when paling stars are twinkling
  In the twilight of the morn,
Thou may'st hear his bell a-tinkling
  'Midst the snows of Wetterhorn.
And the kindness thou bestowest
  On the helpless, thou shalt prove,
Somehow, when thou little knowest,
  In a blessing from above !

An interesting scene of recluse life is exhibited by many a little pool in tropical America, such as I have seen in Jamaica, and such as I have seen, too, in the parts of the northern continent bordering on the tropics. You penetrate the sombre woods perhaps for miles, and suddenly, in the midst of the most perfect quietude, you see a great light, and open upon an area occupied by a green level, which, from indications here and there, you perceive to be water, covered with a coat of vegetation. The lofty trees rise up in closely-serried ranks all around, from the very margin, and their long branches, as if rejoicing in the unwonted room and light, stretch out over the water, and dip their twigs into it. The long, pendent strings of parasites hang down, and lightly touch the surface, whipping the floating duck-weed aside when a storm agitates the great trees. From time to time, one and another have been prostrated before the tempest, and, falling into the pond, project their half-decayed trunks in great snags from the sluggish surface, or form piers, which stretch away from the banks into the midst of the lake, and precarious bridges across different portions.

If we make our way by the starlight of the early morning to such a forest-pond as this, arriving silently and cautiously at its margin, before the light of the advancing dawn has yet struggled into the little inclosure, and take our station behind the shelter of a leafy bush, we shall discern that the spot is instinct with life. A loud clanging cry is uttered, like the note of a child's trumpet, which is immediately taken up in response from the opposite side of the pool. Then a whirring of wings, and much splashing of water. More of the loud clangours, and more splashing; and now the increasing light enables us to discern a dozen or a score of tiny black objects sitting on the surface, or hurrying to and fro. They look like the tiniest of ducks, but are jet black; some are sitting on the points of the projecting snags; and, by their erect attitude, we readily recognise that they are grebes.

Now it is light enough to see clearly, and the suspicious birds do not yet seem to be aware of our presence. Yonder, on the branch of a half-submerged tree, is a great dark mass, and a little bird sitting in it; it must surely be her nest. We must examine it.

Yet, stay! What is that serpent-like object that so quietly sits on yonder overhanging bough? Is it indeed a black snake reposing, with elevated neck, upon the horizontal limb? It moves! It is a bird! The lithe and slender neck is thrown round, and we see the head and beak of a bird, which begins to preen and arrange the plumage of a black body, which is squatted close to the bough. Mark that sudden start! The neck is elevated to the utmost; the head is raised in an attitude of attention; and the bird remains in the most absolute stillness. It was that leaf that we rustled, in the nervousness of our desire to see him more distinctly; he heard it, and is on the watch. Lo, he is gone! he dropped, like a stone, perpendicularly into the pool below; and yet not like a stone, for he made no splash, and we are amazed that so large a body could be immersed from so great a distance. and yet produce scarcely a perceptible disturbance of the surface.

The little grebes, too, have taken the warning; they are gone, all but the faithful mother on the nest. She yet lingers; but we shew ourselves, and advance; and now she jumps into the green water, and disappears; and all is as still and sombre as if we were gazing on a grave.

In our sequestered rural districts we have a little animal not uncommon, almost the tiniest of all quadrupeds, the water-shrew, whose graceful form and pleasing habits are very seldom seen, because of its cautious timidity. With great care it may, however, be occasionally detected in its gambols, and, with due precaution, watched. The following charming picture of the little creature at freedom, all unconscious of observation, has been drawn by Mr Dovaston :—" On a delicious evening, far in April 1825, a little before sunset, strolling in my orchard, beside a pool, and looking into the clear water for insects I expected about that time to come out, 1 was surprised by seeing what I momentarily imagined to be some very large beetle, dart with rapid motion, and suddenly disappear. Laying myself down, cautiously and motionless, on the grass, I soon, to my delight and wonder, observed it was a mouse.   I repeatedly marked it glide from the bank under water, and bury itself in the mass of leaves at the bottom ; I mean the leaves that had fallen off the trees in autumn, and which lay very thick over the mud. It very shortly returned, and entered the bank, occasionally putting its long, sharp nose out of the water, and paddling close to the edge.   This it repeated at very frequent intervals, from place to place, seldom going more than two yards from the side, and always returning in about half a minute.   I presume it sought and obtained some insect or food among the rubbish and leaves, and retired to consume it.   Sometimes, it would run a little on the surface, and sometimes, timidly and hastily, come ashore, but with the greatest caution, and instantly plunge in again.

" During the whole sweet spring of that fine year I constantly visited my new acquaintance.   When under water he looks gray, on account of the pearly cluster of minute air-bubbles that adhere to his fur, and bespangle him all over.   His colour, however, is very dark brown." . . . .

After entering into some descriptive details of the specimen, Mr Dovaston proceeds :—" This minute description I am enabled to give, having caught it in an angler's landing-net, and carefully inspected it in a white basin of water. The poor creature was extremely uneasy under inspection, and we soon, with great pleasure, restored it to liberty and love, for he had a companion, which, from her paler colour and more slender form, we doubted not was his mate, and we were fearful, by our intrusion, of giving offence to either.

" He swims very rapidly; and though he appears to dart, his very nimble wriggle is clearly discernible. He is never seen till sunset; but I saw him every evening I watched, with the most perfect facility. They are easily discovered about the going down of the sun, on still evenings, by the undulating semicircles quickly receding from the bank of the pool, when they are dabbling at the side. I believe this to be the animal said to be so long lost in England, the water-shrew (*Sorex fodiens* of Pennant) . . . .

" I have said he only appears at evening, and such are his habits. Once, at broad and bright noon, while leaning on a tree, gazing on the sun-sparkles passing (like fairy lights) in numberless and continual succession under the gentlest breath of air, I was aware of my little friend running nimbly on the surface among them. My rapture caused me to start with delight, on which he vanished to security, within his rush-fringed bank. . . . I should have mentioned that, on very still evenings, when my ear was close to the ground, I fancied I heard him utter a very short, shrill, feeble sibilation, not unlike that of the grasshopper-lark, in mild, light summer nights, but nothing near so loud, or long continued. Though I have watched for him warily in that and other places, after having, to the end of May, contributed to the myriads of my amusements, I never saw him more." *

* *Mag. Nat. Hist.*, ii., p. 219.

IX

THE WILD.

HAS my reader ever been present at the capture of a shark? If he has crossed the line, or even if he knows what it is to spend a week or two in " the calm latitudes," the debateable border-sea between the ordinary breezes and the trades, he is no stranger to the assiduous attentions of this lank and lithe tenant of the tropical seas. Jack familiarly calls him by the title of " Sea-lawyer," for reasons which are by no means complimentary to the learned profession; and views him with that admixture of hate and fear, with which unsophisticated landsmen are apt to regard his terrestrial representatives. To bait a line and catch the mackerel or the bonito, is always a welcome occupation to the sailor ; but to no amusement does Jack bend himself with such a hearty alacrity as to take the " shirk." When, on approaching the northern tropic,

" Down drops the breeze, the sails drop down,"

'tis not " sad as sad can be ; " for all is hilarity and alertness. Away goes one to the harness-cask, for a junk of salt pork, another is on his knees before the cabin-locker rummaging out an enormous hook, which tradition confidently reports is deposited there ; a third is unreeving the studding-sail halyards to serve as a line, for so tough a customer needs stout gear; a fourth is standing on the taffrail, keeping an eye on the monster, that now drops off, and now comes gliding up, a light-green mass, through the blue water, till his whiteness nearly touches the surface, and telling the villain all the while, with uncouth maledictions, that his time is coming. The mate is on the jib-boom wielding the grains, whose trident-prongs he has been for the last half-hour sharpening with a file, ready to take by force any one of the hated race who may be too suspicious for the bait astern. And now the skipper himself comes up, for even dignity itself cannot resist the temptation, and with his own brawny hands puts on the enticing pork, and lowers away.

'Tis twirling and eddying in the wash of the ship's counter; the crew are divided in their allegiance—half cluster at the quarter to watch the captain's success, half at the cat-heads to see the mate's harpooning. There scuttle up the two little pilot-fishes, in their banded livery of blue and brown, from their station one on each side of the shark's nose: they hurry to the bait, sniff at it, nibble at it, and then back in all haste to their huge patron, giving his grimness due information of the treat that awaits him. See how eagerly he receives it! with a lateral wave of his powerful tail he shoots ahead, and is in an instant at the pork. "Look out there! stand by to take a turn of the line round a belaying pin, for he's going to bite, and he'll give us a sharp tug!" Every pair of eyes is wide open, and every mouth, too; for the monster turns on his side, and prepares to take in the

delicate morsel.   But no ; he smells the rusty iron, perhaps, or perhaps he sees the line ; at any rate he contents himself with a sniff, and drops astern ; coming
forward again, however, the next minute to sniff and
sniff again.   'Tis perilous ; yet 'tis tempting.

A shout forward !   The mate has struck one !   And
away rush the after band to see the sport ; the skipper
himself hauls in the line, and joins the shouting throng.
Yes ; the grains have been well thrown, and are fast in
the fleshy part of the back.   What a monster ! full
fifteen feet long, if he 's an inch ! and how he plunges,
and dives, and rolls round and round, enraged at the
pain and restraint, till you can't discern his body for the
sheet of white foam in which it is enwrapped !   The stout
line strains and creaks, but holds on ; a dozen eager
hands are pulling in, and at last the unwilling victim is
at the surface just beneath the bows, but plunging with
tremendous force.

Now, one of the smarter hands has jumped into the
forechains with a rope made into a noose.   Many efforts
he makes to get this over the tail, without success ; at
length it is slipped over, in an instant hauled taut, and
the prey is secure.

"Reeve the line through a block, and take a run with
it !"   Up comes the vast length, tail foremost, out of the
sea ; for a moment the ungainly beast hangs, twining and
bending his body, and gnashing those horrid fangs, till
half -a-dozen boat-hooks guide the mass to its death-bed
on the broad deck.   Stand clear !   If that mouth get

hold of your leg, it will cut through it, sinew, muscle, and bone ; the stoutest man on board would be swept down if he came within the reach of that violent tail. What reverberating blows it inflicts on the smooth planks !

One cannot look at that face without an involuntary shudder. The long flat head, and the mouth so greatly overhung by the snout, impart a most repulsive expression to the countenance ; and then the teeth, those terrible serried fangs, as keen as lancets, and yet cut into fine notches like saws, lying row behind row, row behind row, six rows deep ! See how the front rows start up into erect stiffness, as the creature eyes you ! You shrink back from the terrific implement, no longer wondering that the stoutest limb of man should be severed in a moment by such chirurgery. But the eyes ! those horrid eyes ! it is the eyes that make the shark's countenance what it is—the very embodiment of Satanic malignity. Half-concealed beneath the bony brow, the little green eye gleams with so peculiar an expression of hatred, such a concentration of fiendish malice,—of quiet, calm, settled villany, that no other countenance that I have ever seen at all resembles. Though I have seen many a shark, I could never look at that eye without feeling my flesh creep, as it were, on my bones.

How *eerie* (to use an expressive northern term, for which we have no equiyalent) must be the scene presented to a few forlorn mariners committed to an open boat in the midst of the broad southern sea, a thousand miles from land, when by night these obscene monsters

come gliding up alongside, keeping hated company!
Cleaving the phosphorescent sea, their bodies are invested
with an elfish light, and a bluish gleam trails behind.
Nothing strikes more terror into the hearts of the poor
ship-bereft seamen than such uninvited companions.
They make no noise : as silently as ghosts they steal
along ; now disappearing for a few minutes ; then there
again ; throughout the dreary night they maintain their
vigil, filling the failing heart with auguries of death.

What do they there? Ah! their horribly unerring
instinct has taught them that such an object too often
yields them the meal they are seeking. They silently
demand the corpse that fatigue and suffering, exposure
and privation, are surely and swiftly preparing for them.
They well deem that by the morning light a sullen plunge
will ease the boat of the night's dead, and they are quite
ready to furnish the living grave.   :

The following vivid picture, though given in a work of
fiction, is so manifestly drawn from the life, that I shall be
pardoned for citing it, the more because I have had some
opportunities of personally verifying this writer's oceanic
delineations, and have observed their remarkable truth-
fulness—

" The night following our abandonment of the ship was
made memorable by a remarkable spectacle. Slumber-
ing in the bottom of the boat, Jarl and I were suddenly
awakened by Samoa. Starting, we beheld the ocean of a
pallid white colour, coruscating all over with tiny golden
sparkles. But the pervading hue of the water cast a

cadaverous gleam upon the boat, so that we looked to each other like ghosts. For many rods astern, our wake was revealed in a line of rushing illuminated foam ; while, here and there beneath the surface, the tracks of sharks were denoted by vivid, greenish trails, crossing and recrossing each other in every direction. Further away, and distributed in clusters, floated on the sea, like constellations in the heavens, innumerable medusæ, a species of small, round, refulgent fish, only to be met with in the South Seas and the Indian Ocean.

" Suddenly, as we gazed, there shot high into the air a bushy jet of flashes, accompanied by the unmistakeable deep-breathing sound of a sperm whale. Soon the sea all round us spouted in fountains of fire ; and vast forms, emitting a glare from their flanks, and ever and anon raising their heads above water, and shaking off the sparkles, shewed where an immense shoal of cachalots had risen from below, to sport in these phosphorescent billows.

" The vapour jetted forth was far more radiant than any portion of the sea ; ascribable, perhaps, to the originally luminous fluid, contracting still more brillancy from its passage through the spouting canal of the whales.

" We were in great fear lest, without any vicious intention, the leviathans might destroy us by coming into close contact with our boat. We would have shunned them, but they were all round and round us. Nevertheless we were safe ; for, as we parted the pallid brine, the peculiar irradiation which shot from about our keel seemed to deter them. Apparently discovering us of a sudden, many of them plunged headlong down into the water, tossing their fiery tails high into the air, and leaving the sea still more sparkling from the violent surging of their descent.

" Their general course seemed the same as our own; to the westward. To remove from them, we at last out oars, and pulled towards the north. So doing, we were steadily pursued by a solitary whale that must have taken our boat for a kindred fish. Spite of all our efforts, he drew near and nearer; at length rubbing his fiery flank against the gunwale, here and there leaving long strips of the glossy transparent substance, which, thin as a gossamer, invests the body of the cachalot.

" In terror at a sight so new, Samoa shrank. But Jarl and I, more used to the intimate companionship of the whales, pushed the boat away from it with our oars; a thing often done in the fishery.

" But, to my great joy, the monster at last departed; rejoining the shoal, whose lofty spoutings of flame were still visible upon the distant line of the horizon, showing there like the fitful starts of the Aurora Borealis.

" The sea retained its luminosity for about three hours, at the expiration of half that period beginning to fade; and, excepting occasional faint illuminations, consequent upon the rapid darting of fish under water, the phenomenon at last wholly disappeared.

" Heretofore, I had beheld several exhibitions of marine phosphorescence, both in the Atlantic and Pacific; but nothing in comparison with what was seen that night. In the Atlantic, there is very seldom any portion of the ocean luminous, except the crests of the waves, and these mostly appear so during wet murky weather. Whereas, in the Pacific, all instances of the sort previously coming under my notice, had been marked by patches of greenish light, unattended with any pallidness of the sea. Save twice on the coast of Peru, when I was summoned from my hammock by the alarming cry of 'All hands ahoy! tack ship!' and rushing on deck, beheld the sea white as a shroud; for which reason it was feared we were on soundings." *

This idea of *unearthliness* is a great element in the Romance of Natural History. Our matter-of-fact age despises and scouts it as absurd, and those who are conscious of such impressions acknowledge that they are unreal, yet feel them none the less. The imaginative Greeks peopled every wild glen, every lonely shore, every obscure cavern, every solemn grove, with the spiritual, only rarely and fitfully visible or audible. So it has been with all peoples, especially in that semi-civilised stage which is so favourable to poetic developments : the elves and fays, the sprites and fairies, the Jack-o'-lanterns, the Will-o'-the-wisps, and Robin-goodfellows, and Banshees,— what are they all but the phenomena of nature, dimly discerned, and attributed by a poetic temperament to beings of unearthly races, but of earthly sympathies? The garish day, with its clearness and perfect definition of

* Melville's *Mardi*, vol. i., p. 187.

P

every object, is far less favourable for these impressions
than night; not only because at the latter season the mind
is solemnised, but also because the obscurity renders
visible objects dim and uncertain; gives to familiar things
strange and fantastic forms; and, while the peculiar conditions of the atmosphere render sounds more distinct,
these are often of an unwonted character, vague in their
origin, and cannot be corrected by the sense of sight.

In the forests of Lower Canada and the New England
States I have often heard in spring a mysterious sound,
of which to this day I know not the author. Soon after
night sets in, a metallic sound is heard from the most
sombre forest swamps, where the spruce and the hemlock
give a peculiar density to the woods, known as the "black
growth." The sound comes up clear and regular, like
the measured tinkle of a cow-bell, or gentle strokes on a
piece of metal, or the action of a file upon a saw. It
goes on, with intervals of interruption, throughout the
hours of darkness. People attribute it to a bird, which
they call the whetsaw; but nobody pretends to have seen
it, so that this can only be considered conjecture, though
a highly probable one. The monotony and pertinacity of
this note had a strange charm for me, increased doubtless
by the mystery that hung over it. Night after night, it
would be heard in the same spot, invariably the most
sombre and gloomy recesses of the black-timbered woods.
I occasionally watched for it, resorting to the woods
before sunset, and waiting till darkness; but, strange to
say, it refused to perform under such conditions. The

shy and recluse bird, if bird it is, was doubtless aware
of the intrusion, and on its guard. Once I heard it under
peculiarly wild circumstances. I was riding late at night,
and just at midnight came to a very lonely part of the
road, where the black forest rose on each side. Everything was profoundly still, and the measured tramp of
my horse's feet on the frozen road was felt as a relief to
the deep and oppressive silence; when, suddenly, from
the sombre woods, rose the clear metallic tinkle of the
whetsaw. The sound, all unexpected as it was, was very
striking, and, though it was bitterly cold, I drew up for
some time to listen to it. In the darkness and silence of
the hour, that regularly measured sound, proceeding too
from so gloomy a spot, had an effect on my mind, solemn
and unearthly, yet not unmingled with pl asure.

It is doubtless the mystery in such cases that mainly
constitutes the charm. In Jamaica I used to hear frequently a querulous cry, "kep, kep, kep,"—uttered in
the air after night-fall by some creature which flew round
in a great circle, but was invisible. Now and then the
utterance was varied by a most demoniac shriek or two,
and then the call went on as before. I was exceedingly
interested in this, till I ascertained that it was the white
owl, and obtained a specimen, after which the romantic
feeling with which I had listened to it was no longer
awakened by the sound.

In some parts of this country the peasantry hear with
superstitious awe the hollow booming note of the bittern,
proceeding from the lonely marsh in the stillness of the

evening.   They attribute the voice to some supernatural
creature of formidable size and powers, which is supposed
to reside at the bottom of the fens, and which they call
the Bull-o'-the-bog.   The sound is sufficiently awful to
excuse the error.

The dreary cypress-swamps of the Southern United
States possess a bird closely allied to our bittern, whose
voice, though destitute of the volume of the European
bird, is startling enough to hear in its savage solitudes.
Nothing can be more dismal, even by day, than the interior of one of those swamps,—half-tepid, stagnant water
covering the ground, the dense timber trees, a hundred
feet in height, whose opaque and sombre-hued foliage
almost shuts out the sky, while the gaunt horizontal
branches are hung with far-pendent ragged bundles of
Spanish moss,* the very type of dreariness and desolation.
Such trees remind one of an army of skeletons, giants of
some remote age, still standing where they had lived, and
still wearing the decaying tatters of the robes which they
had worn of old.   At night, however, these forests are
invested with tenfold gloom, and imagination peoples the
palpable blackness and silence with all sorts of horrors,
as the eye vainly attempts to peer into their depths;
while ever and anon, the melancholy "quah!" hoarse and
hollow, booms out from the solitude, chilling one's spirit,
as if it were the voice of the presiding demon of the place.
Not in vain have the inspired Prophets† made use of the
bittern as one of the elements in their delineations of

---

* *Tillandsia usneoides.*   † Isa. xiv. 23, xxxiv. 11; Zeph. ii. 14.

awful and utter desolation. Take for an example the denunciation upon Idumea, in Isa. xxxiv. :—

"And the streams thereof shall be turned into pitch, and the dust thereof into brimstone, and the land thereof shall become burning pitch.

"It shall not be quenched night nor day; the smoke thereof shall go up for ever: from generation to generation it shall lie waste; none shall pass through it for ever and ever.

"But the cormorant and the bittern shall possess it; the owl also and the raven shall dwell in it: and he shall stretch out upon it the line of confusion, and the stones of emptiness.

"They shall call the nobles thereof to the kingdom, but none shall be there, and all her princes shall be nothing.

"And thorns shall come up in her palaces, nettles and brambles in the fortresses thereof: and it shall be an habitation of dragons, and a court for owls.

"The wild beasts of the desert shall also meet with the wild beasts of the island, and the satyr shall cry to his fellow; the screech-owl also shall rest there, and find for herself a place of rest.

"There shall the great owl make her nest, and lay, and hatch, and gather under her shadow; there shall the vultures also be gathered, every one with her mate."

A fine accumulation is here of wild and dreary images; and I do not know a better exemplification of the category of natural phenomena under consideration than this awful passage of Holy Writ.

Sir Emerson Tennent, in his elaborate volumes on Ceylon, lately published, has alluded to a bird of night which superstition invests with peculiar terrors. He thus speaks of it. Like the whetsaw, it seems to be "*vox et præterea nihil.*"

"Of the nocturnal *accipitres* the most remarkable is the brown owl, which, from its hideous yell, has acquired the name of the 'Devil Bird.' The Singhalese regard it literally with horror; and its scream by night, in the vicinity of a village, is bewailed as the harbinger of approaching calamity."

After alluding to another sound attributed to a bird, but of which the authorship is involved in uncertainty, he adds :—

"Mr Mitford, of the Ceylon Civil Service, to whom I am indebted for many valuable notes relative to the birds of the island, regards the identification of the Singhalese Devil-bird as open to similar doubt: he says, 'The Devil-bird is not an owl. I never heard it until I came to Kornegalle, where it haunts the rocky hill at the back of the Government-house. Its ordinary note is a magnificent clear shout like that of a human being, and which can be heard at a great distance, and has a fine effect in the silence of the closing night. It has another cry, like that of a hen just caught; but the sounds which have earned for it its bad name, and which I have heard but once to perfection, are indescribable, the most appalling that can be imagined, and scarcely to be heard without shuddering; I can only compare it to a boy in torture, whose screams are being stopped by being strangled. I have offered rewards for a specimen, but without success." [*]

The resemblance of this description to that given by Wilson of the performances of the great horned owl of North America, induces a suspicion that Mr Mitford may be in error, in so confidently denying the Ceylon bird to be an owl. Wilson says of his formidable species,—" His favourite residence is in the dark solitudes of deep swamps, covered with a growth of gigantic timber ; and here, as soon as evening draws on, and mankind retire to rest, he sends forth such sounds as seem scarcely to belong to this world, startling the solitary pilgrim as he slumbers by his forest fire,

'Making night hideous.'

Along the mountainous shores of the Ohio, and amidst the deep forests of Indiana, alone, and reposing in the woods, this ghostly watchman has frequently warned me of the approach of morning, and amused me with his singular exclamations, sometimes sweeping down and around my fire, uttering a loud and sudden ' Waugh O ! Waugh O !' sufficient to have alarmed a whole garrison. He has other nocturnal solos, no less melodious, one of which very strikingly resembles the half-suppressed screams of a person suffocating, or throttled, and cannot fail of being exceedingly entertaining to a lonely benighted traveller, in the midst of an Indian wilderness." [†]

I have myself heard the startling call of this fine night-fowl in the Southern States, when, in penetrating through

* Tennent's *Ceylon*, i , p. 167.   † *Amer. Ornithol.*, i., p. 100.

the swamps, covered with gigantic beeches and sycamores, entwined and tangled by the various species of briers and vines that hang in festoons from the trees, and amidst the evergreen bushes of the hystrix fan-palm, this "ghostly watchman" lifts up his hollow voice like a sentinel challenging the intruder. Through the afternoon, and especially as day wanes into evening, they may be heard from all quarters of the swamps; and in the deep solitude and general silence of these gloomy recesses, the cry is peculiarly startling. "Ho! ohó! ohó! waugh hō!" is his call; the last syllable uttered with particular earnestness, and protracted for some seconds, and gradually falling. The whole is given deliberately, in a loud and hollow tone; and one can scarcely be persuaded that it comes from a bird.

I have already alluded to the Guacharo, an extraordinary bird inhabiting a very limited district in the province of Cumana, South America, and entirely confined to caverns. There is, however, so much of romantic interest attached to its habits, that we may glance at a few of the details which Humboldt has given us from his own experience. On his arrival at the valley of Caripe, the people all spoke with superstitious wonder of a cavern several leagues in length, that gave birth to a river, and was haunted by thousands of night-birds, whose fat was used in the Missions instead of butter.

Humboldt made a party to explore this wondrous cavern. After reaching the river which flows out of it, they followed its course upwards by a winding path, till

at length the cave yawned before them in all its grandeur.
It is pierced in the vertical side of a rock, forming a vault
upwards of eighty feet in width, and nearly the same in
height. The face of the rock is clad with gigantic trees,
and all the luxuriant profusion of tropical vegetation.
Beautiful and curious parasitic plants, ferns and orchids,
and elegant creepers and lianes, festooned the rugged
entrance, hanging down in wild drapery, and, what is
remarkable, this *riant* verdure penetrated for some distance
even into the cave. Humboldt beheld with astonishment
noble plantain-like *heliconiæ* eighteen feet high, palms,
and arborescent arums, following the course of the river
even to the subterranean parts. There the vegetation
continues as in the deep crevices of the Andes, half shut
out from the light of day, nor does it disappear till a
distance of thirty or forty paces from the entrance. The
party went forward for about four hundred and thirty
feet, without being obliged to light their torches. Where
the light began to fail, they heard from afar the hoarse
cries of the *guacharo* birds. He states that it is difficult
to form an idea of the horrible noise made by thousands
of these birds in the dark recesses of the cavern, whence
their shrill and piercing cries strike upon the vaulted
rocks, and are repeated by the echo in the depths of the
grotto. He observes that the race of guacharo birds
would probably have been extinct long since, if several
circumstances had not contributed to its preservation.
The natives, withheld by superstitious fears, seldom dare
to proceed far into the recesses of the cavern. Humboldt

had great difficulty in persuading them to pass beyond
the outer part of the cave, the only part of it which they
visit annually to collect the oil; and the whole authority
of the *Padres* was necessary to make them penetrate as
far as the spot where the floor rises abruptly, at an inclination of sixty degrees, and where a small subterraneous
cascade is formed by the torrent. In the minds of the
Indians, this cave, inhabited by nocturnal birds, is
associated with mystic ideas, and they believe that in the
deep recesses of the cavern the souls of their ancestors
sojourn. They say that man should avoid places which
are enlightened neither by the sun nor the moon; and to
" go and join the guacharoes," means to rejoin their
fathers—in short, to die. At the entrance of the cave,
the magicians and poisoners perform their exorcisms, to
conjure the chief of the evil spirits.*

The following incident, which occurred to Mr Atkinson in his travels in Central Asia, is not without a romantic interest :—

" Our course had hitherto been along the middle of the
river, passing on our way several small islands which divided it into different streams. The Cossacks were resting on their oars, not a sound was heard, when we glided
into a narrow channel, between a long island and a thick
bed of reeds. Our canoes had not floated more than fifty
yards, when one of the Cossacks struck the reeds with his
oar, and simultaneously they all gave a loud shout. In a
moment there came a shriek, as if a legion of fiends had

* *Personal Narrative.*

been cast loose, which was followed by a rushing sound
and a flapping of wings on every side, rising high into
mid-air : then the wild concert was taken up and repeated
far above us. We had come suddenly on the covert of
thousands of water-fowl. After this uproar the Cossacks
pulled out into the middle of the stream, and passed
quickly along through some beautiful scenery." *

Those who are familiar with the poulpes and cuttles of
our coasts will readily allow that there is something more
than usually repulsive in their appearance. Their flabby,
corpse-like fleshiness, now lax and soft, now plumping up,
their changes of colour, the livid hue that comes and goes
so strangely, the long lithe arms with their cold adhesive
powers, their uncouth agility, their cunning adroitness
and intelligence, and especially the look of their ghastly
green eyes, make them decidedly "no canny." It does
not need that they should be sufficiently colossal in dimensions to throw their arms over a ship's hull and drag her
under water, as oriental tales pretend, and as old-fashioned
naturalists believed, to induce us to give them a wide
berth. It would not be pleasant to be entwined in the
embrace of those arms ; and we can sympathise with Mr
Beale, who has described his feelings during an encounter
which he had with a beastie of this sort, while engaged in
searching for shells among the rocks of the Bonin Islands.
He was much astonished at seeing at his feet a most extraordinary-looking animal, crawling towards the surf,
which it had only just left. It was creeping on its eight

* Atkinson's *Siberia*, p. 228.

legs, which, from their soft and flexible nature, bent considerably under the weight of its body, so that it was lifted by the efforts of its tentacula only a small distance from the rocks. It appeared much alarmed at seeing him, and made every effort to escape. Mr Beale endeavoured to stop it by pressing on one of its legs with his foot; but, although he used considerable force for that purpose, its strength was so great that it several times liberated its member, in spite of all the efforts he could employ on the wet and slippery rocks. He then laid hold of one of the tentacles with his hand, and held it firmly, so that it appeared as if the limb would be torn asunder by the united efforts of himself and the creature. He then gave it a powerful jerk, wishing to disentangle it from the rocks to which it clung so forcibly by its suckers. This effort it effectually resisted; but, the moment after, the apparently enraged animal lifted its head, with its large projecting eyes, and, loosing its hold of the rocks, suddenly sprang upon Mr Beale's arm, (which he had previously bared to the shoulder for the purpose of thrusting it into holes in the rocks after shells,) and clung to it by means of its suckers with great power, endeavouring to get its beak, which could now be seen between the roots of its arms, in a position to bite. A sensation of horror pervaded his whole frame, when he found that this monstrous animal had fixed itself so firmly on his arm. He describes its cold, slimy grasp as extremely sickening; and he loudly called to the captain, who was similarly engaged at some distance, to come and release him of his disgusting assailant. The captain

quickly came, and, taking him down to the boat, during which time Mr Beale was employed in keeping the beak of the *Octopus* away from his hand, soon released him by destroying his tormentor with the boat-knife, when he disengaged it by portions at a time. This Cephalopod measured across its expanded arms about four feet, while its body was not bigger than a man's fist.*

The shriek of the jackal bursting on the ear in the silence of night has been described by many a dweller in tents in the East as a most appalling sound. But perhaps this yields in effect to the combined efforts of the howling-monkeys in a South American forest. This most striking of all animal voices is heard occasionally at sunrise and sunset, and sometimes in the heat of the day, but more frequently during the darkness of the night. When near, the roar is terrific : a naturalist † has compared it to the tempest howling through rocky caverns. It is a noise so unearthly, that, heard unexpectedly for the first time, it would fill the mind with the most melancholy and fearful forebodings.

A traveller in the western wilds of North America bivouacking on the open prairie, awakened at midnight by the voices of a pack of prairie-wolves giving tongue around him, speaks of the wierd impression made on him by hearing a pack in full cry at the dead of the night, and compares it to the phantom hounds and huntsman of the German legends.‡

What was this, however, to Gordon Cumming's noctur-

* *Hist. of the Sperm Whale.*   † Mr Bates, in the *Zoologist*, p. 3593.
    ‡ Sullivan's *Rambles in America*, p. 77.

nal adventure with the *wilde honden* in Africa? He was watching for game in a hole which he had dug by a pool in that romantic fashion already alluded to, and, having shot a gnu, had put down his rifle without reloading it, and dropped asleep.

He had not slept long before his slumbers were disturbed by strange sounds. He dreamed that lions were rushing about in quest of him, till, the sounds increasing, he awoke with a sudden start, uttering a loud shriek. He heard the rushing of light feet on every side, accompanied by the most unearthly noises, and, on raising his head, to his utter horror, saw himself surrounded by troops of what the colonists call wild dogs, a savage animal between a wolf and a hyena. To the right and left, and within a few paces of the bold hunter, stood two lines of these ferocious-looking animals, cocking their ears and stretching their necks to have a look at him; while two large troops, containing forty at least, kept dashing backwards and forwards across his wind, chattering and growling with the most extraordinary volubility. Another troop of the wild dogs were fighting over the gnu that had been shot; and, on beholding them, the expectation of being himself presently torn in pieces made the blood curdle over his cheeks, and the hair bristle on his head.

In this dilemma the experienced hunter bethought himself of the power of the human voice and a determined bearing in overawing brute animals; and, springing to his feet, he stepped upon the little ledge surrounding the hole, when drawing himself up to his full height, he waved his large blanket with both hands, at the same time addressing his certainly attentive audience in a loud and solemn tone. This had the desired effect: the wild dogs shrank to a more respectful distance, barking at him like so many colleys. Upon this he began to load his rifle, and before this was accomplished the entire pack had retreated.*

* *The Lion Hunter*, chap. ix.

X.

THE TERRIBLE.

MAN'S connexion with the creation around him occasionally brings him into circumstances of more serious result than a temporary excitement of the imagination, and a thrilling of the nerves, which might be on the whole rather pleasant than otherwise. He was indeed invested with lordship over the inferior creatures, and in general they own his dominion; but many of them are endowed with powers for evil, to which he can oppose no effectual resistance; at least, none so invariably effectual, but that occasions occur in which the mastery is reversed. Some are furnished with enormous weight and strength, able to crush him with mere brute momentum; others carry formidable weapons, horns and hoofs, claws and teeth, tusks and fangs, wielded with consummate skill, and made more effective by the aid of muscular strength, fleetness of pace, agility, instinct of combination, or cunning strategy. Others, small and apparently contemptible, are yet armed with implements so terribly lethal, that the slightest puncture of the skin by one of them, darted too with lightning-like rapidity and almost unerring precision, is inevitably and immediately followed by the most horrid form of death.

And the creatures are conscious of their own powers; and, though they will often tacitly own man's supremacy by declining a contest with him, yet there are circumstances ever and anon occurring,—hunger sometimes, sometimes rage, or the desperation induced by escape being cut off, or the στοργή which makes the helpless bold,—in which they are willing to try "the wager of battle" with their liege.

The stern conflict for life, when man stands face to face with his bestial foes, has given many a romantic page to the annals of natural history; and too many such pages are stained with the harrowing record of their grim victory, and his bloody death. We cannot therefore ignore them in the aspect of natural science which we are considering; but we may content ourselves with a few examples of the terrible: the difficulty lies in the selection from the profusion of *matériel.*

Throughout the north temperate zone the wolf is a cruel and bloodthirsty foe of man, making up by a scent like that of the hound, a patient perseverance, and a habit of combining in numbers in common pursuit, what it lacks in individual power. Yet, individually, a wolf is able to pull down an unarmed man, and, when pressed with famine in severe winters, it becomes very daring. In our own island its ravages have long ago induced its extirpation; but in a remote era houses were erected at certain intervals by the road-sides, to serve as places of refuge against the assaults of the wolves; and January was by our Anglo-Saxon ancestors called, " Wolf-mouat,"

Q

(Wolf-month,) because more people were devoured by wolves in that month than at other times.

In the north and east of Europe, the danger incurred by travellers in sledges of being hunted by packs of hungry wolves is very great; and many dreadful incidents bear witness to their success. A very horrible one is narrated by Mr Lloyd. A woman accompanied by three of her children was one day travelling in this mode, when she discovered that she was pursued by these gaunt foes in full pack. She immediately put the horse into a gallop, and drove towards her home, from which she was not far distant, with all possible speed. All, however, would not avail, for the ferocious animals gained upon her, and at last were on the point of rushing on the sledge. For the preservation of her own life, and that of the remaining children, the poor frantic creature now took one of the babes and cast it a prey to her blood-thirsty pursuers. This stopped their career for a moment, but, after devouring the little innocent, they renewed their pursuit, and a second time came up with the vehicle. The mother, driven to desperation, resorted to the same horrible expedient, and threw her ferocious assailants another of her offspring. To cut short this melancholy story, her third child was sacrificed in a similar manner. Soon after this the wretched being, whose feelings may more easily be conceived than described, reached her home in safety.

Mr Atkinson has sketched,* with his usual graphic

* *Siberia*, p. 401.

vigour, the situation of himself and his party of Kalmucks, when surrounded by wolves in Mongolia. They were encamped for the night on the open steppe on the banks of a little lake, when suddenly the howling of the terrible wolves was heard at a distance. The men quickly collected the horses, and prepared to receive the assailants. The fire was nearly out, but it was thought best to allow them to approach, and then by a little fresh fuel obtain light enough for a fair shot. It was not long before the padding of their many feet was heard as they galloped towards the party, and presently a savage howl arose. The men threw some dry bushes on the embers, and blew up a bright flame, which sent its red glare far around, disclosing the pack with ears and tails erect, and flashing eyes. At a signal, five rifles and a double-barrel poured in a volley with deadly effect, as the horrible howling revealed. Snarling and shrieking, the pack drew off, but the Kalmucks declared they would return.

Soon the terror of the horses announced the re-approach of the marauders, and they could be heard stealing round between the encampment and the lake, dividing into two packs, so as to approach on opposite sides. Presently the glare of their eyeballs was seen, and their grizzly forms pushing one another on. Again the bullets sped, and the shrieking packs again retreated, but only to keep watch at a little distance.

The night now grew very dark, and all the fuel was exhausted. Presently, a distant howling announced the approach of a new pack, on whose arrival the old ones, which had been silently biding their time, began to manifest their presence by jealous growls, which soon gave way to a general fight among themselves. Some of the men now, well armed, crept along the margin of the lake to collect more fuel, which was then placed on the fire. The flame was blown up, and a group of eight or ten wolves was seen within fifteen paces, with others beyond. The rifles once more cracked, and the packs with a frightful howl scampered off.

In the morning eight wolves were lying dead, and the bloody tracks shewed that many others had carried away mortal wounds, the reminiscences of this fearful night.

The brown bear of Europe is of formidable strength, and sufficiently bold occasionally to be a serious antagonist, as numerous adventures of Mr Lloyd and other northern sportsmen testify. Though it can subsist on fruits, grain, and honey, which involve no destruction of animal life, yet it is predaceous and ferocious too. The ancient Romans made use of Scottish bears to augment the horrors of public executions :—

> " Nuda Caledonio sic pectora præbuit urso,
> Non falsâ pendens in cruce, Laureolus."

The ferocity of the Syrian bear is illustrated by many passages of Sacred Writ, and in particular by the narrative which records the slaughter of the forty-two youths, who mocked Elisha, by two she-bears.* And the Polar bear is a truly savage and powerful animal.

But no species of the genus can compare with the

* 2 Kings ii. 24.

grizzly bear of the North American prairies, for either size, strength, or ferocity. The names of *Ursus ferox* and *U. horribilis*, which have been given to it, re-echo the prevailing ideas of its terrible character. Even the savage bison, vast and mighty as he is, falls a prey to the grizzly bear, which can drag the carcase, though a thousand pounds in weight, to its haunt. Lewis and Clarke measured one which was nine feet in length.

The hunters and trappers of the Rocky Mountains delight to tell, over their camp fires, stories of personal encounters with this formidable savage. Many of these stirring incidents have found their way into print, and one of them I shall here condense.

A Canadian named Villandrie, pursuing his occupation of a free trapper on the Yellow-stone River, had acquired by his skill and daring the reputation of the best white hunter in the region. One morning, when he was riding out to have a look at his beaver traps, he had to break his way through some thick bushes that grew on a high bank above a small river. He was going along, pushing back the twigs with the barrel of his rifle, and keeping an eye on the bank, when all at once he found himself close to an old she grizzly bear, which rose instantly and dashed furiously at the horse, as he was struggling with the shrubs and bushes. One blow of her colossal paw was enough to break his back, and to throw Villandrie down the bank, his rifle falling into the water. Three half-grown cubs now occupied themselves with the poor struggling horse, while the raging mother rushed towards the trapper, who was just getting up; but before he had well drawn his long knife, the bear's claws were on his left arm and shoulder. His right arm he could still move freely, and he inflicted stab after stab in the neck of his fierce enemy, which did not on that account relax her gripe, but tried to catch the knife with her teeth. At every movement he made, she seemed to dig deeper into his shoulder and loins.

The struggle had not lasted a minute, when the sandy bank suddenly gave way, and down the combatants went into the water. Fortunately for Villandrie, the sudden cold bath made the bear loose her hold: she returned to her cubs, and left her mangled antagonist to get away as well as he could. The next day he reached a Sioux village, very much exhausted from loss of blood; but he got his wounds tolerably healed, and still maintained his character of the best white trapper on the Yellowstone.*

Recent travellers in Africa have made us somewhat familiar with the mighty and ferocious brutes of that arid continent, the very metropolis of bestial power. Not only have the missionary, the colonist, and the soldier encountered the lordly animals in their progress into the wilderness, but hunters, either for sport or profit, have gone in search of them, bearded the lion by his midnight fountain, and provoked the elephant to single combat in his forest fastnesses. Fearful adventures have hence ensued, the records of which have thrilled us dwellers at

* Möllhausen's *Journey to the Pacific*, i., p. 103.

home by our winter firesides. One or two of these I may select for illustration of the terrible in natural history.

Nothing is more appalling in the way of animal voices than the scream, or "trumpeting," as it is called, of an enraged elephant. The hunting of this animal in South Africa is awful work. To stand in front of a creature twelve feet high, infuriated to the utmost, to hear his shriek of rage, to see him come crashing on with an impetus that throws the very trees out of the ground, needs all the nerve and all the courage that man can bring to the conflict. Livingstone says that the terrible "trumpet" is more like what the shriek of a French steam-whistle would be to a man standing on a railway, than any other earthly sound. So confounding is it, that a horse unused to the chase will sometimes stand shivering, and unable to move, instead of galloping from the peril. Gordon Cumming has depicted a stirring scene, in which, having dismounted to fire at an elephant, he was immediately charged by another; his horse, terrified by being thus placed between two enraged monsters, refused to be mounted; and it was only when he expected to feel a trunk clasping his body, that he managed to spring into the saddle.

Even when mounted, the legs of the steed will sometimes fail from terror, and he falls with his rider; or, from the character of the forest, the latter may be dragged from his seat during the flight, and thus be left helpless before the furious beast, exposed to be impaled by the long tusks, or crushed into a mummy by the enormous feet.

An adventure of this sort with an elephant befel one
who has had more narrow escapes than any man living,
but whose modesty has always prevented him from pub-
lishing anything about himself.   On the banks of the
Zouga, in 1850, Mr Oswell pursued one of these animals
into the dense, thick, thorny bushes met with on the
margin of that river, and to which the elephant usually
flees for safety.   He followed through a narrow pathway,
by lifting up some of the branches and forcing his way
through the rest; but when he had just got over this
difficulty, he saw the elephant, whose tail he had got
glimpses of before, now rushing towards him.   There was
then no time to lift up branches, so he tried to force the
horse through them.   He could not effect a passage; and,
as there was but an instant between the attempt and
failure, the hunter tried to dismount; but, in doing this,
one foot was caught by a branch, and the spur drawn
along the animal's flank; this made him spring away
and throw the rider on the ground, with his face to the
elephant, which being in full chase, still went on.   Mr
Oswell saw the huge fore-foot about to descend on his
legs, parted them, and drew in his breath as if to resist
the pressure of the other foot, which he expected would
next descend on his body.   He saw the whole length of
the under part of the enormous brute pass over him; the
horse got away safely.   Dr Livingstone, who records the
anecdote, has heard but of one other authentic instance
in which an elephant went over a man without injury;
and, for any one who knows the nature of the bush in

which this occurred, the very thought of an encounter in it with such a foe is appalling. As the thorns are placed in pairs on opposite sides of the branches, and these turn round on being pressed against, one pair brings the other exactly into the position in which it must pierce the intruder. They cut like knives. Horses dread this bush extremely ; indeed, most of them refuse to face its thorns.*

Occasionally, however, the elephant-hunter falls a victim to his daring. A young and successful ivory-hunter, named Thackwray, after numberless hair-breadth escapes, at length lost his life in the pursuit. On one occasion, a herd pursued him to the edge of a frightful precipice, where his only chance of safety consisted in dropping down to a ledge of rock at some distance below. Scarcely was he down before one of the elephants was seen above, endeavouring to reach him with its trunk. The hunter could easily have shot the brute while thus engaged, but was deterred by the fear of the huge car-case falling down on him, which would have been certain destruction. He escaped this danger, but soon afterwards, almost at the very same spot, he met the fatal rencontre. With one attendant Hottentot, Thackwray had engaged a herd of elephants, one of which he had wounded. The Hottentot, seeing it fall, supposed that it was dead, and approached it, when the animal rose and charged furiously. The lad threw himself upon the ground, and the infuriated beast passed without noticing him, tearing up the trees and scattering them in its blind rage ; but, rushing into

* Livingstone's *South Africa*, p. 580.

a thicket where Thackwray was reloading his rifle, it
caught sight of him, and in an instant hurled him to the
earth, thrusting one of its tusks through his thigh.   It
then caught the wretched man in its trunk, and elevating ·
him in the air, dashed him with great force upon the
ground, kneeling and trampling upon him, and as it were
kneading his crushed and flattened corpse into the dust,
with an implacable fury.   The remains, when discovered,
presented a most appalling spectacle." *   More recently,
another ivory-hunter, named Wahlberg, met a fate almost
precisely parallel.

Little inferior to the elephant in strength, though by no
means approaching it in sagacity, the different species of
African rhinoceros manifest an irascibility against man
which waits not for provocation ; or rather the sight of a
man is itself a sufficient provocation to excite a paroxysm of
restless fury.   Steedman † mentions a Hottentot who had
acquired a reputation as a bold elephant-hunter, who on
one occasion had had his horse killed under him by a
rhinoceros.   Before he could raise his gun, the enormous
beast rushed upon him, thrust its sharp-pointed horn into
the horse's chest, and threw him bodily, rider and all,
over its back.   The savage animal then, as if satisfied,
went off, without following up its victory, and before the
Hottentot could recover himself sufficiently for an aveng-
ing shot.

Mr Oswell met with a similar rencontre.   He was once
stalking two of these beasts, and, as they came slowly to

* Steedman's *Wanderings*, p. 74.   † Ibid . p. 69.

him, he, knowing that there is but little chance of hitting the small brain of this animal by a shot in the head, lay, expecting one of them to give his shoulder, till he was within a few yards. The hunter then thought that by making a rush to his side he might succeed in escaping; but the rhinoceros, too quick for that, turned upon him, and though he discharged his gun close to the animal's head he was tossed in the air. "My friend," adds Dr Livingstone, who gives the account, "was insensible for some time, and on recovering found large wounds on the thigh and body. I saw that on the former part, still open, and five inches long." The white species, though less savage than the black, is not always quite safe, for one, even after it was mortally wounded, attacked Mr Oswell's horse, and thrust the horn through to the saddle, tossing at the same time both horse and rider.*

The buffalo of the same regions is another animal of remarkable savageness of disposition, making an encounter with him a formidable affair. The eminent Swedish botanist, Thunberg, was collecting plants in a wood with two companions, when a buffalo bull rushed on the party with a deafening roar. The men just saved their lives by springing into the trees, while two horses were speedily pierced through by the powerful horns, and killed.

Captain Methuen has given us the following graphic account of an encounter with this most vicious herbivore, which the Cape colonists consider a more dangerous foe than the lion himself. The gallant captain and his party

* Livingstone's *Travels in Africa*, p. 611.

had discovered a herd of buffaloes, and had wounded some, but they had escaped to cover. He had climbed on the low boughs of a small *wait-a-bit* thorn, whence he struck another bull. The wounded animal " ran towards the report, his ears outstretched, his eyes moving in all directions, and his nose carried in a right line with the head, evidently bent on revenge ;—he passed within thirty yards of me, and was lost in the bush. Descending from my frail perch, Frolic [the Hottentot attendant] again discovered this buffalo standing amongst some small thick bushes, which nearly hid him from view ; his head was lowered, not a muscle of his body moved, and he was without doubt listening intently. We crept noiselessly to a bush, and I again fired. The huge brute ran forwards up the wind, fortunately not in our direction, and stood still again. No good screen being near, and his nose facing our way, prudence bade us wait patiently for a change in the state of affairs. Presently he lay gently down, and knowing that buffaloes are exceedingly cunning, and will adopt this plan merely to escape notice and entrap their persecutors, we drew near with great caution. I again fired through his shoulder, and concluding from his not attempting to rise, that he was helpless, we walked close up to him ; and never can the scene which followed be erased from my memory. Turning his ponderous head round, his eye caught our figures ; I fired the second barrel of my rifle behind his horns, but it did not reach the brain. His wounds gave him some difficulty in getting up, which just afforded Moneypenny and myself time to ensconce ourselves behind the slender shrubs that grew round the spot, while Frolic unwisely took to his heels. The buffalo saw him, and uttering a continued unearthly noise, between a grunt and a bellow, advanced at a pace at which these unwieldy creatures are rarely seen to run, unless stirred by revenge.

" Crashing through the low bushes, as if they were stubble, he passed me, but charged quite over Money-penny's lurking-place, who aimed at him as he came on, and lodged the ball in the rocky mass of horn above his head : the buffalo was so near at the time of his firing, that the horn struck the gun-barrels at the next instant; but whether the noise and smoke confused the animal, or he was partially stunned by the bullet, he missed my friend, and continued his pursuit of Frolic.

" The Hottentot dodged the enraged and terrific-looking brute round the bushes, but through these slight obstacles he dashed with ease, and gained ground rapidly. Speech-less, we watched the chase, and, in the awful moment, regardless of concealment, stood up, and saw the buffalo overtake his victim and knock him down. At this crisis, my friend fired his second barrel into the beast, which gave Frolic one or two blows with his fore-feet, and push-ing his nose under, endeavoured to toss him; but the Hottentot, aware of this, lay with much presence of mind perfectly still.

" Moneypenny now shouted to me, ' The buffalo is com-ing ;' and, in darting round a bush, I stumbled on my rifle, cutting my knee very badly. This proved a false alarm ;

and directly after the buffalo fell dead by Frolic, who then rose and limped towards us. He was much hurt, and a powder-flask which lay in his game-bag was stamped flat. The buffalo was too weak to use his full strength upon him, having probably exhausted all his remaining energy in the chase : otherwise the Hottentot would undoubtedly have been killed, since a man is safer under the paws of a wounded lion, than under the head of an infuriated buffalo. Never did I feel more grateful to a protecting Providence, than when this poor fellow came to us ; for his escape without material injury was little short of miraculous." *

Who, that has looked on the meek, deer-like face of a kangaroo, would imagine that any danger could attend a combat with so gentle a creature? Yet it is well known that strong dogs are often killed by it, the kangaroo seiz-ing and hugging the dog with its fore-paws, while with one kick of its muscular hind-leg, it rips up its antagonist, and tears out its bowels. Even to man there is peril, as appears from the following narrative. One of the hunter's dogs had been thus despatched, and he thus proceeds :—

"Exasperated by the irreparable loss of my poor dog, and excited by the then unusual scene before me, I hastened to revenge ; nothing doubting, that, with one fell swoop of my formidable club, my enemy would be prostrate at my feet. Alas ! the fates, and the still more remorseless white ants, frustrated my murderous inten-sions, and all but left me a victim to my strange and

* *Life in the Wilderness*, p. 178.

active foe.   No sooner had the heavy blow I aimed descended on his head, than my weapon shivered into a thousand pieces,* and I found myself in the giant embrace of my antagonist, who was hugging me with rather too warm a demonstration of friendship, and ripping at me in a way by no means pleasant.   My only remaining dog, too, now thoroughly exhausted by wounds and loss of blood, and apparently quite satisfied of her master's superiority, remained a mute and motionless spectator of the new and unequal contest.

"Notwithstanding my utmost efforts to release myself from the grasp of the brute, they were unavailing; and I found my strength gradually diminishing, whilst, at the same time, my sight was obscured by the blood which now flowed freely from a deep wound, extending from the back part of my head over the whole length of my face. I was, in fact, becoming an easy prey to the kangaroo, who continued to insert, with renewed vigour, his talons into my breast, luckily, however, protected by a loose coarse canvas frock, which, in colonial phrase, is called a 'jumper,' and but for which I must inevitably have shared the fate of poor Trip.   As it was, I had almost given myself up for lost; my head was pressed, with surpassing strength, beneath my adversary's breast, and a faintness was gradually stealing over me, when I heard a long and heart-stirring shout.   Was I to be saved?   The thought gave me new life: with increased power I grappled and succeeded in casting from me my determined foe; and,

* The reader will find an explanation of this fact at page 106, *supra.*

seeing a tree close at hand, I made a desperate leap to procure its shelter and protection. I reached, and clung to it for support; when the sharp report of a rifle was heard in my ear, and the bark, about three inches above my head, was penetrated by the ball. Another shot followed, with a more sure aim, and the exasperated animal (now once more within reach of me) rolled heavily over on its side. On the parties nearing, I found them to be my brother and a friend, who had at first mistaken me for the kangaroo, and had very nearly consummated what had been so strangely begun. However, a miss is always as good as a mile; and having recruited my spirits and strength with a draught from the never-failing brandy-flask, and sung a requiem over poor old Trip, my companions shouldered the fallen foe, by means of a large stake, one carrying each end, while I followed with weak and tottering steps. You may imagine that the little beauty I ever had is not much improved by the wound on my face, which still remains, and ever will. I am now an older hand at kangaroo-hunting, and never venture to attack so formidable an antagonist with an ant-eaten club; my dogs, also, have grown too wary to rush heedlessly within reach of his deadly rips. We have killed many since, but rarely so fine a one as that which first tried our mettle on the plains of New Holland." *

The equatorial coast of Africa has recently yielded to European science a gigantic kind of man-like ape, which affords a curious confirmation of an old classic story. Somewhere about the sixth century before the Christian

* *Sporting Review*, ii., p. 343.

era, one Hanno is reported to have sailed from Carthage, through the Pillars of Hercules, on a voyage of exploration along the coast of Africa. In the record of this voyage there occurs the following passage :—"Passing the Streams of Fire, we came to a bay called the Horn of the South. In the recess there was an island like the first, having a lake, and in this there was another island full of wild men. But much the greater part of them were women, with hairy bodies, whom the interpreters called 'Gorillas.' But pursuing them, we were not able to take the men ; they all escaped, being able to climb the precipices; and defended themselves with pieces of rock. But three women, who bit and scratched those who led them, were not willing to follow. However, having killed them, we flayed them, and conveyed the skins to Carthage; for we did not sail any further, as provisions began to fail."＊

The "wild men" of the ancient navigator were doubtless identical with the great anthropoid ape lately re-discovered, to which, in allusion to the old story, the name of Gorilla has been given. The region in question is a richly wooded country, extending about a thousand miles along the coast from the Gulf of Guinea southward ; and as the gorilla is not found beyond these limits, so we may pretty conclusively infer that the extreme point of Hanno was somewhere in this region.

This great ape makes the nearest approach of any brute-animal to the human form ; it is fully equal to man in

＊ *Periplus.*

R

stature, but immensely more broad and muscular; while
its strength is colossal. Though exclusively a fruit-eater,
it is described as always manifesting an enraged enmity
towards man; and no negro, even if furnished with fire-
arms, will willingly enter into conflict with an adult male
gorilla. He is said to be more than a match for the lion.

The rivalry between the mighty ape and the elephant
is curious, and leads to somewhat comic results.   The old
male is always armed with a stout stick when on the
scout, and knows how to use it.   The elephant has no
intentional evil thoughts towards the gorilla, but unfortunately they love the same sorts of fruit.   When the
ape sees the elephant busy with his trunk among the
twigs, he instantly regards it as an infraction of the laws
of property; and, dropping quietly down to the bough, he
suddenly brings his club smartly down on the sensitive
finger of the elephant's proboscis, and drives off the alarmed
animal trumpeting shrilly with rage and pain.

There must be something so wild and unearthly in the
appearance of one of these apes, so demon-like in hideous-
ness, in the solemn recesses of the dark primeval forest,
that I might have told its story in the preceding chapter.
The terrors with which it is invested are, however, more
than imaginary.   The young athletic negroes, in their
ivory hunts, well know the prowess of the gorilla.   He
does not, like the lion, sullenly retreat on seeing them,
but swings himself rapidly down to the lower branches,
courting the conflict, and clutches at the foremost of his
enemies.   The hideous aspect of his visage, his green eyes

flashing with rage, is heightened by the thick and prominent brows being drawn spasmodically up and down,
with the hair erect, causing a horrible and fiendish scowl.
Weapons are torn from their possessors' grasp, gun-barrels
bent and crushed in by the powerful hands and vice-like
teeth of the enraged brute. More horrid still, however,
is the sudden and unexpected fate which is often inflicted
by him. Two negroes will be walking through one of the
woodland paths, unsuspicious of evil, when in an instant
one misses his companion, or turns to see him drawn up
in the air with a convulsed choking cry; and in a few
minutes dropped to the ground a strangled corpse. The
terrified survivor gazes up, and meets the grin and glare
of the fiendish giant, who, watching his opportunity,
had suddenly put down his immense hind-hand, caught
the wretch by the neck with resistless power, and dropped
him only when he ceased to struggle. Surely a horrible
improvised gallows this! *

The pursuit of the whale, whether that species which
our hardy mariners seek amidst the ice-floes of the Polar
Seas, or the still huger kind which wallows in the boundless Pacific, is one full of peril, and its annals are crowded
with strange and terrible adventures. Swift and sudden
deaths; the shattering of a boat into fragments, and the
immersion of the crew in the freezing sea; the dragging
of a man into the depths, by a turn of the tangled line
round his leg or arm; are but too common incidents in
this warfare with the leviathan. One instance of this last-

* See Prof. Owen on the Gorilla (*Proc. Zool. Soc.*, 1859).

named accident is on record, in which the sufferer escaped with life, to tell the harrowing tale of his own sensations.

An American whaling captain in the Pacific was fast to a sperm whale, which "sounded," or descended nearly perpendicularly. The line in swiftly running out became suddenly entangled; the captain was seen to stoop in order to clear it, and in a moment disappeared over the bow. The boat-steerer seized an axe, and instantly cut the line, in hope that, by the slackening, the unfortunate man might become freed.

Several minutes had elapsed, and hope had wellnigh become extinguished, when an object was seen to rise to the surface a little way off. It was the body of the captain, which in a few seconds was lifted into the boat. Though senseless and motionless, life seemed to be not extinct, and the usual remedies being applied, he revived, and became, to use his own phrase, "as good as new," when he gave an account of his singular escape.

It appears that in attempting to throw the line clear from the *chock*, a turn caught his left wrist, and he was dragged overboard by the descending whale. He was perfectly conscious as he was rushing down with immense rapidity, and it seemed to him as if his arm would be torn from its socket, from the resistance of his body to the water. Well aware of his peril, he knew that his only chance was to cut the line, but with his utmost efforts he could not raise his right hand from his side, to which it was pressed by the force with which he was dragged through the water.

On first opening his eyes it appeared as if a stream of
fire was passing before them; but, as he descended, it
grew dark, and he felt a terrible pressure on his brain,
and there was a roaring as of thunder in his ears. Yet
he still remained conscious, and still made vain efforts to
reach the knife that was in his belt. At length, as he
felt his strength failing, and his brain reeling, the line for
an instant slackened by the whale's pausing in its descent;
he reached and drew his knife; the line again became
tight, but the edge of the keen blade was across it, and in
an instant he was freed. From this moment he remembered nothing, until he awoke to light and life and
agonising pain, in his bed.

Perhaps the reader is familiar with a dreadful example
of the voracity of the great white shark. About thirty
natives of the Society Islands were proceeding from isle
to isle in one of their large double canoes. A storm
coming on, the lashings of the two canoes were torn apart
by the violence of the sea, and they were separated.
Their depth and narrowness rendered them incapable of
floating upright when single; and, though the crew strove
hard to keep them on an even keel by balancing the
weight, they were every moment capsized. In these circumstances, they endeavoured to form a raft of the loose
spars and beams, the boards and paddles, which they could
get at, hoping to drift ashore thereon. From their
numbers, however, compared with the small size of the
raft, the latter was pressed so deep, that the waves washed
above their knees. At length they saw the horrid sharks

begin to collect around them, which soon grew so bold as to seize one of the shipwrecked wretches, and drag him into the abyss. Another and another followed; for the poor islanders, destitute of any weapons, and almost exhausted with hunger and fatigue, and crowded together on their submerged narrow platform, could neither defend themselves nor evade their ferocious assailants. Every moment made the conflict more unequal, for the sharks, attracted by the scent of blood, gathered in greater numbers to the spot, and grew more and more audacious, until two or three of the mariners only remaining, the raft floated so as to elevate them beyond reach of the savage monsters, which continued to threaten them, and lingered around, until the waves at lengh bore the survivors to the beach.

Among reptiles, the mailed crocodiles may be mentioned as formidable foes to man. Vast in bulk, yet grovelling with the belly on the earth; clad in bony plates with sharp ridges, the long tail bearing a double row of teeth, like two parallel saws; splay feet terminating in long diverging hooked talons; green eyes with a peculiar fiery glare, gleaming out from below projecting orbits; lips altogether wanting, displaying the long rows of interlocking teeth even when the mouth is closed, so that, even when quiet, the monster seems to be grinning with rage (" his teeth are terrible round about," Job xli. 14),—it is no wonder that the crocodile should be, in all countries which it inhabits, viewed with dread.

Nor is this terror groundless. The crocodiles, both of the Nile and of the West Indian Isles, are well known to make man their victim; and the alligators of continental America are not behind them. Those of the great rivers of South America appear to be more savage than their northern congener. Waterton and other observers have recorded terrible examples of their voracity; and I will add one from a more recent traveller, an officer engaged in the wars which liberated the South American provinces from the Spanish supremacy.

During Morillo's campaign in the Apúri country, three officers were on their route with despatches from Colonel Rangel's camp at Congrial, to General Paëz's head-quarters at Caña Fistola; and, not being able to procure a canoe, were obliged to swim their horses over a small branch of the lagoon of Cunavichi, which lay across the road, carrying as usual their saddles on their heads. Two of the party were brothers, by name Gamarra, natives of Varinas. One of them, a lieutenant of Paëz's Lancers, loitered so long on the bank, as only to have just entered the water at the moment his comrades had reached the opposite side. When he was nearly half-way across, they saw a large *caÿmàn*, which was known to infest this pass, issuing from under the mangrove-trees. They instantly warned their companion of his danger; but it was too late for him to turn back. When the alligator was so close as to be on the point of seizing him, he threw his saddle to it. The ravenous animal immediately caught the whole bundle in its jaws, and disappeared for a few moments; but soon discovered its mistake, and rose in front of the horse, which, then seeing it for the first time, reared and threw its rider. He was an excellent swimmer, and had nearly escaped by diving towards the bank ; but, on rising for breath, his pursuer also rose, and seized him by the middle. This dreadful scene, which passed before their eyes, without the least possibility of their rendering any assistance, was terminated by the alligator, having previously drowned the unfortunate man, appearing on an opposite sand-bank with the body, and there devouring it.[*]

It is in this class of animals that we find the most terrible of all creatures ; more potent than the roused lion, the enraged elephant, the deadly shark, or the mailed alligator. In the whole range of animal existence, there is none that can compare with the venomous snakes for the deadly fatality of their enmity ; the lightning stroke of their poisonous fangs is the unerring signal of a swift dissolution, preceded by torture the most horrible. The bite of the American rattlesnake has been known to produce death in two minutes. Even where the consummation is not so fearfully rapid, its delay is but a brief prolongation of the intense suffering. The terrible symptoms are thus described :—a sharp pain in the part, which becomes swollen, shining, hot, red ; then livid, cold, and insensible. The pain and inflammation spread, and become more intense ; fierce shooting pains are felt in other parts, and a burning fire pervades the whole body. The eyes begin to water abundantly ; then come swoonings, cold sweats, and sharp pains in the loins. The skin be-

* *Campaigns and Cruises in Venezuela,* vol. i., p. 59.

comes deadly pale or deep yellow, while a black watery blood runs from the wound, which changes to a yellowish matter. Violent headache succeeds, and giddiness, faintness, and overwhelming terrors, burning thirst, gushing discharges of blood from the orifices of the body, intolerable fetor of breath, convulsive hiccoughs, and death.

Mr Francis T. Buckland * has described the awful effects of a dose of poison received from the cobra-di-capello in his own person. Fortunately it was a most minute dose, or we should not have received the account. A rat which had been struck by the serpent, Mr Buckland skinned after its death. He scraped the interior of the skin with his finger-nail, forgetting that he had an hour before been cleaning his nails with his penknife. In so doing, he had slightly separated the nail from the quick, and into this little crack the poison had penetrated. Though the orifice was so small as to have been unnoticed, and though the venom was not received direct from the serpent, but had been diffused through the system of the rat, the life of the operator was all but sacrificed.

A few years ago the people of London were shocked by the sudden death of Curling, one of the keepers of the Zoological Gardens, from the bite of a cobra.

In India, where the species is common, its propensity to haunt houses frequently brings it under notice, and many accidents occur. 'It seems, however, on some occasions to be placably disposed, if not assaulted; and some singular escapes are on record of persons who have had

* Curiosities of Nat. Hist., p. 223.

presence of mind enough to let it alone.   One is told of
an officer who, having some repairs done to his bungalow,
was lying on a mattress in the verandah, reading, nearly
undressed.   Perhaps his book was of a soporific tendency,
for he dropped asleep, and awaked with a chilly sensation
about his breast.   Opening his eyes, he beheld, to his
horror, a large cobra coiled up on his bosom, within his
open shirt.   He saw, in a moment, that to disturb the
creature would be highly perilous, almost certainly fatal,
and that it was at present doing no harm, and apparently
intending none.   With great coolness therefore he lay perfectly still, gazing on the bronzed and glittering scales of
the intruder.   After a period which seemed to him an
age, one of the workmen approached the verandah, and
the snake at his footsteps left its warm berth, and was
gliding off, when the servants at the cry of the artisan
rushed out and destroyed it.

It curiously happens that in some of the creatures whose
rage is likely to be fatal to man, there should be something in the physiognomy which puts him on his guard.
We have seen that it is so in the sharks; we have seen
that it is so in the crocodiles; it is so pre-eminently in
the venomous serpents.   There is in most of these an
expression of malignity, which well indicates their deadly
character.   Their flattened head, more or less widened
behind, so as to approach a triangular figure; their wide
gape, and the cleft tongue ever darting to and fro; and,
above all, the sinister expression of the glaring lidless eye,
with its linear pupil; are sufficient to cause the observer

to retreat with shuddering precipitancy. Darwin, speaking of a sort of viper which he found at Bahia Blanca, says : " The expression of this snake's face was hideous and fierce ; the pupil consisted of a vertical slit in a mottled and coppery iris ; the jaws were broad at the base, and the nose terminated in a triangular projection. I do not think I ever saw anything more ugly, excepting, perhaps, some of the vampyre bats."

Many of the snakes of South America are highly venomous. One of these is called, from its prowess and power, the bush-master. Frightful accidents occur in the forests of Guiana by this terrible species. Sullivan * gives us the following : his host, a few days before, had sent a negro to open some sluices on his estate ; but, as he did not return, the master, thinking he had run away, sent another negro to look after him ; this negro went to the place directed, and found the man quite dead, and swollen up to a hideous size. He was bitten in two places, and death must have been instantaneous, as he was not more than three feet from the sluice. They supposed that it must have been a bush-master that had killed him. The couni-couchi, or bush-master, is the most dreaded of all the South American snakes, and, as his name implies, he roams absolute master of the forest. They will not fly from man, like all other snakes, but will even pursue and attack him. They are fat, clumsy-looking snakes, about four feet long, and nearly as thick as a man's arm ; their mouth is unnaturally large, and their fangs are from one

* *Rambles in America*, p. 406.

to three inches in length. They strike with immense force; and a gentleman who had examined a man after having been struck in the thigh and died, told the narrator that the wound was as if two four-inch nails had been driven into the flesh. As the poison oozes out from the extremity of the fang, any hope of being cured after a bite is small, as it is evident that no external application could have any immediate effect on a poison deposited an inch and a half or two inches below the surface; the instantaneousness of the death depends upon whether any large artery is wounded or not.

The same traveller records the following shocking story about a very deadly snake, called the manoota, that infests the borders of the Lake of Valencia, in Venezuela :—

"An American we met related an anecdote of this snake, which, if true, was very frightful. He had gone in a canoe one night with a father and son, intending to shoot deer next morning on one of the islands in the lake. When they reached the island, the son, notwithstanding the repeated warnings of his father, jumped out; but he had no sooner done so, than he gave an agonised yell, and fell back; the father immediately sprung out, but was also struck by the snake, but not so severely. They got the young man into the boat, but he swelled to a horrible size, and, bleeding at eyes, nose, and mouth, died in less than half-an-hour. Our friend and the father now set out on their return to Valencia with the dead body. A storm had in the meantime arisen, and they were in the greatest danger of being capsized.

The old man was suffering fearful agony from his bite, and had nearly gone out of his mind; and the narrator described in graphic terms the horrors of his situation, in a frail canoe, in a dark night during a severe storm, and the momentary expectation of being capsized, his only companion being a mad father lamenting over the body of his dead son." *

Even the most insignificant of creatures may be the scourge of the most exalted. We have seen some examples of insect pests in a former chapter, and of their ravages and successful assaults against man; but that he should be actually slain in mortal conflict with a fly is something unusual. Yet last summer this happened in India.

" Two European gentleman belonging to the Indian Railway Company,—viz., Messrs Armstrong and Bodding-ton—were surveying a place called Bunder Coode, for the purpose of throwing a bridge across the Nerbudda, the channel of which, being in this place from ten to fifty yards wide, is fathomless, having white marble rocks rising perpendicularly on either side from a hundred to a hundred and fifty feet high, and beetling fearfully in some parts. Suspended in the recesses of these marble rocks are numerous large hornets' nests, the inmates of which are ready to descend upon any unlucky wight who may venture to disturb their repose. Now, as the boats of these European surveyors were passing up the river, a cloud of these insects overwhelmed them; the boatmen as well as the two gentlemen jumped overboard, but,

* Sullivan's *Rambles in N. and S. America*, p. 409.

alas! Mr Boddington, who swam and had succeeded in clinging to a marble block, was again attacked, and being unable any longer to resist the assaults of the countless hordes of his infuriated winged foes, threw himself into the depths of the water, never to rise again. On the fourth day his corpse was discovered floating on the water, and was interred with every mark of respect. The other gentleman, Mr Armstrong, and his boatmen, although very severely stung, are out of danger."

Such is the story as narrated in the *Times* of Jan. 28, 1859. But I have the pleasure of being personally acquainted with some of the members of the family of Mr Armstrong, who have assured me that the insects were not hornets, as represented, but honey-bees; it may be not the hive-bee domesticated with us, but a species well known as making honey. Whatever the true nature of the insect, it affords an apt illustration of such passages of Holy Scripture as the following :—"The Lord shall hiss for . . . the bee that is in the land of Assyria." (Isa. vii. 18.) "The Lord thy God will send the hornet among them, until they that are left, and hide themselves from thee, be destroyed." (Deut. vii. 20.)

And with this we shut up our " chamber of horrors."

XI

THE UNKNOWN.

LETOUILLANT tells us, in his "Travels in the East," that whenever he arrived at an eminence, whence he could behold a distant mountain range, he felt an irrepressible desire to reach it; an unreasoning persuasion that it would afford something more interesting, more delightful, than anything which he had yet attained. The charm lay here, that it was *unknown:* the imagination can people the unexplored with whatever forms of beauty or interest it pleases; and it does delight to throw a halo round it, the halo of hope.

> "'Tis distance lends enchantment to the view,
> And clothes the mountain in its azure hue."

One of the greatest pleasures of the out-of-door naturalist depends upon this principle. There is so great variety in the objects which he pursues, and so much uncertainty in their presence at any given time and place, that hope is ever on the stretch. He makes his excursions not knowing what he may meet with; and, if disappointed of what he had pictured to himself, he is pretty sure to be surprised with something or other of interest that he had not anticipated. And much more does the romance of the unknown prevail to the natural history collector in a new and unexplored country. It has been my lot' to pursue various branches of zoology, in regions where the productions were to science largely, to myself wholly, unknown. In a rich tropical island, such as Jamaica, where nature is prodigal in variety and beauty, and where, throughout the year, though there is change, there is no cessation of animal or vegetable activity, there was novelty enough in every day's *opima spolia* to whet the expectation of to-morrow. Each morning's preparation was made with the keenest relish, because there was the undefined hope of good things, but I knew not what; and the experience of each day, as the treasures were gloated over in the evening, was so different in detail from that of the preceding, that the sense of novelty never palled. If the walk was by the shore, the state of the tide, the ever varying wave-washings, the diverse rocks with their numerous pools and crannies and recesses, the cliffs and caves, the fishes in the shallows, the nimble and alert crustacea on the mud, the shelled mollusca on the weed-beds, the echinoderms on the sand, the zoophytes on the corals, continually presented objects of novelty. If I rode with vasculum and insect-net and fowling-piece into the mountain-woods, there was still the like pleasing uncertainty of what might occur, with the certainty of abundance. A fine epiphyte orchid scents the air with fragrance, and it is discovered far up in the fork of some vast tree; then there is the palpitation of hope and fear as we discuss the possibility of getting it down ; then come contrivances and efforts,—pole after pole is cut and tied together with

the cords which the forest-climbers afford. At length the
plant is reached, and pushed off, and triumphantly bagged ;
but lo ! while examining it, some elegant twisted shell is
discovered, with its tenant snail, crawling on the leaves.
Scarcely is this boxed, when a gorgeous butterfly rushes
out of the gloom into the sunny glade, and is in a moment
seen to be a novelty ; then comes the excitement of pursuit; the disappointment of seeing it dance over a thicket
out of sight; the joy of finding it reappear; the tantalising
trial of watching the lovely wings flapping just out of
reach ; the patient waiting for it to descend ; the tiptoe
approach as we see it settle on a flower ; the breathless
eagerness with which the net is poised ; and the trium-
phant flush with which we contemplate the painted wings
within the gauze ; and the admiration with which we
gaze on its loveliness when held in the trembling fingers.
Another step or two, and a gay-plumaged bird rises
from the bush, and falls to the gun ; we run to the spot
and search for the game among the shrubs and moss ; at
last it is found, admired, and committed to a little pro-
tective cone of paper. Now a fern of peculiar delicacy
appears ; then a charming flower, of which we search for
ripe seed : a glittering beetle is detected crawling on the
gray bark of a lichened tree ; here is a fine caterpillar
feeding ; yonder a humming-bird hovering over a brilliant
blossom ; and here a female of the same spangled bird
sitting in her tiny nest. By and by we emerge into a
spot where, for some cause or other, insects seem to have
specially congregated ; a dozen different kinds of butter-

s

flies are flitting to and fro in bewildering profusion of beauty, and our collecting-box is half · filled in the course of an hour. Meanwhile we have shot two or three more birds; caught a pretty lizard; seen a painted tree-frog, which escaped to be captured another day; obtained some strange nondescript creatures under stones; picked a beautiful spider from a web; taken a host of banded shells;—and so the day wears on. And then in the evening what a feasting of the eager eyes as they gloat over the novelties, assigning each to its place, preparing such as need preparation, and recording the facts and habits that help to make up the as yet unwritten history of all.

I turn from my own experience to that of those who have, with similar tastes and similar pursuits, rifled still more prolific regions. Let us hear Mr Bates, who for the last eleven years has been exploring the very heart of South America in the service of natural history, chiefly devoting himself to the gorgeous entomology of the great Valley of the Amazon. He has drawn a picture of an average day's proceedings, such as makes a brother natu-ralist's mouth water, and almost induces him to pack up his traps, and look out in *The Times'* shipping column for the next ship sailing for Parà :—

"The charm and glory of the country are its animal and vegetable productions. How inexhaustible is their study! Remember that, as to botany, in the forest scarcely two trees of the same species are seen growing together. It is not as in temperate countries (Europe), a forest of oak, or birch, or pine—it is one dense jungle;

the lofty forest trees, of vast variety of species, all lashed and connected by climbers, their trunk covered with a museum of ferns, tillandsias, arums, orchids, &c. The underwood consists of younger trees—great variety of small palms, mimosas, tree-ferns, &c.; and the ground is laden with fallen branches—vast trunks covered with parasites, &c. The animal denizens are in the same way of infinite variety; not numerous, as to give the appearance at once of tumultuous life, being too much scattered for that; it is in course of time only that one forms an idea of their numbers. Four or five species of monkey are constantly seen. The birds are in such variety that it is not easy to get two or three of the same species. You see a trogon one day; the next day and the day after, another each day; and all will be different species. Quadrupeds or snakes are seldom seen, but lizards are everywhere met with; and sometimes you get tortoises, tree-frogs, &c. Insects, like birds, do not turn up in swarms of one species; for instance, you take a dozen longicorns one day, and they are sure to be of eight or ten distinct species. One year of daily work is scarcely sufficient to get the majority of species in a district of two miles' circuit.

"Such is the scene of my present labours; and all the rest of the Amazon is similar, though less rich; the river Tapajos alone differing, being a mountainous country. Having thus my work at hand, I will tell you how I proceed. My house is in the centre of the town, but even thus only a few minutes' walk from the edge of the forest. I keep an old and a young servant, on whom I rely for getting eatables and preparing my meals, so as to leave me unembarrassed to devote all my thoughts to my work. Between nine and ten A.M. I prepare for the woods; a coloured shirt, pair of trousers, pair of common boots, and an old felt hat, are all my clothing; over my left shoulder slings my double-barrelled gun, loaded, one with No. 10, one with No. 4 shot. In my right hand I take my net, on my left side is suspended a leathern bag with two pockets, one for my insect-box, the other for powder and two sorts of shot; on my right side hangs my " game-bag," an ornamental affair, with red leather trappings and thongs to hang lizards, snakes, frogs, or large birds. One small pocket in this bag contains my caps; another, papers for wrapping up the delicate birds; others for wads, cotton, box of powdered plaster; and a box with damped cork for the Micro-Lepidoptera; to my shirt is pinned my pin-cushion, with six sizes of pins. A few minutes after entering the edge of the forest, I arrive in the heart of the wilderness; before me nothing but forest for hundreds of miles. Many butterflies are found on the skirts of the forest; in the midst of numbers flitting about, I soon distinguish the one I want—often a new one—*Erycinide, Hesperia, Thecla,* or what not. *Coleoptera* you see nothing fine of at first; a few minute *Halticæ* on the leaves, or small *Curculios,* or *Eumolpi.* When you come to the neighbourhood of a newly-fallen tree, is soon enough to hunt closely for them; not only wood-eating species, but all kinds seem to congregate there; *Agras* and *Lebias* in the folded leaves.

grand *Cassidæ*, and *Erotyli, Rutelæ,* or *Melolonthids, Gymnetis,* &c. ; often a *Ctenostoma* running along some slender twig. It requires a certain kind of weather for *Coleoptera,* and some days all seem to be absent at once.

" Whilst I am about these things, I often hear the noise of birds above—pretty tanagers, or what not. You cannot see the colours of red, cobalt-blue, or beryl-green, when they are up in the trees ; and it takes months of experience to know your bird. I have sometimes shot at small, obscure-looking birds up the trees, and when they have fallen, have been dazzled by their exquisite beauty.

" I walk about a mile straight ahead, lingering in rich spots, and diverging often. It is generally near two P.M. when I reach home, thoroughly tired. I get dinner, lie in hammock a while reading, then commence preparing my captives, &c. ; this generally takes me till five P.M. In the evening I take tea, write and read, but generally in bed by nine." *

I might quote similar details from Mr Wallace's letters, written while engaged in similar pursuits in a neighbouring part of the same mighty continent. But I prefer citing, in illustration of our subject, his observations made when, after having satiated himself in the west, he turned to the gorgeous east, and set himself to explore the virgin treasures of the remotest parts of the Indian Archipelago. Who cannot sympathise with his enthusiasm, when he says :—" I look forward with unmixed satisfaction to my visit to the rich and almost unexplored Spice Islands

* *Zoologist,* p. 5659.   •

the land of the lories, of the coc'.atoos and the birds of paradise, the country of tortoise-shell and pearls, of beautiful shells and rare insects"? And when, having visited them, and swept into his cabinet their riches, his eye is still towards the rising sun, and the gorgeous spoils of the unknown Papuan group are firing his imagination, he thus jots down his undefinable expectations :—

"I am going another thousand miles eastward to the Arru Islands, which are within a hundred miles of the coast of New Guinea, and are the most eastern islands of the Archipelago. Many reasons have induced me to go so far now. I must go somewhere to escape the terrific rainy season here. I have all along looked to visiting Arru as one of the great objects of my journey to the East; and almost all the trade with Arru is from Macassar. I have an opportunity of going in a *proa*, owned and commanded by a Dutchman, (Java-born,) who will take me and bring me back, and assist me in getting a house, &c., there; and he goes at the very time I want to leave. I have also friends here with whom I can leave all the things I do not want to take with me. All these advantageous circumstances would probably never be combined again; and were I to refuse this opportunity I might never go to Arru at all; which, when you consider it is the nearest place to New Guinea where I can stay on shore and work in perfect safety, would be much to be regretted. What I shall get there it is impossible to say Being a group of small islands, the immense diversity and richness of the productions of New Guinea will, of course, be wanting; yet I think I may expect some approach to the strange and beautiful natural productions of that unexplored country. Very few naturalists have visited Arru. One or two of the French discovery ships have touched it. M. Payen, of Brussels, was there, but stayed probably only a few days; and I suppose not twenty specimens of its birds and insects are positively known. Here, then, I shall have tolerably new ground, and if I have health I shall work it well. I take three lads with me, two of whom can shoot and skin birds." *

Such men as these are fast beating up the untrodden ground, and gathering into our museums and cabinets the natural history harvest of every land. Already we know the *characteristic forms* of almost all the regions of the earth; and, though there yet remain great tracts unexplored, and these in the most teeming climes, yet from the productions of surrounding or contiguous districts we can pretty surely conjecture what forms they will yield,— what *sorts* of forms, at least, though there may remain much of novelty in detail. When we consider that an ardent and most indefatigable entomologist, after spending eleven years in one region—the Valley of the Amazon,— devoting his whole time and energy to searching after butterflies, yet finds new species turning up, in almost unabated profusion, and that every little district visited, though but a few miles distant from the last, has its own peculiar, though allied kinds, we may form some idea of the vast variety and abundance of unknown insects which

* *Zoologist*, pp. 5117, 5656.

the almost boundless forests of South America have yet
to yield to scientific enterprise.

Yet in all this profusion, it is almost wholly new species
of already recognised genera that constitute the reward
of perseverance. It is comparatively rare to capture a
butterfly so different from anything before known as to
warrant the formation of a new genus; and the occurrence
of a new family is almost out of the question.

Then, again, throughout that immense region, so little
explored by competent naturalists, we can assert with a
measure of confidence that no great mammal, scarcely any
conspicuous bird, is at all likely to be added to those
already known, with the exception of additional species
of characteristic and large groups, such as the trogons,
the tanagers, the toucans, or the humming-birds. At the
same time, we may well believe that many of the smaller
mammalia, and a still greater number of the sombre-
coloured birds, have been as yet unnoticed.

It is, however, possible that a great anthropoid ape
may exist, as yet unrecognised by zoologists. On the
cataracts of the upper Orinoco, Humboldt heard reports
of a "hairy man of the woods," which was reputed to
build huts, to carry off women, and to devour human
flesh. The first and second of these attributes are so
characteristic of the great anthropoid *Simiæ* of Africa,
that, unless the belief has been transferred from the one
continent to the other, (a circumstance little probable,
when we think of the seat of the report, in the very heart
of the forests of Venezuela,) their adduction gives a

measure of authority to the statement; while the third would be a very natural inference from such ferocity as animates the gorilla. Both Indians and missionaries firmly believe in the existence of this dreaded creature, which they call *vasitri*, or "the great devil." Humboldt suggests that the original of what he boldly calls "the fable," may exist in the person of "one of those large bears, the footsteps of which resemble those of man, and which are believed in every country to attack women;" and he seems to claim credit for being the only person to doubt the existence of the great anthropomorphous monkey of America. But it might be permitted, in return, to ask what "large bear" is known to inhabit Venezuela; and whether it is true that bears' footsteps have a signal resemblance to those of men; and that bears specially attack women. Is not such a bear in South America quite as gratuitous as the monkey himself? And, since species of *Quadrumana* are characteristic of the forests of that region, may it not be possible that some one rivalling man in stature and strength, may there exist, as well as in Africa and the Oriental Archipelago? The mighty gorilla himself has only just been introduced to us.

The immense, almost continental, islands of the eastern hemisphere, Java, Sumatra, Borneo, and, above all, Papua, hold, it is likely, more unknown animals than the Western Continent. Yet the remark just made will hold good here also,—that we may rather expect new species of well-known genera, than any really new forms. Again, nearly half of the Australian continent is within the tropics, and this is absolutely virgin ground to the naturalist; but what we know of the poverty of the Australian fauna does not encourage any extravagant expectation of novelties, even from so vast an expanse of intertropical country: some new genera of marsupial mammalia, and a good many birds and reptiles, may possibly remain to be discovered. Papua, if it is indeed continuous land and not a group of islands, is the most promising region in this quarter to the naturalist: it is a land of hope, immense in area, and covered with virgin forest, producing birds and insects the most magnificent in the world, and yet only just glimpsed here and there on the coast. We may expect great things from it when explored; and cannot but hope that Mr Wallace, whose longings have just been recorded, may yet find opportunity, with safety to himself, of satisfying the desire of his heart.

The interior of China is a great region scarcely seen by an European eye; and its mountainous districts especially are doubtless rich in animal and vegetable productions as yet unknown to science. But the incredibly crowded condition of its human population, and the diligence with which every available inch of land is cultivated, are circumstances which militate against the existence of wild animals and plants.* Japan will probably fall under the

---

* Mr Wallace, writing from Lombok, one of the Sunda Isles, removed but a few degrees from the equator, thus complains of the antagonism of cultivation to natural history :—" There is nothing but dusty roads and paddy fields for miles around, producing no insects or birds worth collecting. It is really astonishing, and will be almost incredible to many persons at home, that a tropical country, when cultivated, should

same conditions; and, in a less degree, the further peninsula of India. But of this last considerable portions are
mountainous, well watered with great rivers, and covered
with forests; all circumstances favourable to natural history. The jealousy of the native governments has tended
to shut up these regions from Europeans, and we may
reasonably expect that important discoveries may yet remain in the immense intertropical countries of Cochin
China, Cambodia, Siam, Laos, and Burmah; countries
where the elephant attains his most colossal dimensions,
where the two-horned rhinoceros roams the jungle, and
where the camphor and the gutta-percha grow.

Madagascar is another land of promise. Here, too,
mountain and forest prevail; situation is favourable; and
we know almost nothing of the interior. It appears to
be remarkably destitute of the greater *Mammalia*, but Mr
Ellis's late researches shew how rich it is in strange forms
of vegetation; and doubtless it will prove to be the home
of many unknown birds, reptiles, and insects.

Africa is the land of wild beasts. The grandest forms

produce so little for the collector. The worst collecting-ground in
England would produce ten times as many species of beetles as can be
found here; and even our common English butterflies are finer and
more numerous than those of Ampanam in the present dry season. A
walk of several hours with my net will produce, perhaps, two or three
species of *Chrysomela*, and *Coccinella*, and a *Cicindela*, and two or three
Hemiptera and flies; and every day the same species will occur. In
an uncultivated district which I have visited, in the south part of the
island, I did indeed find insects rather more numerous, but two months'
assiduous collecting have only produced me eight species of *Coleoptera*.
Why, there is not a spot in England where the same number could not
be obtained in a few days in spring."—*Zoologist*, p. 5415.

of the terrestrial creation have their habitation in that continent. The elephant, the hippopotamus, several different sorts of rhinoceros, the zebra, the quagga, the giraffe; multitudes of antelopes, some of them of colossal dimensions; the buffalo; the gorilla, the chimpanzee, the mandril, and other baboons and monkeys; the lion, the panther, the leopard;—these are only the more prominent of the quadrupeds which roam the plains and woods of Africa. Thinly peopled and little cultivated; a region enclosed between sixty degrees of latitude, bisected by the equator, and (in its widest part) between as many of longitude; of which, perhaps, more than three-fourths are only now just beginning to be penetrated by the straggling foot of the European explorer and missionary;—what may we not expect of the vast, the uncouth, the terrible, among the creatures which lurk as yet unsuspected in the teeming wilds of Central Africa? Perhaps less, however, after all, than at first view appears probable. It is remarkable that the explorations of the adventurous Livingstone from the south, and of Barth and others from the north—explorations which have immensely diminished the extent of absolutely unknown land—have contributed almost nothing to what we previously knew of the natural history of the continent. The most important recent addition to zoology is, undoubtedly, the gorilla; but this discovery was not the result of geographic extension, the animal inhabiting the forests of a line of coast frequented for centuries by European traders. The great pioneers alluded to were not strictly naturalists, it is true; and their immediate object was not to make discoveries in zoology; nay, their interest would lie in avoiding, so far as possible, the haunts of unknown savage animals; but, in the case of Dr Livingstone particularly, his frequent encounters with such as were already well known, and his intelligent spirit of inquiry, leave no room for supposing that any conspicuous forms inhabit the regions through which he penetrated, different from those.

I am therefore inclined to believe, that whatever discoveries of importance are yet to be made in African zoology, will be in the very central district; the region, that is, which lies south of Lake Tchad and Abyssinia, and extends to the equator. There is reason to suppose that lofty mountain-chains exist here, and geographical discovery has not yet even approached these parts. Many forms of high interest, and some of them of vast dimensions, may yet be hidden there.

It is highly probable that an animal of ancient renown, and one in which England has (or ought to have) a peculiar interest, resides in the region just indicated. I refer to one of the supporters of Britain's shield, the famed Unicorn. We may not, to be sure, find him exactly what the heraldic artists delight to represent him—a sort of mongrel between a deer and a horse, with cloven hoofs, a tuft-tipped tail, and a horn spirally twisted to a point; but there may be the original of the traditionary portrait of which this is the gradually corrupted copy.

Dr Andrew Smith, an able and sober zoologist, who has investigated with much enterprise and success the zoology of South Africa, has collected a good deal of information about a one-horned animal which is yet unknown to Europeans, and which appears to occupy an intermediate rank between the massive rhinoceros and the lighter form of the horse. Cavassi, cited by Labat, heard of such a beast in Congo under the name of *Abada;* and Rüppel mentions it as commonly spoken of in Kordofan, where it is called *Nillekma,* and sometimes *Arase*—that is, *unicorn.* Mr Freeman, the excellent missionary whose name is so intimately connected with Madagascar, received the most particular accounts of the creature from an intelligent native of a region lying northward from Mozambique. According to this witness, an animal called the Ndzoodzoo is by no means rare in Makooa. It is about the size of a horse, extremely fleet and strong. A single horn projects from its forehead from two feet to two and a-half feet in length. This is said to be flexible when the animal is asleep, and can be curled up at pleasure, like an elephant's proboscis; but it becomes stiff and hard under the excitement of rage. It is extremely fierce, invariably attacking a man whenever it discerns him. The device adopted by the natives to escape from its fury, is to climb a thick and tall tree out of sight. If the enraged animal ceases to see his enemy, he presently gallops away; but, if he catches sight of the fugitive in a tree, he instantly commences an attack on the tree with his frontal horn, boring and ripping it till he brings it down, when the wretched man is presently gored to death. If the tree is not very bulky, the perseverance of the creature usually succeeds in overturning it. His fury spends itself in goring and mangling the carcase, as he never attempts to devour it. The female is altogether without a horn.*

When in the neighbourhood of the tropic, Dr Smith himself heard reports of a similar creature inhabiting the country north of that parallel. The persons who professed to be personally familiar with it, as well as a new kind of rhinoceros allied to *R. Keitloa,* were only visitors in the country it was said to inhabit, and, therefore, were unable to afford any very circumstantial evidence. It was, however, described as very different from any species of rhinoceros they had ever seen, with a single long horn situated towards the forehead. Dr Smith then cites the particulars given by Mr Freeman, introducing them with the following just observations :—

" Now, though descriptions of objects by such persons are often inaccurate, from the circumstance of their not having been favourably situated for making correct observations, as well as from a deficiency of language calculated to convey the information they actually possess, I have always remarked, that even a hasty examination seemed to supply the savage with more accurate notions of the general character of animals, than it did the civilised man ; and, therefore, I do not despair of species such as these mentioned being yet discovered. It is in regard to the species with the single horn that we experience the greatest hesitation in receiving their evidence as credible ; and therefore, it is agreeable to have it corroborated by

* *South Afr. Christian Recorder,* vol. i.

the testimony of a man from a very different part of the country, as obtained and published by a missionary of great research, who resided a long time in Madagascar." *

The rude drawings made by savages are often faithful delineations of the salient features of the objects familiar to them. Sir J. Barrow, in his *Travels in Africa*, has given the head of an unicorn, answering well to the *ndzoo-dzoo*, which was copied from a charcoal sketch made by a Caffre in the interior of a cavern. The copy was made by Daniell; and Colonel Hamilton Smith mentions having seen, among the papers of this artist, another drawing likewise copied from the walls of an African cave. In this were represented, with exceedingly characteristic fidelity, several of the common antelopes of the country, such as a group of elands, the hartebeest, and the springbok; while among them appeared, with head and shoulders towering above the rest, an animal having the general character of a rhinoceros, but, in form, lighter than a wild bull, having an arched neck, and a long nasal horn projecting in the form of a sabre. "This drawing," observes the Colonel, "is no doubt still extant, and should be published; but, in confirmation of the opinion that truth exists to a certain extent in the foregoing remarks, it may be observed that we have seen, we believe in the British Museum, a horn brought from Africa, unlike those of any known species of rhinoceros: it is perfectly smooth and hard, about thirty inches in length, almost equally thick throughout, not three inches in its greatest diameter, nor less than two

* *Illustr. of Zool. of South Africa.*

in its smaller, and rather sharp pointed at top : from the narrowness of the base, its great length and weight, the horn must evidently stand moveable on the nasal bones, until excitement renders the muscular action more rigid, and the coriaceous sole which sustains it more firm,—circumstances which may explain the repeated assertion of natives, that the horn, or rather the agglutinated hair which forms that instrument, is flexible.*

Much more recently, accounts have reached Europe of the same nature, confirmatory of the former, inasmuch as much of the value of such evidence consists in its cumulative character; but still only hearsay report. M. Antoine d'Abbadie, writing to the *Athenæum* from Cairo, gives the following account of an animal new to European science, which account he had received from Baron Von Müller, who had recently returned to that city from Kordofan:— "At Melpes, in Kordofan," said the Baron, "where I stopped some time to make my collections, I met, on the 17th of April 1848, a man who was in the habit of selling to me specimens of animals. One day he asked me if I wished also for an A'nasa, which he described thus :—It is the size of a small donkey, has a thick body and thin bones, coarse hair, and tail like a boar. It has a long horn on its forehead, and lets it hang when alone, but erects it immediately on seeing an enemy. It is a formidable weapon, but I do not know its exact length. The A'nasa is found not far from here, (Melpes,) towards the S.S.W. I have seen it often in the wild grounds, where the

* *Cyclop. Bibl. Lit.*, Art. REEM.

T

negroes kill it, and carry it home to make shields from
its skin.

"*N.B.*—This man was well acquainted with the rhinoceros, which he distinguished, under the name of Fetit,
from the A'nasa. On June the 14th I was at Kursi,
also in Kordofan, and met there a slave-merchant who
was not acquainted with my first informer, and gave me
spontaneously the same description of the A'nasa, adding
that he had killed and eaten one not long ago, and that its
flesh was well flavoured." *

Almost as little known as the heart of Africa are the
depths of ocean. The eye penetrates in the clear crystalline sea a few fathoms down, and beholds mailed and
glittering forms flitting by; the dredge gathers its scrap-
ings; divers plunge out of sight, and bring up pearls;
and the sounding-lead goes down, down, down, hundreds
of fathoms, and when it comes up, we gaze with eager
eyes to see what adheres to the tallow "arming;" the tiny
shells, the frustules of diatoms, even the atoms of coral
sand,—curious to learn what is at the bottom of the deep.
But, after all, it is much like the brick which the Greek
fool carried about as a sample of the house he had to let.

Who can penetrate into the depths of the ocean to trace
the arrowy course of the mailed and glittering beings
that shoot along like animated beams of light? Who can
follow them to their rocky beds and coral caverns? The
wandering mariner sees with interested curiosity the flying-
fishes leaping in flocks from the water, and the eager

* *Athenæum*, Jan. 1849.

bonito rushing after them in swift pursuit; but who can tell what the flying-fish is doing when not pursued, or how the bonito is engaged when the prey is not before him? How many pleasing traits of conjugal or parental attachment the waves of the fathomless sea may conceal, we know not: what ingenious devices for self-protection; what structures for the concealment of eggs or offspring; what arts of attack and defence; what manœuvrings and stratagems; what varied exhibitions of sagacity, forethought, and care; what singular developments of instinct;—who shall tell?

The aquarium has, indeed, already enlarged our acquaintance with the curious creatures that inhabit the waters; and not a few examples of those habits and instincts that constitute animal *biography*, have by this means been brought to light. Much more will doubtless be learned by the same instrumentality; but there will still remain secrets which the aquarium will be powerless to resolve. From its very nature it can deal only with the small, and those which are content with little liberty; for the multitude of large, unwieldy, swift-finned races, which shoot athwart the deep, and for the countless hosts of tiny things, to whose organisation even the confinement of a vessel is speedy death, we must find some other device before we can cultivate acquaintance with them.

It is true, we can put together a goodly number of individual objects, which various accidents have from time to time revealed to us from the depths, and form them into an imaginary picture. Schleiden has done this, and a lovely delineation he has made. You have only to gaze on it, to admire it: I would not abate your admiration; I admire it too :—but remember, after all, it is but a fancy sketch of the unknown; it is only *"founded* on fact."

"We dive," he observes, "into the liquid crystal of the Indian Ocean, and it opens to us the most wondrous enchantments of the fairy tales of our childhood's dreams. The strangely branching thickets bear living flowers. Dense masses of Meandrinas and Astræas contrast with the leafy, cup-shaped expansions of the Explanarias, the variously-ramified Madrepores, which are now spread out like fingers, now rise in trunk-like branches, and now display the most elegant array of interlacing branches. The colouring surpasses everything: vivid green alternates with brown or yellow; rich tints of purple, from pale red-brown to the deepest blue. Brilliant rosy, yellow, or peach-coloured Nullipores overgrow the decaying masses, and are themselves interwoven with the pearl-coloured plates of the Retipores, resembling the most delicate ivory carvings. Close by, wave the yellow and lilac fans, perforated like trellis-work, of the Gorgonias. The clear sand of the bottom is covered with the thousand strange forms and tints of the sea-urchins, and star-fishes. The leaf-like Flustras and Escharas adhere like mosses and lichens to the branches of the corals; the yellow, green, and purple-striped Limpets cling like monstrous cochineal insects upon their trunks. Like gigantic cactus-blossoms, sparkling in the most ardent colours, the Sea-anemones expand their crowns of tentacles upon the broken rocks, or more modestly embellish the bottom, looking like beds of variegated ranunculuses. Around the blossoms of the coral shrubs play the humming-birds of the ocean,—little fish sparkling with red or blue metallic glitter, or gleaming in golden green, or in the brightest silvery lustre.

" Softly, like spirits of the deep, the delicate milk-white or bluish bells of the jelly-fishes float through this charmed world. Here the gleaming violet and gold-green Isabelle, and the flaming yellow, black, and vermilion-striped Coquette, chase their prey; there the band-fish shoots, snake-like, through the thicket, like a long silver ribbon, glittering with rosy and azure hues. Then come the fabulous cuttle-fish, decked in all colours of the rainbow, but marked by no definite outline, appearing and disappearing, intercrossing, joining company and parting again, in most fantastic ways; and all this in the most rapid change, and amid the most wonderful play of light and shade, altered by every breath of wind, and every slight curling of the surface of the ocean. When day declines, and the shades of night lay hold upon the deep, this fantastic garden is lighted up in new splendour. Millions of glowing sparks, little microscopic Medusas and Crustaceans, dance like glow-worms through the gloom. The Sea-feather, which by daylight is vermilion-coloured, waves in a greenish, phosphorescent light. Every corner of it is lustrous. Parts which by day were dull and brown, and retreated from the sight amid the universal brilliancy of colour, are now radiant in the most wonderful play of green, yellow, and red light; and to complete the wonders of the enchanted night, the silver disc, six feet across, of the moon-fish,* moves, slightly luminous, among the crowd of little sparkling stars.

"The most luxuriant vegetation of a tropical landscape cannot unfold as great wealth of form, while in the variety and splendour of colour it would stand far behind this garden landscape, which is strangely composed exclusively of animals, and not of plants; for, characteristic as the luxuriant development of vegetation of the temperate zones is of the sea-bottom, the fulness and multiplicity of the marine Fauna is just as prominent in the regions of the tropics. Whatever is beautiful, wondrous, or uncommon in the great classes of fish and echinoderms, jelly-fishes and polypes, and the molluscs of all kinds, is crowded into the warm and crystal waters of the tropical ocean,—rests in the white sands, clothes the rough cliffs, clings where the room is already occupied, like a parasite, upon the first comers, or swims through the shallows and depths of the element—while the mass of the vegetation is of a far inferior magnitude. It is peculiar in relation to this, that the law valid on land, according to which the animal kingdom, being better adapted to accommodate itself to outward circumstances, has a greater diffusion than the vegetable kingdom;—for the Polar Seas swarm with whales, seals, sea-birds, fishes, and countless numbers of the lower animals, even where every trace of vegetation has long vanished in the eternally frozen ice, and the cool sea fosters no sea-weed;—that this law, I say, holds good

* *Orthagoriscus mola.*

also for the sea, in the direction of its depth ; for when we descend, vegetable life vanishes much sooner than the animal, and, even from the depths to which no ray of light is capable of penetrating, the sounding-lead brings up news at least of living infusoria." *

Who has not felt, when looking over a boat's side into the clear crystal depth, a desire to go and explore ? Even on our own coasts, to see the rich luxuriant forests of *Laminaria* or *Alaria*, waving their great brown fronds to and fro, over which the shell-fishes crawl, and on which the green and rosy-fingered Anemones expand like flowers, while the pipe-fishes twine about, and the brilliant wrasses dart out and in, decked in scarlet and green,—is a tempting sight, and one which I have often gazed on with admiration.

"Nothing can be more surprising and beautiful," says Sir A. de Capell Brooke, " than the singular clearness of the water of the Northern Seas. As we passed slowly over the surface, the bottom, which here was in general a white sand, was clearly visible, with its minutest objects, where the depth was from twenty to twenty-five fathoms. During the whole course of the tour I made, nothing appeared to me so extraordinary as the inmost recesses of the deep unveiled to the eye. The surface of the ocean was unruffled by the slightest breeze, and the gentle splashing of the oars scarcely disturbed it. Hanging over the gunwale of the boat, with wonder and delight I gazed on the slowly moving scene below. Where the bottom was sandy, the different kinds of *Asterias*, *Echinus*, and

* Schleiden's *Lectures,* pp. 403–406.

even the smallest shells, appeared at that great depth conspicuous to the eye ; and the water seemed, in some measure, to have the effect of a magnifier, by enlarging the objects like a telescope, and bringing them seemingly nearer.   Now, creeping along, we saw, far beneath, the rugged sides of a mountain rising towards our boat, the base of which, perhaps, was hidden some miles in the great deep below.   Though moving on a level surface, it seemed almost as if we were ascending the height under us ; and when we passed over its summit, which rose in appearance to within a few feet of our boat, and came again to the descent, which on this side was suddenly perpendicular, and overlooking a watery gulf, as we pushed gently over the last point of it, it seemed as if we had thrown ourselves down this precipice ; the illusion, from the crystal clearness of the deep, actually producing a start.   Now we came again to a plain, and passed slowly over the submarine forests and meadows, which appeared in the expanse below ; inhabited, doubtless, by thousands of animals, to which they afford both food and shelter—animals unknown to man ; and I could sometimes observe large fishes of singular shape gliding softly through the watery thickets, unconscious of what was moving above them.   As we proceeded, the bottom became no longer visible ; its fairy scenes gradually faded to the view, and were lost in the dark green depths of the ocean."*

* *Travels in Norway*, p. 195.

XII.

THE GREAT UNKNOWN.

A SAILOR lad, after his first voyage, having returned to his country home, was eagerly beset for wonders. "What hast t' seen in furrin parts?" Among other things he reported having been where the rum flowed like rivers, and sugar formed whole mountains. At last, his inventive powers being exhausted, he began to speak of the shoals of tropical flying-fishes, a phenomenon which his familiar sight had long ceased to regard as a wonder. But here his aged mother thought reproof needful; raising her horn spectacles, and frowning in virtuous indignation, she said, "Nae, nae, Jock! mountains o' sugar may be, and rivers o' rum may be; but fish to flee ne'er can be!"

Old Dame Partlet did only what philosophers in all ages have done; she had formed her schedule of physical possibilities, outside of which nature could not go; nay, *must* not go. It so happened, however, that old Dame Nature was obstreperous, and refused to be confined within possibilities; and the lawless fishes fly to this day, in spite of Dame Partlet's virtuous protest.

There are several questions in natural science which are *questiones vexatæ*, because a certain amount of evidence of facts is on one side, and a certain amount of presump-

tion of impossibility on the other.   If eye-witnesses (or
those who present themselves as such) could decide the
points, they would have been decided long ago ; but those
who are believed to be best acquainted with natural laws
claim that theoretic impossibilities should overpower even
ocular demonstration.   There is far more justice in this
claim than appears at first sight.   The power of drawing
correct inferences from what we see, and even of knowing
what we do really see, and what we only *imagine*, is vastly
augmented by the rigorous training of the faculties which
long habits of observing certain classes of phenomena
induce ; and every man of science must have met with
numberless cases in which statements egregiously false
have been made to him in the most perfect good faith ;
his informant implicitly believing that he was simply
telling what he had seen with his own eyes.   A person
the other day assured me, that he had frequently seen
humming-birds sucking flowers in England : I did not set
him down as a liar, because he was a person of indubitable
honour ; his acquaintance with natural history, however,
was small, and he had fallen into the very natural error
of mistaking a moth for a bird.

It is quite proper that, when evidence is presented of
certain occurrences, the admission of which would over-
turn what we have come to consider as fixed laws, or
against which there exists a high degree of antecedent
improbability,—*that* evidence should be received with
great suspicion.   It should be carefully sifted ; possible
causes of error should be suggested ; the powers of the

observer to judge of the facts should be examined ; the actual bounding line between sensuous perception and mental inference should be critically investigated ; and confirmatory, yet independent, testimony should be sought. Yet, when we have done all this, we should ever remember that truth is stranger than fiction ; that our power to judge of fixed laws is itself very imperfect ; and that indubitable phenomena are ever and anon brought to light, which compel us to revise our code.   It is only a few years since the existence of metamorphosis in the *Crustacea*, when first announced, was scouted as absurd by naturalists of high reputation ; and the wide pre-valence of what is called Parthenogenesis in the *Insecta* is even now laughing to scorn what had seemed one of the most immutable laws of physiology.*

I propose, then, to examine a few questions in natural history, the very mooting of which ‧ is enough with many to convict the inquirer of wrong-headedness and credulity. High authorities—deservedly high, and entitled to speak *ex cathedrá*—have pronounced verdicts on them ; and numbers of inferior name (as usual, going far beyond their teachers,) are ready to treat with ridicule those who venture to think that, in spite of the αὐτὸς ἔφα, any

---

* "Experience," says Sir J. W. Herschell, "once recognised as the fountain of all our knowledge of nature, it follows that, in the study of nature and its laws, we ought at once to make up our minds to dismiss as idle prejudices, or at least suspend as premature, any pre-conceived notion of what *might*, or what *ought to be*, the order of nature in any proposed case, and content ourselves with observing, as a plain matter of fact, what *is*."—*Prelim. Discourse*, p. 79.

other conclusion can possibly be tenable.   I by no means
wish to appear as a partisan in treating such questions;
perversely adducing evidence only on one side, and cu-
shioning or distorting what might be said on the other;
but honestly to weigh the proof on both sides, so that the
reader may be able to determine for himself to which is
the preponderance.

Perhaps the most renowned of all these doubtful questions is the existence of the "Sea-serpent."

For ages, an animal of immense size and serpentine
form has been believed to inhabit the ocean, though to be
but rarely seen.   A strong conviction of its existence has
always prevailed among the inhabitants of Norway; and
the fjords or deep inlets which indent the coast-line of
that mountainous country are the situations in which it
is reported to have been most frequently seen.   The coasts
of New England, in the United States, are also said to
have been favoured with frequent visits from the august
stranger during the present century; and, even recently,
reports by many witnesses of unimpeachable character
have been published of its appearance in the midst of the
ocean, far from land, in various latitudes.

Bishop Pontoppidan, who, about the middle of the last
century, wrote a natural history of Norway, his native
country, collected together a considerable mass of testimony to the occasional appearance of an immense serpentiform marine animal off the shores of northern Europe
before that period.   Among other evidence, he adduces
that of Captain de Ferry, of the Norwegian navy, who saw

the animal, when in a boat rowed by eight men, near Molde, in August 1747. The declaration was confirmed by oath, taken before a magistrate, by two of the crew. The animal was described as of the general form of a serpent, stretched on the surface in receding coils or undulations, with the head, which resembled that of a horse, elevated some two feet out of the water.

The public papers of Norway, during the summer of 1846, were occupied with statements to the following effect :—

Many highly respectable persons, and of unimpeached veracity, in the vicinity of Christiansand and Molde, [the reader will observe that it is the same locality as that mentioned by Captain de Ferry, a hundred years before,] report that they have lately seen the marine serpent. It has been, for the most part, observed in the larger fjords, rarely in the open sea. In the fjord of Christiansand it is believed to have been seen every year, but only in the hottest part of the summer, and when the sea has been perfectly unruffled.

Affidavits of numerous persons are then given in detail, which, with some discrepancies in minute particulars, agree in testifying that an animal of great length (from about fifty to about a hundred feet) had been seen by them at various times—in many cases more than once. The head, which was occasionally elevated, was compared for size to a ten-gallon cask, rather pointed, as described by one witness ; by another, as rounded. All agreed that the eyes were large and glaring ; that the body was dark

brown, and comparatively slender; and that a diffusive
mane of long spreading hair waved behind the head. The
movements were in vertical undulations, according to pre-
ponderating testimony; but some attributed to the animal
lateral undulations also.   The deponents were of various
positions in society,—a workman, a fisherman, a merchant,
a *candidatus theologiæ*, a sheriff, a surgeon, a rector, a
curate, &c.

Later in the season, the Rev. P. W. Deinboll, arch-
deacon of Molde, published the following statement:—
" On the 28th of July 1845, J. C. Lund, bookseller and
printer; G. S. Krogh, merchant; Christian Flang, Lund's
apprentice; and John Elgenses, labourer; were out on
Romsdal-fjord, fishing.   The sea was, after a warm sun-
shiny day, quite calm.   About seven o'clock in the afternoon, a little distance from shore, near the ballast place
and Molde Hooe, they saw a large marine animal, which
slowly moved itself forward; as it appeared to them,
with the help of two fins, on the fore part of the body
nearest the head, which they judged from the boiling of
the water on both sides of it.   The visible part of the
body appeared to be between forty and fifty feet in length,
and moved in undulations like a snake.   The body was
round and of a dark colour, and seemed to be several ells
(an ell=two feet) in thickness.   As they discerned a
waving motion in the water behind the animal, they concluded that part of the body was concealed under water.
That it was one connected animal, they saw plainly from
its movement.   When the animal was about one hundred

yards from the boat, they noticed tolerably correctly its fore-part, which ended in a sharp snout; its colossal head raised itself above the water in the form of a semicircle; the lower part was not visible. The colour of the head was dark brown, and the skin smooth. They did not notice the eyes, or any mane or bristles on the throat. When the serpent came about a musket-shot near, Lund fired at it, and was certain the shots hit it in the head. After the shot he dived, but came up immediately. He raised his head like a snake preparing to dart on its prey. After he had turned and got his body in a straight line, which he appeared to do with great difficulty, he darted like an arrow against the boat. They reached the shore, and the animal, perceiving it had come in shallow water, dived immediately, and disappeared in the deep.

"Such is the declaration of these four men, and no one has any cause to doubt their veracity, or imagine that they were so seized with fear, that they could not observe what took place so near them. There are not many here, or on other parts of the Norwegian coast, who longer doubt the existence of the sea-serpent. The writer of this narrative was a long time sceptical, as he had not been so fortunate as to see this monster of the deep; but after the many accounts he has read, and the relations he has received from creditable witnesses, he does not dare longer to doubt the existence of the sea-serpent."

That I may bring to a point the Norwegian testimony on the subject, I add here a statement made by an English gentleman, and published under the signature of "Oxoni-

ensis " in *The Times* for November 4, 1848, on the occasion of the celebrated account of Captain M'Quhæ, presently to be given.

" There does not appear," says this writer, " to be a
single well-authenticated instance of these monsters having
been seen in any southern latitudes ; but in the north of
Europe, notwithstanding the fabulous character so long
ascribed to Pontoppidan's description, I am convinced that
they both exist and are frequently seen. During three
summers in Norway, I have repeatedly conversed with the
natives on this subject. A parish priest, residing on Romsdal-fjord, about two days' journey south of Drontheim—
an intelligent person, whose veracity I have no reason to
doubt—gave me a circumstantial account of one which
he had himself seen. It rose within thirty yards of the
boat in which he was, and swam parallel with it for a
considerable time. Its head he described as equalling a
small cask in size, and its mouth, which it repeatedly
opened and shut, was furnished with formidable teeth ;
its neck was smaller, but its body—of which he supposed
that he saw about half on the surface of the water—was
not less in girth than that of a moderate-sized horse.
Another gentleman, in whose house I stayed, had also
seen one, and gave a similar account of it ; it also came
near his boat upon the fjord, when it was fired at, upon
which it turned and pursued them to the shore, which
was luckily near, when it disappeared. They expressed
great surprise at the general disbelief attaching to the
existence of these animals amongst naturalists, and assured

me that there was scarcely a sailor accustomed to those inland lakes who had not seen them at one time or another."

The Rev. Alfred Charles Smith, M.A., an excellent naturalist, who passed the three summer months of 1850 in Norway, and who published his observations in a series of papers in the *Zoologist* for that and the following year, thus alludes to his own inquiries, which, if they add nothing to the amount of fact accumulated, add weight to the testimonies already adduced. "I lost no opportunity," he remarks, "of making inquiries of all I could see, as to the general belief in the country regarding the animal in question; but all, with one single exception— naval officers, sailors, boatmen, and fishermen—concurred in affirming most positively that such an animal did exist, and had been repeatedly seen off their coasts and fjords; though I was never fortunate enough to meet a man who could boast of having seen him with his own eyes. All, however, agreed in unhesitating belief as to his existence and frequent appearance; and all seemed to marvel very much at the scepticism of the English, for refusing credence to what to the minds of the Norwegians seemed so incontrovertible. The single exception to which I have alluded, was a Norwegian officer, who ridiculed what he called the credulity or gullibility of his countrymen; though I am bound to add my belief, that he did this, not from any decided opinion of his own, but to make a show of superior shrewdness in the eyes of an Englishman, who, he at once concluded, must undoubtedly disbelieve the

U

existence of the marine monster. That Englishman, however, certainly partakes of the credulity of the Northmen,
and cannot withhold his belief in the existence of some
huge inhabitant of those northern seas, when, to his mind,
the fact of his existence has been so clearly proved by
numerous eye-witnesses, many of whom were too intelligent to be deceived, and too honest to be doubted." *

In 1817, the Linnæan Society of New England published a "Report relative to a large marine animal, supposed to be a serpent, seen near Cape Ann, Massachusetts,
in August" of that year. A good deal of care was taken to
obtain evidence, and the depositions of eleven witnesses of
fair and unblemished characters were taken on the matter,
and certified on oath before magistrates, one of whom
himself saw the creature, and corroborated the statements
of the deponents on the most important points. The
serpent form was attested by all, and the colour, a dark
brown, mottled, according to some, with white on the
under parts of the head and neck. The length was vari-
ously estimated, from fifty to a hundred feet. *No appearance of mane was seen by any.* The head was compared to that of a sea-turtle, a rattlesnake, and a serpent
generally ; and, *for size*, to that of a horse. As to the
form of the body, five deponents speak of dorsal protuberances ; four declare that the body was straight, while two
do not moot the point. The mode of progression is generally spoken of as by vertical undulation, "like that of a
caterpillar,"—probably a looping or geometric caterpillar

* *Zoologist,* p. 3223.

is meant. The magistrate who saw the animal, and to whom the body appeared straight, considers that the appearance of protuberances was due to the vertical bendings of the body during energetic motion.

That there were other witnesses of the same appearance of the stranger in 1817, was generally stated at the time ; and one of these, whose testimony is of value, was brought out by the report of Captain M'Quhæ, and the correspondence that ensued upon it. In the Boston (U.S.) *Daily Advertiser* for November 25, 1848, appeared a long communication from the Hon. T. H. Perkins of that city, attesting his own personal observation of the marine serpent at Gloucester Harbour, near Cape Ann, in 1817. The communication mainly consisted of a copy of a letter which Colonel Perkins had written to a friend in 1820.

" . . . . Wishing to satisfy myself on a subject on which there existed a great difference of opinion, I myself visited Gloucester with Mr Lee. On our way down we met several persons returning, who had visited the place where he was said to have exhibited himself, and who reported to us that he had not been seen for two or three days past. We, however, continued our route to Gloucester, though with fears that we should not be gratified with the sight of the monster which we sought. I satisfied myself, from conversation with several persons who had seen him, that the report in circulation was not a fable. All the town were, as you may suppose, on the alert ; and almost every individual, both great and small, had been gratified, at a greater or less distance, with a sight of him. The

weather was fine, the sea perfectly smooth, and Mr Lee
and myself were seated on a point of land which projects
into the harbour, and about twenty feet above the level
of the water, from which we were distant about fifty or
sixty feet. . . . .

" In a few moments after my exclamation, I saw on
the opposite side of the harbour, at about two miles' distance from where I had first seen, or thought I saw, the
snake, the same object, moving with a rapid motion up the
harbour, on the western shore.   As he approached us, it
was easy to see that his motion was not that of the common snake, either on the land or in the water, but evidently
the vertical movement of the caterpillar.   As nearly as I
could judge, there was visible at a time about forty feet
of his body.   It was not, to be sure, a continuity of body,
as the form from head to tail (except as the apparent
bunches appeared as he moved through the water) was
seen only at three or four feet asunder.   It was very evident, however, that his length must be much greater than
what appeared, as, in his movement, he left a considerable
wake in his rear.   I had a fine glass, and was within from
one-third to half a mile of him.   The head was flat in the
water, and the animal was, as far as I could distinguish,
of a chocolate colour.   I was struck with an appearance
in the front part of the head like a single horn, about
nine inches to a foot in length, and of the form of a mar-
linespike.   There were a great many people collected by
this time, many of whom had before seen the same object,
and the same appearance.   From the time I first saw him

until he passed by the place where I stood, and soon after disappeared, was not more than fifteen or twenty minutes.

"I left the place fully satisfied that the reports in circulation, although differing in details, were essentially correct. I returned to Boston, and having made my report, I found Mrs Perkins and my daughters disposed to make a visit to Gloucester with me when the return of the animal should be again announced. A few days after my return I went again to Cape Ann with the ladies ; we had a pleasant ride, but returned ungratified in the object which carried us there.

"Whilst at Cape Ann I talked with many persons who had seen the serpent, and among others with a person of the name of Mansfield, one of the most respectable inhabitants of the town. His account to me was, that a few days before, as he was taking a ride with his wife in a chair, the road taking them close to a bank which overlooks the harbour, (and is nearly a perpendicular precipiece,) he saw an uncommon appearance, which induced him to descend from the carriage, when he saw the seaserpent, in which until then he had been an unbeliever. The animal was stretched out, partly over the white sandy beach, which had four or five feet of water upon it, and lay partly over the channel. He desired his wife to get out of the chair, which she did. He said he had made up his mind as to the length of the snake, but wished the opinion of his wife on the same subject. He asked her what she should consider his length ; she answered that she could not undertake to say how many feet in length he was, but that she thought him as long as the wharf behind their house, an object with which she had always been familiar. Mr Mansfield said he was of the same opinion. The wharf is one hundred feet in length. It is to be observed that the person above spoken of had been such an unbeliever in the existence of this monster, that he had not given himself the trouble to go from his house to the harbour when the report was first made of such an animal being there. Subsequent to the period of which I have been speaking, the snake was seen by several of the crews of our coasting vessels, and in some instances within a few yards. Captain Tappan, a person well known to me, saw him with his head above water two or three feet, at times moving with great rapidity, and at others slowly. He also saw what explained the appearance which I have described, of a horn on the front of the head. This was doubtless what was observed by Captain Tappan to be the tongue, thrown in an upright position from the mouth, and having the appearance which I have given to it.

"One of the revenue cutters, whilst in the neighbourhood of Cape Ann, had an excellent view of him at a few yards' distance ; he moved slowly, and upon the approach of the vessel, sank and was seen no more."

Though the position and character of some of these witnesses add weight to their testimony, and seem to preclude the possibility of their being either deceived or deceivers, on a matter which depended on the use of their eyes, yet, owing to a habit prevalent in the United States, of supposing that there is somewhat of wit in gross exaggerations, or hoaxing inventions, we do naturally look with a lurking suspicion on American statements, when they describe unusual or disputed phenomena. It may therefore be interesting to give the evidence of five British officers, to the serpent's appearance on the American coast, some fifteen years after the occurrence last mentioned.

"On the 15th of May 1833, a party, consisting of Captain Sullivan, Lieutenants Maclachlan and Malcolm of the Rifle Brigade, Lieutenant Lyster of the Artillery, and Mr Ince of the Ordinance, started from Halifax in a small yacht for Mahone Bay, some forty miles eastward, on a fishing excursion. The morning was cloudy, and the wind at S.S.E., and apparently rising: by the time we reached Chebucto Head, as we had taken no pilot with us, we deliberated whether we should proceed or turn back; but after a consultation, we determined on the former, having lots of ports on our lee. Previous to our leaving town, an old man-of-war's-man we had along with us busied himself in inquiries as to our right course; he was told to take his departure from the Bull Rock off Pennant Point, and that a W.N.W. course would bring us direct on Iron Bound Island, at the entrance of Mahone or Mecklenburgh Bay: he, however, unfortunately told us to steer W.S.W., nor corrected his error for five or six hours; consequently we had gone a long distance off the coast. We had run about half the distance, as we supposed, and were enjoying ourselves on deck, smoking our

cigars, and getting our tackle ready for the approaching
campaign against the salmon, when we were surprised by
the sight of an immense shoal of grampuses, which
appeared in an unusual state of excitement, and which in
their gambols approached so close to our little craft, that
some of the party amused themselves by firing at them
with rifles ; at this time we were jogging on at about five
miles an hour, and must have been crossing Margaret's
Bay.   I merely conjecture where we were, as we had not
seen land since a short time after leaving Pennant Bay.
Our attention was presently diverted from the whales and
'such small deer,' by an exclamation from Dowling, our
man-of-war's-man, who was sitting to leeward, of, 'O
sirs, look here !' We were started into a ready compliance,
and saw an object which banished all other thoughts, save
wonder and surprise.

    "At the distance of from a hundred and fifty to two
hundred yards on our starboard bow, we saw the head
and neck of some denizen of the deep, precisely like those
of a common snake, in the act of swimming, the head so
far elevated and thrown forward by the curve of the neck,
as to enable us to see the water under and beyond it.
The creature rapidly passed, leaving a regular wake, from
the commencement of which, to the fore part, which was
out of water, we judged its length to be about eighty feet ;
and this within, rather than beyond the mark.   We were,
of course, all taken aback at the sight, and, with staring
eyes and in speechless wonder, stood gazing at it for full
half a minute.   There could be no mistake, no delusion

and we were all perfectly satisfied that we had been favoured with a view of the 'true and veritable sea-serpent,' which had been generally considered to have existed only in the brain of some Yankee skipper, and treated as a tale not much entitled to belief. Dowling's exclamation is worthy of record,—' Well, I've sailed in all parts of the world, and have seen rum sights too in my time, but this is the queerest thing I ever see!' and surely Jack Dowling was right. It is most difficult to give correctly the dimensions of any object in the water. The head of the creature we set down at about six feet in length, and that portion of the neck which we saw, at the same; the extreme length, as before stated, at between eighty and one hundred feet. The neck in thickness equalled the bole of a moderate sized tree. The head and neck of a dark brown or nearly black colour, streaked with white in irregular streaks. I do not recollect seeing any part of the body.

" Such is the rough account of the sea-serpent, and all the party who saw it are still in the land of the living,— Lyster in England, Malcolm in New South Wales, with his regiment, and the remainder still vegetating in Halifax.

" W. SULLIVAN, Captain, Rifle Brigade,   June 21, 1831.

A. MACLACHLAN, Lieutenant, ditto,   August 5, 1824.

G. P. MALCOLM, Ensign, ditto,   August 13, 1830.

B. O'NEAL LYSTER, Lieut., Artillery,   June 7, 1816.

HENRY INCE, Ordnance Store-keeper at Halifax." [*]

[*] This account was published in the *Zoologist* for 1847, (page 1715;)

I now come to an incident, which, from the character of the witnesses, the captain, officers, and crew of one of Her Majesty's ships, and from the medium through which it was announced, an official report to the Lords of the Admiralty,—commanded great notoriety and interest, and gave an unwonted impetus to the investigation of the question.

The Times newspaper of October 9, 1848, published the following paragraph : — " When the *Dædalus* frigate, Captain M'Quhæ, which arrived at Plymouth on the 4th instant, was on her passage home from the East Indies, between the Cape of Good Hope and St Helena, her captain, and most of her officers and crew, at four o'clock one afternoon, saw a sea-serpent. The creature was twenty minutes in sight of the frigate, and passed under her quarter. Its head appeared to be about four feet out of the water, and there was about sixty feet of its body in a straight line on the surface. It is calculated that there must have been under water a length of thirty-three or forty feet more, by which it propelled itself at the rate of fifteen miles an hour. The diameter of the exposed part of the body was about sixteen inches, and when it extended its jaws, which were full of large jagged teeth, they seemed sufficiently capacious to admit of a tall man standing upright between them."

and the editor states that he is indebted for it to Mr W. H. Ince, who received it from his brother, Commander J. M. R. Ince, R.N. It was written by their uncle, one of the eye-witnesses, Mr Henry Ince, the Ordnance Store-keeper at Halifax, in Nova Scotia. The dates affixed to the names, are those on which the gentlemen received their respective commissions. The editor is not aware of their present rank.

Some of the details here given were not afterwards substantiated; but popular curiosity was excited. The Admiralty instantly inquired into the truth of the statement, and in *The Times* of the 13th was published the gallant captain's official reply in the following terms :—

"HER MAJESTY'S SHIP DÆDALUS,
HAMOAZE, *Oct.* 11.

"SIR,—In reply to your letter of this date, requiring information as to the truth of a statement published in *The Times* newspaper, of a sea-serpent of extraordinary dimensions having been seen from Her Majesty's ship *Dœdalus*, under my command, on her passage from the East Indies, I have the honour to acquaint you, for the information of my Lords Commissioners of the Admiralty, that at five o'clock P.M., on the 6th of August last, in latitude 24° 44′ S., and longitude 9° 22′ E., the weather dark and cloudy, wind fresh from the N.W., with a long ocean swell from the S.W., the ship on the port tack heading N.E. by N., something very unusual was seen by Mr Sartoris, midshipman, rapidly approaching the ship from before the beam. The circumstance was immediately reported by him to the officer of the watch, Lieutenant Edgar Drummond, with whom and Mr William Barrett, the master, I was at the time walking the quarter-deck. The ship's company were at supper.

"On our attention being called to the object, it was discovered to be an enormous serpent, with head and shoulders kept about four feet constantly above the surface of the sea, and, as nearly as we could approximate by comparing it with the length of what our maintopsail-yard would shew in the water, there was at the very least sixty feet of the animal *à fleur d'eau,*[*] no portion of which was, to our perception, used in propelling it through the water, either by vertical or horizontal undulation. It passed rapidly, but so close under our lee quarter, that had it been a man of my acquaintance, I should easily have recognised his features with the naked eye; and it did not, either in approaching the ship or after it had passed our wake, deviate in the slightest degree from its course to the S.W., which it held on at the pace of from twelve to fifteen miles per hour, apparently on some determined purpose.

"The diameter of the serpent was about fifteen or sixteen inches behind the head, which was, without any doubt, that of a snake; and it was never, during the twenty minutes that it continued in sight of our glasses, once below the surface of the water; its colour a dark brown, with yellowish white about the throat. It had no fins, but something like the mane of a horse, or rather a bunch of sea-weed, washed about its back. It was seen by the quarter-master, the boatswain's mate, and the man at the wheel, in addition to myself and officers above-mentioned.

" I am having a drawing of the serpent made from a sketch taken immediately after it was seen, which I hope

* " *At the surface of the water.*" What need there was to express this by a French phrase in an English report, is not obvious.

to have ready for transmission to my Lords Commissioners of the Admiralty by to-morrow's post.

"PETER M'QUHÆ, Captain.

" To Admiral Sir W. H. Gage, G.C.H., Devonport."

Lieutenant Drummond, the officer of the watch named in the above report, published his own impressions of the animal, in the form of an extract from his own journal, as follows:—"In the four to six watch, at about five o'clock, we observed a most remarkable fish on our lee-quarter, crossing the stern in a S.W. direction; the appearance of its head, which, with the back fin, was the only portion of the animal visible, was long, pointed, and flattened at the top, perhaps ten feet in length, the upper jaw projecting considerably; the fin was perhaps twenty feet in the rear of the head, and visible occasionally; the captain also asserted that he saw the tail, or another fin about the same distance behind it; the upper part of the head and shoulders appeared of a dark brown colour, and beneath the under jaw a brownish white. It pursued a steady undeviating course, keeping its head horizontal with the surface of the water, and in rather a raised position, disappearing occasionally beneath a wave for a very brief interval, and not apparently for purposes of respiration. It was going at the rate of perhaps from twelve to fourteen miles an hour, and when nearest, was perhaps one hundred yards distant. In fact it gave one quite the idea of a large snake or eel. No one in the ship has ever seen anything similar, so it is at least extraordinary. It was visible to the naked eye for five minutes, and with a glass for perhaps fifteen more. The weather was dark and squally at the time, with sea running." [*]

The pictorial sketch alluded to in Captain M'Quhæ's report, as well as one representing the animal in another aspect, was published in the *Illustrated London News*, of October 28, 1848, "under the supervision of Captain M'Quhæ, and with his approval of the authenticity of the details as to position and form." These drawings will be criticised presently.

As I have already said, a good deal of popular curiosity and interest was immediately awakened; and the public papers were for a while filled with strictures, objections, suggestions, and confirmations. Among the last, Captain Beechey, the eminent navigator, mentioned an extraordinary appearance which had occurred to him during the voyage of the *Blossom*, in the South Atlantic. "I took it for the *trunk of a large tree*, and before I could get my glass it had disappeared."

Mr J. D. Morries Stirling, a gentleman long resident in Norway, communicated to the Secretary to the Admiralty important confirmatory evidence of the existence of the animal on the coasts of that country, collected by a scientific body at Bergen, of which he was one of the directors. In the course of this communication, the writer points out certain points of resemblance borne by the Norwegian animal to the great fossil reptiles known to geologists as the *Enaliosauri* :—"In several of

[*] *Zoologist*, p. 2306.

the fossil reptiles somewhat approaching the sea-serpent in size and other characteristics, the orbit is very large; and, in this respect, as well as in having short paws or flappers, the descriptions of the Northern sea-serpents agree with the supposed appearance of some of the antediluvian species." This important identification had been suggested (probably, however, without Mr Stirling's knowledge) nearly two years before, by Mr E. Newman, F.L.S., the able editor of the *Zoologist*.*

The most valuable portion of Mr Stirling's communication is its closing paragraph:—"In concluding this hurried statement, allow me to add my own testimony as to the existence of a large fish or reptile of cylindrical form. (I will not say sea-serpent.) Three years ago, while becalmed in a yacht between Bergen and Sogn in Norway, I saw (at about a quarter of a mile astern) what appeared to be a large fish ruffling the otherwise smooth surface of the fjord, and, on looking attentively, I observed what looked like the convolutions of a snake. I immediately got my glass, and distinctly made out three convolutions, which drew themselves slowly through the water; the greatest diameter was about ten or twelve inches. No head was visible, and from the size of each convolution I supposed the length to be about thirty feet. The master of my yacht, (who, as navigator, seaman, and fisherman, had known the Norwegian coast and North Sea for many

* To the philosophic candour'with which the *Zoologist* has been opened to reports and discussions on such mooted questions as these, natural history is much indebted. Not a little of the evidence adduced in this chapter I have derived thence.

years,) as well as a friend who was with me, an experienced Norwegian sportsman and porpoise shooter, saw the same appearance at the same time, and formed the same opinion as to form and size.   I mention my friend being a porpoise shooter, as many have believed that a shoal of porpoises following each other has given rise to the fable, as they called it, of the sea-serpent." *

A writer in *The Times* of November 2, 1848, under the signature of "F. G. S.," also suggested affinity with the *Enaliosauri*, and particularly adduced the fossil genus *Plesiosaurus* as presenting the closest resemblance. "One of the greatest difficulties," observes this writer, "on the face of the narrative [of Captain M'Quhæ], and which must be allowed to destroy the analogy of the motions of the so-called 'sea-serpent' with those of all known snakes and anguilliform fishes, is that no less than sixty feet of the animal were seen advancing *à fleur d'eau* at the rate of from twelve to fifteen miles an hour, without it being possible to perceive, upon the closest and most attentive inspection, any undulatory motion to which its rapid advance could be ascribed.   It need scarcely be observed that neither an eel nor a snake, if either of those animals could swim at all with the neck elevated, could do so without the front part of its body being thrown into undulation by the propulsive efforts of its tail."

He then inquires to what class of animals it could have belonged, and thus proceeds :—

* *Illustrated London News*, Oct. 28, 1848.

" From the known anatomical character of the *Plesio-sauri*, derived from the examination of their organic remains, geologists are agreed in the inference that those animals carried their necks (which must have resembled the bodies of serpents) above the water, while their progression was effected by large paddles working beneath— the short but stout tail acting the part of a rudder. It would be superfluous to point out how closely the surmises of philosophers resemble, in these particulars, the description of the eye-witnesses of the living animal, as given in the letter and drawings of Captain M'Quhæ. In the latter we have many of the external characters of the former, as predicated from the examination of the skeleton. The short head, the serpent-like neck, carried several feet above the water, forcibly recall the idea conceived of the extinct animal ; and even the bristly mane in certain parts of the back, so unlike anything found in serpents, has its analogy in the *Iguana*, to which animal the *Plesiosaurus* has been compared by some geologists. But I would most of all insist upon the peculiarity of the animal's progression, which could only have been effected with the evenness, and at the rate described, by an apparatus of fins or paddles, not possessed by serpents, but existing in the highest perfection in the *Plesiosaurus*."

A master in science now appeared upon the field,— Professor Richard Owen, who, in a most able article, gave his verdict against the serpentine character of the animal seen, and pronounced it to have been, in his judgment, a

x

seal. This opinion is too important to bear abridgment, and must be given *in extense :—*

"The sketch [a reduced copy of the animal seen by Captain M'Quhæ, attached to the submerged body of a large seal, shewing the long eddy produced by the action of the terminal flippers] will suggest the reply to your query, 'Whether the monster seen from the *Dœdalus* be anything but a saurian?' If it be the true answer, it destroys the romance of the incident, and will be anything but acceptable to those who prefer the excitement of the imagination to the satisfaction of the judgment. I am far from insensible to the pleasures of the discovery of a new and rare animal; but before I can enjoy them, certain conditions—*e. g.*, reasonable proof or evidence of its existence—must be fulfilled. I am also far from undervaluing the information which Captain M'Quhæ has given us of what he saw. When fairly analysed, it lies in a small compass; but my knowledge of the animal kingdom compels me to draw other conclusions from the phenomena than those which the gallant captain seems to have jumped at. He evidently saw a large animal moving rapidly through the water, very different from anything he had before witnessed—neither a whale, a grampus, a great shark, an alligator, nor any of the larger surface-swimming creatures which are fallen in with in ordinary voyages. He writes :—' On our attention being called to the object, it was discovered to be an enormous serpent,' (read 'animal,') ' with the head and shoulders kept about four feet constantly above the surface of the sea. The diameter of the serpent' (animal) 'was about fifteen or sixteen inches behind the head ; its colour a dark brown, with yellowish white about the throat. No fins were seen, (the captain says there were none ; but from his own account, he did not see enough of the animal to prove his negative.) 'Something like the mane of a horse, or rather a bunch of sea-weed washed about its back.' So much of the body as was seen was 'not used in propelling the animal through the water, either by vertical or horizontal undulation.' A calculation of its length was made under a strong preconception of the nature of the beast. The head, *e. g.*, is stated to be, 'without any doubt, that of a snake ;' and yet a snake would be the last species to which a naturalist, conversant with the forms and characters of the heads of animals, would refer such a head as that of which Captain M'Quhæ has transmitted a drawing to the Admiralty, and which he certifies to have been accurately copied in the *Illustrated London News* for October 28, 1848, p. 265. Your Lordship will observe, that no sooner was the captain's attention called to the object, than 'it was discovered to be an enormous serpent,' and yet the closest inspection of as much of the body as was visible, *à fleur d'eau*, failed to detect any undulations of the body, although such actions constitute the very character which would distinguish a serpent or serpentiform swimmer from any other marine species. The foregone conclusion, therefore, of the beast's being a sea-serpent, notwithstanding its capacious vaulted cranium, and stiff, inflexible trunk, must be kept in mind in estimating the value of the approximation made to the **total** length of the animal, as '(at the very least) sixty feet.' This is the only part of the description, however, which seems to me to be so uncertain as to be inadmissible, in an attempt to arrive at a right conclusion as to the nature of the animal. The more certain characters of the animal are these:—Head with a convex, moderately capacious cranium, short obtuse muzzle, gape of the mouth not extending further than to beneath the eye, which is rather small, round, filling closely the palpebral aperture; colour, dark brown above, yellowish white beneath; surface smooth, without scales, scutes, or other conspicuous modifications of hard and naked cuticle. And the captain says, 'Had it been a man of my acquaintance, I should have easily recognised his features with my naked eye.' Nostrils not mentioned, but indicated in the drawing by a crescentic mark at the end of the nose or muzzle. All these are the characters of the head of a warm-blooded mammal—none of them those of a cold-blooded reptile or fish. Body long, dark brown, not undulating, without dorsal or other apparent fins; 'but something like the mane of a horse, or rather a bunch of sea-weed, washed about its back.' The character of the integuments would be a most important one for the zoologist in the determination of the class to which the above-defined creature belonged. If an opinion can be deduced as to the integuments from the above indication, it is that the species had hair, which, if it was too short and close to be distinguished on the head, was visible where it usually is the longest, on the middle line of the shoulders or advanced part of the back, where it was not stiff and upright like the rays of a fin, but 'washed about.' Guided by the above interpretation, of the 'mane of a horse, or a bunch of sea-weed,' the animal was not a cetaceous mammal, but rather a great seal. But what seal of large size, or indeed of any size, would be encountered in latitude 24° 44' south, and longitude 9° 22' east—viz., about three hundred miles from the western shore of the southern end of Africa? The most likely species to be there met with are the largest of the seal tribe, *e. g*, Anson's sea-lion, or that known to the southern whalers by the name of the " sea-elephant," the *Phoca proboscidea*, which attains the length of from twenty to thirty feet. These great seals abound in certain of the islands of the southern and antarctic seas, from which an individual is occasionally floated off upon an iceberg. The sea-lion exhibited in London last spring, which was a young individual of the *Phoca proboscidea*, was actually captured in that predicament; having been carried by the currents that set northward towards the Cape, where its temporary resting-place was rapidly melting away. When a large individual of the *Phoca proboscidea* or *Phoca leonina* is thus borne off to a distance from its native shore, it is compelled to return for rest to its floating abode, after it has made its daily excursions in quest of the fishes or squids that constitute its food. It is thus brought by the iceberg into the latitudes of the Cape, and perhaps further north, before the berg has melted away. Then the poor seal is compelled to swim as long as strength endures ; and in such a predicament I imagine the creature was that Mr Sartoris saw rapidly approaching the *Dœdalus* from before the beam, scanning, probably, its capabilities as a resting place, as it paddled its long stiff body past the ship. In so doing, it would raise a head of the form and colour described and delineated by Captain M'Quhæ, supported on a neck also of the diameter given; the thick neck passing into an inflexible trunk, the longer and coarser hair on the upper part of which would give rise to the idea, especially if the species were the *Phoca leonina*, explained by the similes above cited. The organs of locomotion would be out of sight. The pectoral fins being set on very low down, as in my sketch, the chief impelling force would be the action of the deeper immersed terminal fins and tail, which would create a long eddy, readily mistakeable, by one looking at the strange phenomenon with a sea-serpent in his mind's-eye, for an indefinite prolongation of the body.

"It is very probable, that not one on board the *Dœdalus* ever before beheld a gigantic seal freely swimming in the open ocean. Entering unexpectedly from that vast and commonly blank desert of waters, it would be a strange and exciting spectacle, and might well be interpreted as a marvel; but the creative powers of the human mind appear to be really very limited, and, on all the occasions where the true source of the 'great unknown' has been detected--whether it has proved to be a file of sportive porpoises, or a pair of gigantic sharks—old Pontoppidan's sea-serpent with the mane has uniformly suggested itself as the representative of the portent, until the mystery has been unravelled.

"The vertebræ of the sea-serpent described and delineated in the *Wernerian Transactions*, vol. i., and sworn to by the fishermen who saw it off the Isle of Stronsa, (one of the Orkneys,) in 1808, two of which vertebræ are in the Museum of the College of Surgeons, are certainly those of a great shark, of the genus *Selache*, and are not distinguishable from those of the species called ' basking-shark,' of which individuals from thirty feet to thirty-five feet in length have been from time to time captured or stranded on our coasts.

"I have no unmeet confidence in the exactitude of my interpretation of the phenomena witnessed by the captain and others of the *Dædalus*. I am too sensible of the inadequacy of the characters which the opportunity of a rapidly passing animal, 'in a long ocean swell,' enabled them to note, for the determination of its species or genus. Giving due credence to the most probably accurate elements of their description, they do little more than guide the zoologist to the class, which, in the present instance, is not that of the serpent or the saurian.

"But I am usually asked, after each endeavour to explain Captain M'Quhæ's sea-serpent, ' Why should there not be a great sea-serpent ?'—often, too, in a tone which seems to imply, ' Do you think, then, there are not more marvels in the deep than are dreamt of in your philosophy ?' And, freely conceding that point, I have felt bound to give a reason for scepticism as well as faith.

If a gigantic sea-serpent actually exists, the species must, of course, have been perpetuated through successive generations, from its first creation and introduction into the seas of this planet. Conceive, then, the number of individuals that must have lived, and died, and have left their remains to attest the actuality of the species during the enormous lapse of time, from its beginning, to the 6th of August last! Now, a serpent, being an air-breathing animal, with long vesicular and receptacular lungs, dives with an effort, and commonly floats when dead; and so would the sea-serpent, until decomposition or accident had opened the tough integument, and let out the imprisoned gases. Then it would sink, and, if in deep water, be seen no more until the sea rendered up its dead, after the lapse of the æons requisite for the yielding of its place to dry land—a change which has actually revealed to the present generation the old saurian monsters that were entombed at the bottom of the ocean, of the secondary geological periods of our earth's history. During life the exigencies of the respiration of the great sea-serpent would always compel him frequently to the surface; and when dead and swollen—

'Prone on the flood, extended long and large,'

he would

'Lie floating many a rood; in bulk as huge,
    As whom the fables name of monstrous size,
    Titanian, or Earth-born, that warr'd on Jove.'

Such a spectacle, demonstrative of the species if it existed, has not hitherto met the gaze of any of the countless voyagers who have traversed the seas in so many directions. Considering, too, the tides and currents of the ocean, it seems still more reasonable to suppose that the dead sea-serpent would be occasionally cast on shore. However, I do not ask for the entire carcase. The structure of the back-bone of the serpent tribe is so peculiar, that a single vertebra would suffice to determine the existence of the hypothetical Ophidian ; and this will not be deemed an unreasonable request when it is remembered that the vertebræ are more numerous in serpents than in any other animals. Such large blanched and scattered bones on any sea-shore, would be likely to attract even common curiosity ; yet there is no vertebra of a serpent larger than the ordinary pythons and boas in any museum in Europe.

"Few sea-coasts have been more sedulously searched, or by more acute naturalists (witness the labours of Sars and Lovén) than those of Norway. Krakens and sea-serpents ought to have been living and dying thereabouts from long before Pontoppidan's time to our day, if all tales were true ; yet they have never vouchsafed a single fragment of the skeleton to any Scandinavian collector ; whilst the great denizens of those seas have been by no means so chary. No museums, in fact, are so rich in skeletons, skulls, bones and teeth of the numerous kinds of whales, cachalots, grampuses, walruses, sea-unicorns, seals, &c., as those of Denmark, Norway, and Sweden ; but of any large marine nondescript or indeterminable monster they cannot shew a trace.

" I have inquired repeatedly whether the natural history collections of Boston, Philadelphia, or other cities of the United States, might possess any unusually large ophidian vertebræ, or any of such peculiar form as to indicate some large and unknown marine animal ; but they have received no such specimens.

"The frequency with which the sea-serpent has been supposed to have appeared near the shores and harbours of the United States, has led to its being specified as the 'American sea-serpent ; ' yet out of the two hundred vertebræ of every individual that should have lived and died in the Atlantic since the creation of the species, not one has yet been picked up on the shores of America. The diminutive snake, less than a yard in length, 'killed upon the sea-shore,' apparently beaten to death, ' by some labouring people of Cape Ann,' United States, (see the 8vo pamphlet, 1817, Boston, page 38,) and figured in the *Illustrated London News*, October 28, 1848, from the original American memoir, by no means satisfies the conditions of the problem.　Neither does the *Saccopharynx* of Mitchell, nor the *Ophiognathus* of Harwood—the one four and a half feet, the other six feet long : both are surpassed by some of the congers of our own coasts, and, like other murænoid fishes and the known small sea-snake, *(Hydrophis,)* swim by undulatory movements of the body. ． ． ． ．

"The fossil vertebræ and skull which were exhibited by Mr Koch, in New York and Boston, as those of the great sea-serpent, and which are now in Berlin, belonged to different individuals of a species which I had previously proved to be an extinct whale ; a determination which has subsequently been confirmed by Professors Müller and Agassiz. Mr Dixon, of Worthing, has discovered many fossil vertebræ, in the Eocene tertiary clay at Brack-lesham, which belong to a large species of an extinct genus of serpent (*Palæophis*), founded on similar verte-bræ from the same formation in the Isle of Sheppey. The largest of these ancient British snakes was twenty feet in length ; but there is no evidence that they were marine.

"The sea saurians of the secondary periods of geology have been replaced in the tertiary and actual seas by marine mammals. No remains of *Cetacea* have been found in lias or oolite, and no remains of Plesiosaur, or Ichthyosaur, or any other secondary reptile, have been found in Eocene or later tertiary deposits, or recent, on the actual sea-shores ; and that the old air-breathing saurians floated when they died has been shewn in the *Geological Transactions,* (vol. v., second series, p. 512.) The inference that may reasonably be drawn from no recent carcase or fragment of such having ever been discovered, is strengthened by the corresponding absence of any trace of their remains in the tertiary beds.

"Now, on weighing the question, whether creatures meriting the name of 'great sea-serpent' do exist, or whether any of the gigantic marine saurians of the secondary deposits may have continued to live up to the present time, it seems to me less probable that no part of

the carcase of such reptiles should have ever been discovered in a recent or unfossilised state, than that men
should have been deceived by a cursory view of a partly
submerged and rapidly moving animal, which might only
be strange to themselves. In other words, I regard
the negative evidence from the utter absence of any of
the recent remains of great sea-serpents, krakens, or
Enaliosauria, as stronger against their actual existence,
than the positive statements which have hitherto weighed
with the public mind in favour of their existence. A
larger body of evidence from eye-witnesses might be got
together in proof of ghosts than of the sea-serpent." *

Such was the explanation of the deposed facts offered
by the ablest of living physiologists. Coming as it did
from such a quarter, and supported by so much intrinsic
reason, it is not surprising, that, although the romance
was sadly shorn away, most persons were willing to
acquiesce in the decision.

Captain M'Quhæ, however, promptly replied to Professor
Owen :—" I now assert, neither was it a common seal,
nor a sea-elephant ; its great length, and its totally differing physiognomy precluding the possibility of its being
a *Phoca* of any species. The head was flat, and not a
' capacious vaulted cranium ;' nor had it ' a stiff inflexible
trunk '—a conclusion to which Professor Owen has
jumped, most certainly not justified by the simple statement, that no ' portion of the sixty feet seen by us was

* The *Times,* of November 11, 1848.

used in propelling it through the water, either by vertical
or horizontal undulation.'

"It is also assumed that the 'calculation of its length
was made under a strong preconception of the nature of
the beast; another conclusion quite the contrary to the
fact. It was not until after the great length was developed
by its nearest approach to the ship, and until after that
most important point had been duly considered and
debated, as well as such could be in the brief space of
time allowed for so doing, that it was pronounced to be a
serpent by all who saw it, and who are too well accustomed
to judge of lengths and breadths of objects in the sea to
mistake a real substance and an actual living body, coolly
and dispassionately contemplated, at so short a distance
too, for the 'eddy caused by the action of the deeper
immersed fins and tail of a rapidly-moving gigantic seal
raising its head above the water,' as Professor Owen
imagines, in quest of its lost iceberg.

"The creative powers of the human mind may be very
limited. On this occasion they were not called into
requisition; my purpose and desire being, throughout, to
furnish eminent naturalists, such as the learned Professor,
with accurate facts, and not with exaggerated representations, nor with what could by any possibility proceed
from optical illusion; and I beg to assure him that old
Pontoppidan's having clothed his sea-serpent with a mane
could not have suggested the idea of ornamenting the
creature seen from the *Dædalus* with a similar appendage,
for the simple reason that I had never seen his account,

or even heard of his sea-serpent, until my arrival in London. Some other solution must therefore be found for the very remarkable coincidence between us in that particular, in order to unravel the mystery.

" Finally, I deny the existence of excitement, or the possibility of optical illusion. I adhere to the statements, as to form, colour, and dimensions, contained in my official report to the Admiralty ; and I leave them as data whereupon the learned and scientific may exercise the 'pleasures of imagination' until some more fortunate opportunity shall occur of making a closer acquaintance with the 'great unknown' — in the present instance assuredly no ghost." *

A few months later, the following letter appeared in the *Bombay Bi-monthly Times* for January 1849. It is a very valuable testimony :—

" I see, in your paper of the 30th December, a paragraph in which a doubt is expressed of the authenticity of the account given by Captain M'Quhæ of the 'great sea-serpent.' When returning to India, in the year 1829, I was standing on the poop of the *Royal Saxon*, in conversation with Captain Petrie, the commander of that ship. We were at a considerable distance south-west of the Cape of Good Hope, in the usual track of vessels to this country, going rapidly along (seven or eight knots) in fine smooth water. It was in the middle of the day, and the other passengers were at luncheon ; the man at the wheel, a steerage passenger, and ourselves, being the only

---

* The *Times*, November 21, 1848.

persons on the poop. Captain Petrie and myself, at the same instant, were literally fixed in astonishment by the appearance, a short distance ahead, of an animal of which no more generally correct description could be given than that by Captain M'Quhæ. It passed within thirty-five yards of the ship, without altering its course in the least; but as it came right abreast of us, it slowly turned its head towards us. Apparently about one-third of the upper part of its body was above water, in nearly its whole length, and we could see the water curling up on its breast as it moved along, but by what means it moved we could not perceive. We watched it going astern with intense interest until it had nearly disappeared, when my companion, turning to me with a countenance expressive of the utmost astonishment, exclaimed, 'Good heavens! what can that be?' It was strange that we never thought of calling the party engaged at luncheon to witness the extraordinary sight we had seen; but the fact is, we were so absorbed in it ourselves, that we never spoke, and scarcely moved, until it had nearly disappeared. Captain Petrie, a superior and most intelligent man, has since perished in the exercise of his profession. Of the fate of the others then on deck I am ignorant; so the story rests on my own unsupported word, but I pledge that word to its correctness. Professor Owen's supposition, that the animal seen by the officers of the *Dædalus* was a gigantic seal, I believe to be incorrect, because we saw this apparently similar creature in its whole length, with the exception of a small portion of the tail, which was under water; and, by comparing its length with that of the *Royal Saxon*, (about six hundred feet,) when exactly alongside in passing, we calculated it to be in that, as well as in its other dimensions, greater than the animal described by Captain M'Quhæ. Should the foregoing account be of any interest to you, it is at your service; it is an old story, but a true one. I am not quite sure of our latitude and longitude at the time, nor do I exactly remember the date, but it was about the end of July.— R. DAVIDSON, *Superintending Surgeon, Nagpore Subsidiary Force, Kamptee, 3d January*, 1849."

In the year 1852, the testimony of British officers was again given to the existence of an enormous marine animal of serpent form. The descriptions, however, shew great discrepancy with that of the creature seen from the *Dædalus*, and cannot be considered confirmatory of the former account, otherwise than as proving that immense unrecognised creatures of elongate form roam the ocean.

Two distinct statements of the incident were published, which I cite from the *Zoologist* (p. 3756); but one of them had already appeared in *The Times*.

Lieutenant-Colonel Thomas Steele, of the Coldstream Guards, thus writes:—

" I have lately received the following account from my brother, Captain Steele, 9th Lancers, who, on his way out to India in the *Barham*, saw the sea-serpent. Thinking it might be interesting to you, as corroborating the account of the *Dædalus*, I have taken the liberty of sending you the extract from my brother's letter:—' On the

28th of August, in long. 40° E., lat. 37° 16' S., about half-past two, we had all gone down below to get ready for dinner, when the first mate called us on deck to see a most extraordinary sight. About five hundred yards from the ship there was the head and neck of an enormous snake; we saw about sixteen or twenty feet out of the water, and he *spouted* a long way from his head; down his back he had a crest like a cock's comb, and was going very slowly through the water, but left a wake of about fifty or sixty feet, as if dragging a long body after him. The captain put the ship off her course to run down to him, but as we approached him, he went down. His colour was green, with light spots. *He was seen by every one on board.'* My brother is no naturalist, and I think this is the first time the monster has been ever seen to spout."

The second statement is contained in a letter from one of the officers of the ship :—

" You will be surprised to hear that we have actually seen the great sea-serpent, about which there has been so much discussion. Information was given by a sailor to the captain just as we were going to dinner. I was in my cabin at the time, and from the noise and excitement, I thought the ship was on fire. I rushed on deck, and on looking over the side of the vessel I saw a most wonderful sight, which I shall recollect as long as I live. His head appeared to be about sixteen feet above the water, and he kept moving it up and down, sometimes shewing his enormous neck, which was surmounted with a huge crest

Y

in the shape of a saw. It was surrounded by hundreds of birds, and we at first thought it was a dead whale. He left a track in the water like the wake of a boat, and from what we could see of his head and part of his body, we were led to think he must be about sixty feet in length, but he might be more. The captain kept the vessel away to get nearer to him, and when we were within a hundred yards he slowly sank into the depths of the sea. While we were at dinner he was seen again."

Mr Alfred Newton, of Elveden Hall, an excellent and well-known naturalist, adds the guarantee of his personal acquaintance with one of the recipients of the above letters.*

If it were not for the spouting—which is not mentioned by one observer, and may possibly have been an illusion—I should be inclined to think that this may have been one of the scabbard-fishes, specimens of which inhabit the ocean of immense size. They carry a high serrated dorsal fin, and swim with the head out of water.†

On the 19th February 1849, Mr Herriman, commander of the British ship *Brazilian*, sailed from the Cape of Good Hope, and on the 24th was becalmed almost exactly in the spot where Captain M'Quhæ had seen his monster.

"About eight o'clock on that morning, whilst the

* I note this, because discredit has been undeservedly cast on the phenomena observed, by foolish fabulous stories having been published under fictitious names, for the purpose of *hoaxing.*

† See Colonel Montagu's account, in Yarrell's *British Fishes*, vol. i., p. 199, (edit. 1841.)

captain was surveying the calm, heavy, rippleless swell of
the sea through his telescope, the ship at the same time
heading N.N.W., he perceived something right abeam,
about half a mile to the westward, stretched along the
water to the length of about twenty-five or thirty feet, and
perceptibly moving from the ship with a steady, sinuous
motion. The head, which seemed to be lifted several feet
above the waters, had something resembling a mane, running down to the floating portion, and within about six
feet of the tail it forked out into a sort of double fin.
Having read at Colombo the account of the monster said
to have been seen by Captain M'Quhæ in nearly the same
latitude, Mr Herriman was led to suppose that he had
fallen in with the same animal, or one of the genus; he
immediately called his chief officer, Mr Long, with several of the passengers, who, after surveying the object for
some time, came to the unanimous conclusion that it
must be the sea-serpent seen by Captain M'Quhæ. As
the *Brazilian* was making no headway, Mr Herriman,
determining to bring all doubts to an issue, had a boat
lowered down, and taking two hands on board, together
with Mr Boyd of Peterhead, near Aberdeen, one of the
passengers, who acted as steersman under the direction of
the captain, they approached the monster, Captain Herriman standing on the bow of the boat armed with a har-
poon, to commence the onslaught. The combat, however,
was not attended with the danger which those on board
apprehended, for on coming close to the object it was
found to be nothing more than an immense piece of sea-

weed, evidently detached from a coral reef, and drifting with the current, which sets constantly to the westward in this latitude, and which, together with the swell left by the subsidence of the gale, gave it the sinuous, snake-like motion.

"But for the calm, which afforded Captain Herriman an opportunity of examining the weed, we should have had another 'eye-witness' account of the great sea-serpent, —Mr Herriman himself admitting that he should have remained under the impression that he had seen it. What appeared to be head, crest, and mane of the *immensum volumen*, was but the large root which floated upwards, and to which several pieces of the coral reef still adhered. The captain had it hauled on board, but, as it began to decay, was compelled to throw it over. He now regrets that he had not preserved it in a water-butt for the purpose of exhibition in the Thames, where the conflicting motion produced by the tide and steamers would in all probability give it a like appearance.*

A new and unexpected interpretation was thus given to the observed phenomena; an interpretation which has been recently revived. For a statement published in *The Times* of February 5, 1858, by Captain Harrington of the ship *Castilian*, brought out another witness on the sea-weed hypothesis.

The statement alluded to was couched in the form of an extract from a Meteorological Journal kept on board the ship, the original of which was sent to the Board of

* *Sun,* July 9, 1849.

Trade. It was authenticated by Captain Harrington, and his chief and second officers.

" Ship *Castilian*, Dec. 12, 1857; N.E. end of St Helena, distant ten miles.   At 6·30 P.M., strong breezes and cloudy, ship sailing about twelve miles per hour.   While myself and officers were standing on the lee side of the poop, looking towards the island, we were startled by the sight of a huge marine animal, which reared its head out of the water within twenty yards of the ship, when it suddenly disappeared for about half a minute, and then made its appearance in the same manner again, shewing us distinctly its neck and head about ten or twelve feet ·out of the water.   Its head was shaped like a long nun buoy, and I suppose the diameter to have been seven or eight feet in the largest part, with a kind of scroll, or tuft of loose skin, encircling it about two feet from the top ; the water was discoloured for several hundred feet from its head, so much so, that, on its first appearance, my impression was that the ship was in broken water, produced, as I supposed, by some volcanic agency since the last time I passed the island, but the second appearance completely dispelled those fears, and assured us that it was a monster of extraordinary length, which appeared to be moving slowly towards the land,   The ship was going too fast to enable us to reach the mast-head in time to form a correct estimate of its extreme length, but from what we saw from the deck, we conclude that it must have been over two hundred feet long.   The boatswain and several of the

crew who observed it from the top-gallant forecastle, state
that it was more than double the length of the ship, in
which case it must have been five hundred feet; be that
as it may, I am convinced that it belonged to the serpent
tribe; it was of a dark colour about the head, and was
covered with several white spots. Having a press of
canvas on the ship at the time, I was unable to round to
without risk, and therefore was precluded from getting
another sight of this leviathan of the deep.

> " GEORGE HENRY HARRINGTON, Commander.
> WILLIAM DAVIES, Chief Officer.
> EDWARD WHEELER, Second Officer."

This document was immediately answered by Captain
Fred. Smith, of the ship *Pekin*, in the following announce-
ment :—·

" On Dec. 28, 1848, being then in lat. 26° S., long. 6° E.,
nearly calm, saw about half a mile on port beam, a very
extraordinary-looking thing in the water, of considerable
length. With the telescope we could plainly discern a
huge head and neck, covered with a long shaggy-looking
kind of mane, which it kept lifting at intervals out of the
water. This was seen by all hands, and declared to be
the great sea-serpent. I determined on knowing something about it, and accordingly lowered a boat, in which
my chief officer and four men went, taking with them a
long small line in case it should be required. I watched
them very anxiously, and the monster seemed not to regard
their approach. At length they got close to the head.

They seemed to hesitate, and then busy themselves with the line, the monster all the time ducking its head, and shewing its great length. Presently the boat began pulling towards the ship, the monster following slowly. In about half an hour they got alongside; a tackle was got on the mainyard and it was hoisted on board. It appeared somewhat supple when hanging, but so completely covered with snaky-looking barnacles, about eighteen inches long, that we had it some time on board before it was discovered to be a piece of gigantic seaweed, twenty feet long, and four inches diameter; the root end appeared when in the water like the head of an animal, and the motion given by the sea caused it to seem alive. In a few days it dried up to a hollow tube, and as it had rather an offensive smell was thrown overboard. I had only been a short time in England when the *Dædalus* arrived and reported having seen the great sea-serpent,—to the best of my recollection near the same locality, and which I have no doubt was a piece of the same weed. So like a huge living monster did this appear, that had circumstances prevented my sending a boat to it, I should certainly have believed I had seen the great sea-snake."

The last imputation called up "An officer of H.M.S. *Dædalus*," whose testimony puts *hors de combat* the seaweed hypothesis in that renowned case. I need not give it at length, the following sentences sufficing:—"The object seen from H.M. ship was, beyond all question, a living animal, moving rapidly through the water against

a cross sea, and within five points of a fresh breeze, with
such velocity that the water was surging under its chest,
as it passed along at a rate probably of ten miles per
hour. Captain M'Quhæ's first impulse was to tack in
pursuit, . . . but he reflected that we could neither lay up
for it nor overhaul it in speed.   There was nothing to be
done, therefore, but to observe it as accurately as we could
with our glasses, as it came up under our lee quarter and
passed away to windward, at its nearest position being
not more than two hundred yards from us ; *the eye, the
mouth, the nostril, the colour and form, all being most
distinctly visible to us.* . . . My impression was that it
was rather of a lizard than a serpentine character, as its
movement was steady and uniform, *as if propelled by fins,*
not by any undulatory power." *

Further correspondence ensued, but no additional light
of any importance was shed on the matter, except that
Captain Smith stated that the diameter of his sea-weed
capture in the water, before it was " divested of its extraordinary-looking living appendages," was three feet.

———

A large mass of evidence has been accumulated ; and
I now set myself to examine it.   In so doing, I shall
eliminate from the inquiry, all the testimony of Norwegian
eye-witnesses, that obtained in Massachusetts in 1817,
and various statements made by French and American
captains since.   Confining myself to *English* witnesses
of known character and position, most of them being

* The *Times* of Feb. 16, 1858.

officers under the crown, I have adduced the following testimonies :—

1. That of five British officers, who saw the animal at Halifax, N.S., in 1833.

2. That of Captain M'Quhæ and his officers, who saw it from the *Dædalus* in 1848.

3. That of Captain Beechey, who saw something similar from the *Blossom.*

4. That of Mr Morries Stirling, who saw it in a Norwegian fjord.

5. That of Mr Davidson, who saw it from the *Royal Saxon*, in 1829.

6. That of Captain Steele and others, who saw it from the *Barham*, in 1852.

7. That of Captain Harrington and his officers, who saw it from the *Castilian*, in 1857.

Carefully comparing these independent narratives, we have a creature possessing the following characteristics :

1. The general form of a serpent (1, 2, 3,* 4, 5, 6, 7).

2. Great length, say above sixty feet, (1, 2, 5, 6, 7†).

3. Head considered to resemble that of a serpent, (1, 2, 5, 6, 7 ‡).

4. Neck from twelve to sixteen inches in diameter, (1, § 2, 4, 5).

---

* Captain Beechey's view was too momentary to be of much value; the object he saw he compares to the trunk of a tree, which, so far as it goes, agrees with the serpent shape.

† From two hundred to five hundred feet (7).

‡ " Like a long nun-buoy" (7).

§ " That of a moderate-sized tree" (1).

5. Appendages on the head (7), neck (6). or back (2, 5), resembling a crest or mane. (Considerable discrepancy in details.)

6. Colour dark brown (1, 2, 5, 7), or green (6) ; streaked or spotted with white (1, 2, 5, 6, 7).

7. Swims at surface of the water (1, 2, 3, 4, 5, 6, 7), with a rapid (1, 2, 5), or slow (4, 6, 7), movement; the head and neck projected and elevated above the surface (1, 2, 5, 6, 7).

8. Progression steady and uniform ; the body straight (2, 5, 6), but capable of being thrown into convolutions (4).

9. Spouts in the manner of a whale (6).

To which of the recognised classes of created beings can this huge rover of the ocean be referred? And, first, is it an animal at all? That there are immense algæ in the ocean, presenting some of the characters described, has been already shewn ; and on two occasions an object supposed to be the "sea-serpent" proved on examination to be but a sea-weed floating ; the separated and inverted roots of which, projecting in the roll of the swell, seemed a head, and the fronds (in the one case) and (in the other) a number of attached barnacles, resembled a shaggy mane washed about in the water.

But surely it must have been a very dim and indistinct view of the floating and ducking object, which could have mistaken this for a living animal ;* and it would be

* The distance is estimated at half a mile on both occasions. (See the accounts of Captains Herriman and Smith.)

absurd in the highest degree to presume that of such a
nature could be the creatures, going rapidly through the
water at ten or twelve miles an hour, with the head and
neck elevated, so distinctly seen by Captain M'Quhæ and
Mr Davidson, the former at two hundred, the latter at
thirty-five yards' distance. We may fairly dismiss the
sea-weed hypothesis.

Among animals, the *Vertebrata* are the only classes
supposable. But of these, which? Birds are out of the
question ;—but *Mammalia, Reptilia, Pisces,*—there is
no antecedent absurdity in assigning it to either of these.
Each of these classes contains species of lengthened form,
of vast dimensions, of pelagic habit ; and to each has
the creature been, by different authorities, assigned.

Let us, then, look at the *Mammalia.* Here Professor
Owen would place it ; and his opinion on a zoological
question has almost the force of an axiom. I trust I shall
not be accused of presumption if I venture to examine
the decision of one whom I so greatly respect. It is true,
his reasoning applies directly only to the creature seen
from the *Dædalus;* but we are bound to consider the
exigencies not only of that celebrated case, but of all the
other well-authenticated cases.

Professor Owen thus draws up the characters of the
animal:—" Head with a *convex, moderately capacious
cranium,* short obtuse-muzzle, *gape not extending further
than the eye ;* eye rather small, round, *filling closely the
palpebral aperture ;* colour dark brown above, yellowish
white beneath ; surface smooth, *without scales, scutes,* or

other conspicuous modifications of hard and naked cuticle, nostrils not mentioned, but indicated in the drawing by *a crescentic mark at the end of the nose or muzzle ;* body long, dark brown, not undulating, without dorsal or other apparent fins ;—'but something like the mane of a horse, or rather a bunch of sea-weed washed about its back.'"

The earlier of these characters are those " of the head of a warm-blooded mammal ; none of them those of a cold-blooded reptile or fish." The comparison of the dimly-seen something on the back to a horse's mane or sea-weed, seems to indicate a clothing of hair ; and, guided by this interpretation, the Professor judges that the animal was not a cetacean, but rather a great seal.

Now, it is manifest that it was from the pictorial sketches, more than from the verbal description of Captain M'Quhæ, that this diagnosis was drawn up. And if the drawings had been made *from the life,* under the direction of a skilful zoologist, nothing could be more legitimate than such a use of them. But surely it has been overlooked that they were made under no such circumstances. Only one of the published representations was original ; and this was taken "immediately *after* the animal was seen." * That is, one of the officers, who could draw, went below immediately, and attempted to reproduce what his eye was still filled with. Now, what

---

* The enlarged view of the head was no doubt made up from one of the other drawings expressly for the *Illustrated London News,* and therefore claims no independent value.

could one expect under such conditions? Of course, the
artist was not a zoologist, or we should have had a
zoologist's report. Would the drawing so produced be of
any value? Surely yes; of great value. It would doubtless be a tolerably faithful representation of the *general
appearance* of the object seen, but nothing more; its
form, and position, and colour, and *such* of the details *as
the observer had distinctly noticed, and marked down,*
so to speak, *in his mind,* would be given; but a great
deal of the details would be put in by mere guess.
When a person draws from an object before him, he
measures the various lines, curves, angles, relative dis-
tances, and so on, with his eye, one by one, and puts them
down *seriatim;* ever looking at the part of the original
on which he is working, for correction. But no possibility
of doing this was open to the artistic midshipman; he
had merely his vivid, but necessarily vague, idea of the
whole before him as the original from which he drew.
Who is there that could carry all the details of an object
in the memory, after a few minutes' gaze, and that, too,
under strong excitement? This was not the case even of
a cool professional artist, called in to view an object for
the purpose of depicting it; in all probability the officer
had not thought of sketching it till all was over, and
had made no precise observations, his mind being mainly
occupied by wonder. He sits down, pencil in hand; he
dashes in the general outline at once; now he comes to
details,—say the muzzle, the facial angle;—of course, his
figure must have *some* facial angle, *some* outline of

muzzle ; but probably he had not particularly noticed that point. What shall he do? there is no original before him, a glance at which would decide ; he sketches on a scrap of paper by his side two or three forms of head ; perhaps he shews the paper to a brother officer, with a question, " Which of these do you think most like the head?" and then he puts the one selected in his sketch, and so of other details.

Those who are not used to drawing will think I am making a caricature. I am doing no such thing. I have been accustomed for nearly forty years to draw animals from the life; and the public are able to judge of my power of representing what I see ; but I am quite sure that if I were asked to depict an object unfamiliar to me, which I had been looking at for a quarter of an hour, without thinking that 1 should have to draw it, I should do, in fifty points of detail, just what I have supposed the officer to have done. Let my reader try it. Get hold of one of your acquaintances, whom you know to be a skilful, but non-professional artist, whose attention has never been given to flowers ; take him into your green-house, and shew him some very beautiful thing in blossom; keep him looking at it for some ten minutes without a hint of what you are thinking of, then take him into your drawing-room, put paper and colours before him, and say, " Make me a sketch of that plant you have just seen!" When it is done, take it to a botanist, and ask him to give you the characters of the genus and species from the sketch ; or compare it yourself with the original, and note how many and what ludicrous blunders had been made in details, while there was a fair general correctness.

Viewed in this light, it will be manifest how inefficient the sketch made on board the *Dædalus* must be for minute characters ; and particularly those which in the diagnosis above I have marked with italics. Yet these are the characters mainly relied on to prove the mammalian nature of the animal. Some of these characters could not possibly have been determined at two hundred yards' distance. I say "*mainly* relied on ;" because there is the mane-like appendage yet to be accounted for. This is a strong point certainly in favour of a mammalian, and of a phocal nature ; whether it decides the question, however, I will presently examine.

The head in either of the large sketches (those, I mean, in which the creature is represented in the sea) does not appear to me at all to resemble that of a seal ; nor do I see a "vaulted cranium." The summit of the head does not rise above the level of the summit of the neck ; in other words, the *vertical* diameter of the head and neck are equal, while there are indications that the occiput considerably exceeds the neck in *transverse* diameter. This is not the case with any seal, but it is eminently characteristic of eels, of many serpents, and some lizards. Let the reader compare the lower figure (*Illustrated London News*, Oct. 28, 1848) with that of the Broad-nosed Eel in Yarrell's *British Fishes*, (Ed. ii., vol. ii., p. 396.) The head of some of the scincoid lizards (the

Jamaican *Celestus occiduus*, for instance) is not at all
unlike that represented ; it is full as vaulted, and as short,
but a little more pointed, and with a flatter facial angle.
On this point the Captain's assertion corrects the drawing;
for in reply to Professor Owen he distinctly asserts that
"the head was *flat*, and not a capacious vaulted cranium;"
and the description of Lieutenant Drummond, *published
before any strictures were made on the point*, says,
"the head : . . . was long, pointed, and flattened at
the top, perhaps ten feet in length, the upper jaw projecting considerably."

With regard to the "mane." The great *Phoca proboscidea* is the only seal which will bear comparison with
the *Dædalus* animal in dimensions, reaching from twenty
to thirty feet. H. M. officers declare that upwards of
sixty feet of their animal were visible at the surface ; but
Mr Owen supposes, not improbably, that the disturbance
of the water produced by progression induced an illusive
appearance of a portion of this length. But how much ?
Suppose all behind thirty feet, the extreme length of the
elephant seal. Then it is impossible the animal could
have been such a seal, for the following reason. The
fore paws of the seal are placed at about one-third of the
total length from the muzzle ; that is, in a seal of thirty
feet long, at ten feet behind the muzzle. But *twenty* feet
of the "serpent" were projected from the water, and yet
no appearance of fins was seen. Lieutenant Drummond
judges the head to have been ten feet in length (with
which the lower figure, assuming sixty or sixty-five feet

as the total length drawn, well agrees;) and besides this, at least an equal length of neck was exposed.

But the great *Phoca proboscidea* has no *mane* at all. For this, we must have recourse to other species, known as sea-lions. Two kinds are recognised under this name, *Otaria jubata* and *Platyrhynchus leoninus ;* though there is some confusion in the names. Neither of these ever exceeds sixteen feet in total length, of which, about five feet would be the utmost that could project from the water in swimming. Suppose, however, the eyes of the gallant officers to have magnified the leonine seal to sufficient dimensions; I fear even then it will not do. For the mane in these animals is a lengthening and thickening of the hair on the occiput and on the neck, just as in the lion. But the "serpent's" mane was not there, but "perhaps twenty feet in the rear of the head," says Lieutenant Drummond; it "washed about its back," says Captain M'Quhæ.

I do not hesitate to say, therefore, that on data we at present possess the seal hypothesis appears to me quite untenable.

It is by no means impossible that the creature may prove to belong to the *Cetacea* or whale tribe. I know of no reason why a slender and lengthened form should not exist in this order. The testimony of Colonel Steele, who represents his animal as spouting, points in this direction.

As to its place among Fishes, Dr Mantell and Mr Melville* consider that the *Dædalus* animal may have

* See *Zoologist*, p. 2310.

Z

been one of the sharks; and there is no doubt that the celebrated Stronsa animal, which was considered by Dr Barclay as the Norwegian sea-serpent, was really the *Selache maxima* or basking shark.   But the identification of Captain M'Quhæ's figure and description with a shark is preposterous.

There are, however, the ribbon-fishes; and some of these, as the hair-tail, the *Vaegmaer*, and the *Gymnetrus*, are of large size, and slender sword-like form.   Several kinds have been found in the North Atlantic, and wherever seen they invariably excite wonder and curiosity.   All of these are furnished with a back-fin; but in other respects they little correspond with the descriptions of the animal in question.   One of their most striking characteristics, moreover, is, that their surface resembles polished steel or silver.

A far greater probability exists, that there may be some oceanic species of the eel tribe, of gigantic dimensions.   Our own familiar conger is found ten feet in length.   Certainly, Captain M'Quhæ's figures remind me strongly of an eel; supposing the pectorals to be either so small as to be inconspicuous at the distance at which the animal was seen, or to be placed more than commonly far back.

To the Reptiles, however, popular opinion has pretty uniformly assigned this denizen of the sea; and his accepted title of "sea-serpent" sufficiently indicates his zoological affinities in the estimation of the majority of those who believe in him.   Let us, then, test his claims to be a serpent.

The marine habit presents no difficulty. For, in the Indian and Pacific Oceans, there are numerous species of true snakes (*Hydrophidæ*), which are exclusively inhabitants of the sea. They are reported to remain much at the sur'ace, and even to sleep so soundly there that the passing of a ship through a group sometimes fails to awaken them.

None of these are known to exceed a few feet in length, and, so far as we know, none of them have been found in the Atlantic. It is remarkable, however, that a record exists of a serpent having been seen in the very midst of the North Atlantic. The *Zoologist* (p. 1911) has published a communication signed, "S. H. Saxby, Bonchurch, Isle of Wight," containing an extract from the log-book of a very near relative, dated August 1, 1786, on board the ship *General Coole*, in latitude 42° 44′ N., and longitude 23° 10′ W.; that is, a little to the northeast of the Azores. It is as follows:—"A very large *snake* passed the ship: it appeared to be about sixteen or eighteen feet in length, and three or four feet in circumference; the back of a lightish colour, and the belly thereof yellow." According to the log, the ship was becalmed at the time. Mr Saxby vouches for the correctness of the statement, and adds, that any one is welcome to see the original record. It augments very considerably the value of this incident, that no suggestion of identity with the Norwegian dragon appears to have occurred to the observer: he speaks of it as "a snake," and nothing more; the dimensions alone appear to have excited surprise, "sixteen or eighteen feet," and these are by no means extravagant.

On the whole, I am disposed to accept this case as that of a true serpent—perhaps the *Boa murina,* one of the largest known, and of very aquatic habits—carried out to sea by one of the great South American rivers, and brought by the gulf stream to the spot where it was seen. If I am warranted in this conclusion, it affords us no help in the identification of the *great unknown.*

I do not attach much value to the assertions of observers, that the head of the animal seen by them respectively was "undoubtedly that of a snake." Such comparisons made by persons unaccustomed to mark the characteristic peculiarities which distinguish one animal from another, are vague and unsatisfactory. Their value, at all events, is rather negative than positive. For example; if a person of liberal education and general information, but no naturalist, were to tell me he had seen a creature with a head "exactly like that of a snake;" I should understand him, that the head was not that of an ordinary beast, nor of a bird, nor that of the generality of fishes; but I should have no confidence at all that it was not as like that of a lizard as of a serpent; and should entertain doubts whether, if I shewed him the form of head, even of certain fishes, he would not say,—"Yes, it was something like *that.*"

There does not seem, then, any sufficient evidence that the colossal animal seen from the *Dædalus,* and on other occasions, is a serpent, in the sense in which zoologists use that term. A lengthened cylindrical form it seems to have; but, for anything that appears, it may as well be a monstrous eel, or a slender cetacean, as anything. All analogies and probabilities are against its being an ophidian.

It yet remains to consider the hypothesis advanced by Mr E. Newman, Mr Morries Stirling, and "F. G. S.,"[*] that the so-called sea-serpent will find its closest affinities with those extraordinary animals, the *Enaliosauria*, or Marine Lizards, whose fossil skeletons are found so abundantly scattered through the oolite and the lias. The figure of *Plesiosaurus*, as restored in Professor Ansted's *Ancient World* has a cranium not less capacious or vaulted than that given in Captain M'Quhæ's figures; to which, indeed, but that the muzzle in the latter is more abbreviate, it bears a close resemblance. The head was fixed at the extremity of a neck, composed of thirty to forty vertebræ, which, from its extraordinary length, slenderness, and flexibility, must have been the very counterpart of the body of a serpent. This snake-like neck merged insensibly into a compact and moderately slender body, which carried two pairs of paddles, very much like those of a sea-turtle, and terminated behind in a gradually attenuated tail.

Thus, if the *Plesiosaur* could have been seen alive, you would have discerned nearly its total length at the surface of the water, propelled at a rapid rate, without any undulation, by an apparatus altogether invisible,—the powerful paddles beneath; while the entire serpentine

[*] See *supra*, pp 318, 320.

neck would probably be projected obliquely, carrying the reptilian head, with an eye of moderate aperture, and a mouth whose gape did not extend behind the eye. Add to this a covering of the body not formed of scales, bony plates, or other form of solidified integument, but a yielding, leathery skin, probably black and smooth, like that of a whale; give the creature a length of some sixty feet or more, and you would have before you almost the very counterpart of the apparition that wrought such amazement on board the *Dædalus*. The position of the nostrils at the summit of the head indicates, that, on first coming to the surface from the depths of the sea, the animal would spout in the manner of the whales,—a circumstance reported by some observers of the sea-serpent.

I must confess that I am myself far more disposed to acquiesce in this hypothesis than in any other that has been mooted. Not that I would identify the animals seen with the actual *Plesiosaurs* of the lias. None of them yet discovered appear to exceed thirty-five feet in length, which is scarcely half sufficient to meet the exigencies of the case. I should not look for any species, scarcely even any genus, to be perpetuated from the oolitic period to the present. Admitting the actual continuation of the order *Enaliosauria*, it would be, I think, quite in conformity with general analogy to find important generic modifications, probably combining some salient features of several extinct forms. Thus the little known *Pliosaur* had many of the peculiarities of the *Plesiosaur*, without its extraordinarily elongated neck, while it vastly

exceeded it in dimensions. What if the existing form should be essentially a *Plesiosaur*, with the colossal magnitude of a *Pliosaur* ?

There seems to be no real structural difficulty in such a supposition except the " mane," or waving appendage, which has so frequently been described by those who profess to have seen the modern animal. This, however, is a difficulty of ignorance, rather than of contradiction. We do not *know* that the smooth integument of the *Enaliosaurs* was destitute of any such appendage, and I do not think there is any insuperable improbability in the case. The nearest analogy that I can suggest, however, is that of the *Chlamydosaur*, a large terrestrial lizard of Australia, whose lengthened neck is furnished with a very curious plaited frill of thin membrane, extending like wings or fins to a considerable distance from the animal.*

Two strong objections, however, stand in the way of our acceptance of the present existence of *Enaliosauria;* and these are forcibly presented by Professor Owen. They are,—1. The hypothetical improbability of such forms having been transmitted from the era of the secondary strata to the present time; and, 2. The entire absence of any parts of the carcases or unfossilised skeletons of such animals in museums.

My ignorance of the details of palæontology makes me

---

* It was not till after this paragraph was written that I noticed the very close similarity of the fins with which Hans Egede has adorned his figure of the sea-serpent, (copied in the *Illustrated London News*, Oct. 28, 1848,) to the frill of the *Chlamydosaurus.*

feel very diffident in attempting to touch the former point, especially when so great an authority has pronounced an opinion; still I will modestly express one or two thoughts on it.

There does not seem any *à priori* reason why early forms should not be perpetuated; and examples are by no means rare of animals much anterior, geologically, to the *Enaliosaurs*, being still extant. The very earliest forms of fishes are of the *Placoïd* type, and it is remarkable, that not only is that type still living in considerable numbers, but the most gigantic examples of this class belong to it,—viz., the sharks and rays; and these exhibiting peculiarities which by no means remove them far from ancient types. The genus *Chimœra* appears in the oolite, the wealden, and the chalk; disappears (or rather is not found) in any of the tertiary formations, but reappears, somewhat rarely, in the modern seas. It is represented by two species inhabiting respectively the Arctic and Antarctic Oceans.

Now, this is exactly a parallel case to what is conjectured of the *Enaliosaurs*. They appear in the oolite and the chalk, are not found in the tertiary strata, but reappear, rarely, in the modern seas, represented by two or more species inhabiting the Northern and Southern Oceans.

Among Reptiles, the curious family of river tortoises named *Trionychidœ*, distinguished by their long neck, and a broad cartilaginous margin to the small back-shell, appears first in the wealden. No traces occur of it in any subsequent formation, till the present period, when we find it represented by the large and savage inhabitants of the Mississippi, the Nile, and the Ganges.

What is still more to the purpose is, that the *Iguanodon*, a vast saurian which was contemporary with the *Plesiosaur* and *Ichthyosaur*, though transmitting no observed representative of its form through the tertiary era, is yet well represented by the existing *Iguanadæ* of the American tropics.

It is true the *Iguana* is not an *Iguanodon;* but the forms are closely allied. I do not suppose that the so-called sea-serpent is an actual *Plesiosaur,* but an animal bearing a similar relation to that ancient type. The *Iguanodon* has degenerated (I speak of the type, and not of the species) to the small size of the *Iguana;* the *Plesiosaurus* may have become developed to the gigantic dimensions of the sea-serpent.

A correspondent of the *Zoologist* (p. 2395) adduces the great authority of Professor Agassiz to the possibility of the present existence of the *Enaliosaurian* type. That eminent palæontologist is represented as saying, that "it would be in precise conformity with analogy that such an animal should exist in the American seas, as he had found numerous instances in which the fossil forms of the Old World were represented by living types in the New. He instanced the gar-pike of the Western rivers, and said he had found several instances in his recent visit to Lake Superior, where he had detected several fishes belonging to genera now extinct in Europe."

On this point, however, an actual testimony exists, to which I cannot but attach a very great value. Mr Edward Newman, in the same volume of the *Zoologist* that I have just cited, (p. 2356,) records what he considers "in all respects the most interesting natural-history fact of the present century." It is as follows :—

"Captain the Hon. George Hope states, that, when in H.M.S. *Fly*, in the Gulf of California, the sea being perfectly calm and transparent, he saw at the bottom a large marine animal, with the head and general figure of an alligator,* except that the neck was much longer, and that instead of legs the creature had four large flappers, somewhat like those of turtles, the anterior pair being larger than the posterior. The creature was distinctly visible, and all its movements could be observed with ease. It appeared to be pursuing its prey at the bottom of the sea. Its movements were somewhat serpentine, and an appearance of annulations or ring-like divisions of the body were distinctly perceptible. Captain Hope made this relation in company, and as a matter of conversation. When I heard it from the gentleman to whom it was narrated, I inquired whether Captain Hope was

---

* Mr Marshall, in his interesting "Four Years in Burmah," just published, mentions his having seen an "alligator" *forty-five feet* in length, swimming in the Irawaddy, with the *head and nearly half of the body out of the water.* He is confident that it was travelling at the rate of at least *thirty miles an hour,* and this against a *very strong tide!* What could this have been? Surely no Crocodilian; for the great Gavial, the largest of known Saurians, is little more than one-third of this length. MM. Dumeril and Bibron give the dimensions of the largest on record as 5 met. 40 centim., or about 17½ feet.

acquainted with those remarkable fossil animals, *Ichthyosauri* and *Plesiosauri*, the supposed forms of which so nearly correspond with what he describes as having seen alive, and I cannot find that he had heard of them,—the alligator being the only animal he mentioned as bearing a partial similarity to the creature in question." *

Now, unless this officer was egregiously deceived, he saw an animal which could have been no other than an *Enaliosaur,*—a marine reptile of large size, of sauroid figure, with turtle-like paddles.† It is a pity that no estimate, even approximate, of the dimensions is given ; but as the alligator affords the comparison as to form, it is most probable that there was a general agreement with it in size. This might make it some twelve or fifteen feet in length.

I cannot, then, admit that either the *general* substitution of *Cetacea* for *Enaliosauria* in our era, or the ab-

---

* *Zoologist*, p. 2356.

† Dr J. E. Gray long ago expressed his opinion, that some undescribed form exists, which is intermediate between the tortoises and the serpents. " There is every reason to believe, from general structure, that there exists an affinity between the tortoises and the snakes; but the genus that exactly unites them is at present unknown to European naturalists; which is not astonishing when we consider the immense number of undescribed animals which are daily occurring. Mr Macleay thought that those two orders might be united by means of *Emys longicollis* (the long-necked tortoise) of Shaw; but the family to which this animal belongs appears to be the one which unites this class to the crocodile. If I may be allowed to speculate from the peculiarities of structure which I have observed, I am inclined to think that the union will most probably take place by some newly discovered genera allied to the marine or fluviatile soft-skinned turtles, and the marine serpent." *

* *Synopsis of Gen of Reptiles*, in *Ann. of Philos.*, 1825.

sence of remains of the latter in the tertiary deposits, is sufficient evidence of their non-existence in our seas ; any more than the general replacement of *Placoïd* and *Ganoïd* fishes by the Cycloïds and Ctenoïds, or the absence of the former two from the tertiaries, is proof of *their* present non-existence.

It must not be forgotten, as Mr Darwin has ably insisted, that the specimens we possess of fossil organisms are very far indeed from being a complete series. They are rather fragments accidentally preserved, by favouring circumstances, in an almost total wreck. The *Enaliosauria*, particularly abundant in the secondary epoch, may have become sufficiently scarce in the tertiary to have no representative in these preserved fragmentary collections, and yet not have been absolutely extinct.*

But Professor Owen presses also the absence of any recognised recent remains of such animals. Let us test this evidence first by hypothesis, and then by actual fact.

It may be that a true serpent, with large vesicular lungs, would float when dead, and be liable to be seen by navigators in that condition, or to be washed ashore, where its peculiar skeleton would be sure to attract notice. But, as I have before said, I do not by any means believe that the unknown creature is a *serpent* in the zoological sense. Would a *Plesiosaurus* float when dead ? I think not. It is supposed to have had affinities with the whales.

* I reason as a geologist, on geological premises,—reserving my own convictions on the subject of *prochronism,* which would not affect this argument.

Now, a whale sinks like lead as soon as the blubber is removed; the surface-fat alone causes a whale to float. But we have no warrant for assuming that the *Plesiosaur* was encased in a thick blanket of blubber; no geologist has suggested any such thing, and the long neck forbids it; and if not, doubtless it would sink, and not float, when dead. Therefore the stranding of such a carcase, or the washing ashore of such a skeleton, would most probably be an extremely rare occurrence, even if the animal were as abundant as the sperm-whale; but, on the supposition that the species itself is almost extinct, we ought not to expect such an incident, perhaps, in a thousand years. If we add to this the recollection, how small a portion of the border of the ocean is habitually viewed by persons able to discriminate between the vertebræ of an *Enaliosaur* and those of a *Cetacean*, we shall not, I think, attach great importance to this objection.

The only region of the globe, in which the unknown monster is reputed to be in any sense common, is the coast of Norway. Now this, it is true, is fortunately within the ken of civilised and scientific man; and, confessedly, no enormous ophidian or saurian carcases have ever been recognised on that shore. But the shore of Norway is, perhaps, the least favourable in the world for such a *jetsam*. Such a thing as a sand or shingle beach is scarcely known; the coast is almost exclusively what is called iron-bound; the borders· of the deeply indented fjords rise abruptly out of the sea, so that there is generally from fifty to three hundred fathoms' depth of water within a boat's length of the shore. How could a carcase or a skeleton be cast up here, even if it floated?

But, secondly, as to facts. Is it true, that of all the larger oceanic animals we find the carcases or skeletons cast up on the shore? Is it true even of the *Cetacea*, whose blubber-covered bodies invariably ensure their floating, and whose bones are so saturated with oil that they are but little heavier than water?

In September, 1825, a cetacean was stranded on the French coast which was previously unknown to naturalists. It was so fortunate as to fall under the examination of so eminent an zoologist as De Blainville; and hence its anatomy was well investigated. It has become celebrated as the Toothless Whale of Havre *(Aodon Dalei)*. Yet *no other example of this species is on record;* and, but for this accident, a whale *inhabiting the British Channel* would be quite unrecognised.

Of another whale *(Diodon Sowerbyi), likewise British,* *our entire knowledge rests on a single individual* which was cast on shore on the Elgin coast, and was seen and described by the naturalist Sowerby.

There is a species of sperm-whale *(Physeter tursio)* affirmed to be frequently seen about the Shetland Islands; a vast creature of sixty feet in length, and readily distinguishable from all other *Cetacea* by its lofty dorsal, and, according to old Sibbald, by other remarkable peculiarities in its anatomy. Yet *no specimen of this huge creature has fallen under modern scientific observation;*

and zoologists are not yet agreed among themselves, whether the High-finned Cachalot is a myth or a reality!

M. Rafinesque Smaltz, a Sicilian naturalist, described a Cetacean which, he said, he had seen in the Mediterranean, possessing *two dorsals*. The character was so abnormal that his statement was not received ; but the eminent zoologists attached to one of the French exploring expeditions,—MM. Quoy and Gaimard,—saw a school of cetacea around their ship in the South Pacific, having this extraordinary character,—the supernumerary fin being placed on the back of the head. Here is the evidence of competent naturalists to the existence of a most remarkable whale, *no carcase* of which, *no skeleton, has ever been recognised.*

The last example I shall adduce is from my own experience. During my voyage to Jamaica, when in lat. 19° N., and long. from 46° to 48° W., the ship was surrounded for *seventeen continuous hours* with a troop of whales, of a species which is certainly undescribed. I had ample opportunity for examination, and found that it was a *Delphinorhynchus*, thirty feet in length, black above and white beneath, with the swimming paws white on the upper surface, and isolated by the surrounding black of the upper parts,—a very remarkable character. This could not have been the Toothless Whale of Havre; and there is no other with which it can be confounded. *Here, then, is a whale of large size, occurring in great numbers in the North Atlantic, which on no other occasion has fallen under scientific observation.*

Are not these facts, then, sufficiently weighty to restrain us from rejecting so great an amount of testimony to the so-called sea-serpent, merely on the ground that its dead remains have not come under examination?

In conclusion, I express my own confident persuasion, that there exists some oceanic animal of immense proportions, which has not yet been received into the category of scientific zoology; and my strong opinion, that it possesses close affinities with the fossil *Enaliosauria* of the lias.

INDEX.

2 A

LECTURES ON METAPHYSICS. By SIR WILLIAM HAMILTON With Notes from original materials. 8vo, cloth. $3.00.

LECTURES ON LOGIC. By SIR WILLIAM HAMILTON. With an Appendix, containing the author's latest development of his new Logical theory. 8vo, cloth.

ELEMENTS OF MORAL SCIENCE. By FRANCIS WAYLAND, D. D., late President of Brown University. 12mo, cloth. $1.25.

THE SAME, Abridged for Schools and Academies, half morocco. 50 cents.

ELEMENTS OF POLITICAL ECONOMY. By FRANCIS WAYLAND, D. D. 12mo, cloth. $1.25.

THE SAME, Abridged for Schools and Academies, half morocco. 50 cents.

MENTAL PHILOSOPHY; including the Intellect, the Sensibilities, and the Will. By JOSEPH HAVEN, D. D. 12mo, cloth. $1.50.

MORAL PHILOSOPHY; including Theoretical and Practical Ethics. By JOSEPH HAVEN, D. D. 12mo, cloth. $1.25.

THE EARTH AND MAN; Lectures on Comparative Physical Geography in its relation to the History of Mankind. By ARNOLD GUYOT. 12mo, cloth. $1.25.

THE ELEMENTS OF GEOLOGY; adapted to Schools and Colleges. With numerous Illustrations. By J. R. LOOMIS, President of Lewisburg University. 12mo, cloth. 75 cents.

PRINCIPLES OF ZOÖLOGY; for the use of Schools and Colleges. With numerous Illustrations By LOUIS AGASSIZ and AUGUSTUS A. GOULD. M. D. 12mo, cloth. $1.00.

PALEY'S NATURAL THEOLOGY. Illustrated by forty Plates. Edited by JOHN WARE, M. D. 12mo, cloth. $1.25.

GUYOT'S MURAL MAPS; A series of elegant colored maps, exhibiting the Physical Phenomena of the Globe.

MAP OF THE WORLD, mounted. $10.00

MAP OF NORTH AMERICA, mounted. $9.00.

MAP OF SOUTH AMERICA, mounted. $9.00.

MAP OF GEOGRAPHICAL ELEMENTS, mounted. $9.00

GEOLOGICAL MAP OF THE UNITED STATES AND BRITISH PROVINCES; with Geological Sections and Fossil Plates. By JULES MARCOU. 2 vols., 8vo, cloth. $3.00.

Gould and Lincoln's Publications.

(SCIENTIFIC.)

ANNUAL OF SCIENTIFIC DISCOVERY. 11 vols., from 1850—1860. By D. A. WELLS, A. M. With Portraits of distinguished men. 12mo. $1.25 each.

THE PLURALITY OF WORLDS; a new edition, with the author's reviews of his reviewers. 12mo. $1 00.

COMPARATIVE ANATOMY OF THE ANIMAL KINGDOM. By Profs. SIEBOLD and STANNIUS. Translated by W. I. BURNETT, M. D. 8vo. $3.00

HUGH MILLER'S WORKS. TESTIMONY OF THE ROCKS. With Illustrations. 12mo, cloth. $1.25.

————————————————— *FOOTPRINTS OF THE CREATOR.* With Illustrations. Memoir by LOUIS AGASSIZ. 12mo, cloth. $1.00.

————————————————— *THE OLD RED SANDSTONE.* With Illustrations, etc. 12mo, cloth. $1.25.

————————————————— *MY SCHOOLS AND SCHOOLMASTERS.* An Autobiography. Full-length Portrait of Author. 12mo, cloth. $1 25

————————————————— *FIRST IMPRESSIONS OF ENGLAND AND ITS PEOPLE.* With fine Portrait. 12mo, cloth. $1 00.

————————————————— *CRUISE OF THE BETSEY.* A Ramble among the Fossiliferous Deposits of the Hebrides. 12mo, cloth. $1 25

————————————————— *POPULAR GEOLOGY.* 12mo, cloth. $1.25.

HUGH MILLER'S WORKS, 7 vols., embossed cloth, with box, $8.25.

UNITED STATES EXPLORING EXPEDITION, under CHARLES WILKES. Vol. XII., Mollusca and Shells. By A. A. GOULD, M. D. 4to. $10 00.

LAKE SUPERIOR. Its Physical Character, Vegetation, and Animals. By L. AGASSIZ. 8vo. $3.50.

THE NATURAL HISTORY OF THE HUMAN SPECIES. By C. HAMILTON SMITH. With Elegant Illustrations. With Introduction, containing an abstract of the views of eminent writers on the subject, by S. KNEELAND, M. D. 12mo. $1.25.

THE CAMEL. His organization, habits, and uses, with reference to his introduction into the United States. By GEORGE P. MARSH. 12mo. 63 cents.

INFLUENCE OF THE HISTORY OF SCIENCE UPON INTELLECTUAL EDUCATION. By W. WHEWELL, D. D. 12mo. 25 cents.

SPIRITUALISM TESTED; or, the Facts of its History Classified, and their causes in Nature verified from Ancient and Modern Testimonies. By GEO. W. SAMSON, D. D. 16mo, cloth. 38 cents.

CYCLOPÆDIA OF ANECDOTES OF LITERATURE AND THE FINE ARTS. Containing a copious and choice Selection of Anecdotes of the various forms of Literature, of the Arts, of Architecture, Engravings, Music, Poetry, Painting, and Sculpture, and of the most celebrated Literary Characters and Artists of different Countries and Ages, etc. By KAZLITT ARVINE, A. M. Numerous Illustrations. Octavo, cl. $3.00.

> This is unquestionably the choicest collection of *Anecdotes* ever published. It contains *three thousand and forty Anecdotes:* and such is the wonderful variety, that it will be found an almost inexhaustible fund of interest for every class of readers.

KNOWLEDGE IS POWER. A View of the Productive Forces and the Results of Labor, Capital, and Skill. By CHARLES KNIGHT. With numerous Illustrations. Revised by DAVID A. WELLS. 12mo, cloth. $1.25.

LANDING AT CAPE ANNE; or, The Charter of the First Permanent Colony on the Territory of the Massachusetts Company. By J. WINGATE THORNTON. 8vo, cloth. $1.50.

> ☞ " A rare contribution to the early history of New England."— *Mercantile Journal.*

THE CRUISE OF THE NORTH STAR. Excursion to England, Russia, Denmark, France, Spain, Italy, Malta, Turkey, Madeira, etc. By Rev. JOHN O. CHOULES, D. D. With Illustrations, etc. 12mo, cloth, gilt. $1.50.

PILGRIMAGE TO EGYPT. A Diary of Explorations on the Nile, the Manners, Customs, and Institutions of the People, the condition of the Antiquities and Ruins. By Hon. J. V. C. SMITH. Numerous Engravings. 12mo, cloth. $1.25.

VISITS TO EUROPEAN CELEBRITIES. Graphic and life-like Personal Sketches of the most distinguished men and women of Europe. By the Rev. WILLIAM B. SPRAGUE, D. D. 12mo, cloth. $1.00.

THOUGHTS ON THE PRESENT COLLEGIATE SYSTEM in the United States. By FRANCIS WAYLAND, D. D. 16mo, cloth. 50 cents.

SACRED RHETORIC; or, Composition and Delivery of Sermons. By H. J. RIPLEY, D. D. With Dr. WARE's Hints on Extemporaneous Preaching. 12mo, cloth. 75 cents.

MANSEL'S MISCELLANIES; including "Prolegomina Logica," "Metaphysics," "Limits of Demonstrative Evidence," "Philosophy of Kant," etc. 12mo, cloth. *In preparation.*

MACAULAY ON SCOTLAND. A Critique, from HUGH MILLER'S "Edinburgh Witness." 16mo, flexible cloth. 25 cents.

NOTES ON THE UNITED STATES OF AMERICA. By T. H. GRAND PIERRE, D. D., Pastor of the Reformed Church, Paris. 16mo, cloth. 50 cts.

HISTORY OF CHURCH MUSIC IN AMERICA. Peculiarities; its legitimate use and its abuse; with notices of Composers, Teachers, Schools, Choirs, Societies, Conventions, Books, etc. By N. D. GOULD. 12mo, cloth. 75 cents.

THE CAPTIVE IN PATAGONIA; or, Life among the Giants. A Personal Narrative. By B. FRANKLIN BOURNE. With Illustrations. 12mo, cloth. 85 cents.

www.ingramcontent.com/pod-product-compliance
Lightning Source LLC
Chambersburg PA
CBHW032317280326
41932CB00009B/848